# LOYALISTS AND LONERS

## Books by Michael Foot

Armistice: 1918–1939
Guilty Men (*with others*)
The Trial of Mussolini
Brendan and Beverley
Who are the Patriots? (*with Donald Bruce*)
Still at Large (*Tribune pamphlet*)
Full Speed Ahead (*Tribune pamphlet*)
The Pen and the Sword
Guilty Men, 1957 (*with Mervyn Jones*)
Aneurin Bevan: 1897–1945
Aneurin Bevan: 1945–1960
Debts of Honour
Another Heart and Other Pulses

# LOYALISTS AND LONERS

*Michael Foot*

COLLINS
8 Grafton Street, London W1
1986

William Collins Sons and Co Ltd
London · Glasgow · Sydney · Auckland
Toronto · Johannesburg

Foot, Michael
Loyalists and loners.
1. Political parties – Great Britain – History
2. Party affiliation – Great Britain – History
I. Title
324.241    JN1117

ISBN 0 00 217583 5

First published 1986
© Michael Foot 1986

Set in Linotron Sabon by
Rowland Phototypesetting Ltd,
Bury St Edmunds, Suffolk
Made and Printed in Great Britain by
William Collins Sons and Co Ltd, Glasgow

## To Jill

and to the people of Blaenau Gwent,
including for this purpose, the people
of Rhymney and Abertysswg, shamefully
severed from the old Ebbw Vale constituency
by the barbarian boundary commissioners.

My special thanks are due to Una Cooze
and Enid Hutchinson, who have given me
expert, indispensable assistance in
preparing this book for the publisher.
Elizabeth Thomas has read the proofs and
devised the index, and deep thanks are
due to her too.

# Acknowledgements

I must offer my thanks to a number of editors or ex-editors in whose columns these pieces or parts of them first appeared. The newspapers or magazines involved are as follows: the *Observer*, the *Evening Standard*, *Tribune*, the *Listener*, the *Spectator*, *Books and Bookmen*, the *Hampstead and Highgate Express*, the *Jewish Chronicle*.

The Vicky cartoons are reprinted from originals left to us at the time of his death.

A note on the title page of each separate article gives some indication of the books involved and the circumstances in which they were published or reviewed. However, in several instances, something quite different from a book review is attempted, more a biographical essay, and I trust these distinctions are fairly indicated in the notes.

# Contents

## Some True Prophets

# *Foreword*

Party loyalty has never been a popular virtue, even in the land which invented the idea. A mere mention of 'party politics' can unloose floods of hypocrisy and absurdity. Party politics are dismissed as a dirty game or a puerile distraction or a downright menace to state and public alike, while party politicians, with no more than a slight twist in the invective, are damned to all eternity. How to explain such a widely-held piece of populist sophistry? A better case can be made for the claim that it is party politics which, over a period of nearly three centuries, have provided the distinctive flavour and vitality of British freedom. And without the loyalists, even the ultra-loyalists, how would the parties survive?

One explanation of this contrast may be that the greatest polemicist who ever used the English language for his purpose devoted much energy to the propagation of the myth. Jonathan Swift's first political pamphlet took the form of a denunciation of party politicians: 'Man is so apt to imitate, so much a sheep that whoever is so bold to give the first great leap over the heads of those about him (though he be the worst of the flock) shall quickly be followed by the rest. Besides, when parties are once formed, the struggles look so ridiculous and become so insignificant, that they have no other way but to run with the herd, which at least will hide and protect them; and where to be much considered, requires only to be very violent.' And, of course, when he wrote *Gulliver's Travels* some twenty-five years later, whole chunks of that child's guide were directed, in anger or derision, at the same victims. It may be recalled of one of the few heroes of the book, the King of Brobdingnag: 'The prejudices of his education prevailed so far, that he could not forbear taking me up in his right hand, and stroking me gently with the other, after an hearty fit of laughing, asked me, whether I were a Whig or a Tory.'

*Whig* and *Tory* were, as every schoolchild is taught, originally terms of abuse. How, with such a shameful pedigree, did they endure at all; how could they fail to be consumed by the combined fury and comic genius of Swift, especially since his dazzling denunciations were quickly adopted by others? Alexander Pope spoke for many of his contemporaries: 'A curse on the word *party* which I have been forced to use so often in this period! I wish the present reign may put an end to the distinction . . .' A few years later William Cowper forecast (in a highly biased book entitled *The Impartial History of Parties*) that George I would 'extinguish the being and the very name of party among us'. How frequently that old, stuffy, Hanoverian appeal has been renewed throughout the ensuing centuries! The first plaintive cries usually appear in *The Times* or the *Telegraph* correspondence columns, but soon thereafter they will be heard in the editorial columns: how intolerably long must the nation wait before the moderate men of all parties or of none come together to save the liberties which in years gone by the moderate men etc. . . Inevitably this sentence fades into incoherence since precious few of our liberties were first established or best defended by the so-called moderate men. More often the name of moderation was the cloak used a few generations later by the men who had executed revolutionary deeds themselves or who had cherished the achievements of their forebears. For a few decisive decades Roundheads had to fight physically for our liberties against Royalists. For nearly a couple of decisive centuries, Whigs had to fight for our liberties against the Tories; but, thanks chiefly to 'party politics', the fights could be conducted without bloodshed. Thereafter, from round about the 1830s, in the age of Peterloo, Tolpuddle and the Chartists, other elements (certainly not moderates under any form of nomenclature) had to fight for our liberties against Whigs and Tories combined in temporary, terrified alliance. But here again, thanks to 'party politics', the contest was mostly conducted by peaceful means. And out of these struggles new parties, new loyalties, were born. These new struggles showed also how great changes could be digested peaceably or at least without an unconscionable plunge into violence. The English people have never quite unlearnt the habit – which is why it was never truly so presumptuous when, according to Milton's magnificent instruction, they could never forget their precedence in teaching the nations how to live.

These peaceful possibilities and achievements – George Orwell saw this comparative gentleness almost as part of the English character – need to be stressed all the more since in modern times, even after genuine democratic institutions have been established, the right to settle matters at the ballot box instead of by fighting is occasionally derided or despised. A kind of bastard Marxism or Trotskyism has sought to spread the doctrine that since all capitalist states are by definition repressive, any form of resistance is equally legitimate. Neither Karl Marx nor Leon Trotsky, we must hastily add, ever said anything quite so demonstrably and dangerously foolish. Indeed, Marx and Engels learnt more from the Chartists than the Chartists learnt from them. They sensed some of the potentialities of real democracy long before Britain could be called a democracy or anything like it. Some of those who had to practise politics before Marx appeared on the scene to preach it understood these realities in their bones, and had the courage to speak out. Witness both the life of William Lovett and the tribute later paid him by the leaders of 'physical-force' Chartists. In other words, there was a case – albeit not necessarily a conclusive one, in all circumstances – for 'moral force' methods even before the appeal to the ballot was in operation. How much stronger still the case against the resort to violence became, once the democratic argument of, say, the Chartists or the Suffragettes had been translated into law, into new democratic rights.

However, occasionally in recent times these arguments have been distorted beyond recognition by the defence of terrorism even in societies which can truly be called democratic. The records of past oppressions combined with the continuing existence of capitalist power in, say, West Germany or the Punjab or Northern Ireland, is held to justify or excuse the wanton killings of the Bader Meinhof Group or the Sikh extremists or the IRA. It is necessary for democratic Socialists to repudiate these doctrines with all the power at their command, especially in view of the way these three groups of killers take special steps to glory in the very wantonness of their choice of victims. No Socialist in the past would ever have justified the resort to these perverted means to secure his ends; no nationalist pursuing legitimate nationalist aims would have favoured such indiscriminate violence; no attempt to invoke Marxist authority would have been tolerated by Karl Marx himself or anyone truly speaking in his name. Alexander Herzen would have made a comparable repudiation for those who conspired to overthrow the

Tsars, and Michael Davitt would have done the same to keep clean the cause of Ireland. And in societies which have built, or seriously started to build, democratic institutions, the readiness to condone the resort to such measures injures the democratic case, and for no purpose. These pleas might just be dismissed as political tomfoolery were it not that the advocates of these measures do take themselves seriously. To make the point specific: no defence of the kind of methods adopted by terrorists in Northern Ireland is justified. No comparison with South Africa can be substantiated; there the oppressed majority has no vote. Above all, such methods have nothing to do with Socialism; they have a much closer kinship with Fascism, which makes no pretence about any method of operations except for its actual preference for violence, the fiercer the better. But, let no one forget: it is the tradition of party politics, the existence of effective parties, which makes possible the peaceful development towards democracy and its proper protection thereafter.

One might have supposed that a tradition so beneficent, so productive of new benefits, would always have been guarded and extolled by political philosophers and practising politicians, or even the two speaking in unison. Yet, as we have already noted, the exact opposite is the case. Those who are ready to denounce 'party politics' and party loyalties are numerous and vocal, in every period, with the editorials in most newspapers offering the ever-open column. It is the defenders of the parties who are the rare birds, and therefore all the more to be treasured. I offer two specimens, one Whig and one Tory, before we come to modern times.

Just over two hundred years ago Edmund Burke wrote the first and still the most formidable defence of party loyalty as the essential political virtue. 'When bad men combine,' he said, 'the good must associate: else they will fall, one by one, an unpitied sacrifice in a contemptible struggle.' At once, in that first classical statement, he dealt with the objection that public men should rather be concerned to act according to their conscience on all issues, and that party allegiance would interfere with this primary demand. 'It is not enough in a situation of public trust in the Commonwealth that a man means well to his country; it is not enough that in his single person he never did an evil act, but always voted according to his conscience . . . This innoxious and ineffectual character, that seems formed on a plan of apology and disculpation, falls miserably short of the mark of public duty. That duty demands and requires that what is right should not only be made known but made prevalent; that what is evil should not only be detested, but defeated . . . It is surely no very rational account of a man's life that he always acted right, but has taken care to act in such a manner that his endeavours could not possibly be productive of any consequence.' Thus the great Whig philosopher, in his best Whig days, bestowed his blessing on those, the much-scorned partisan activists, who dare to descend into the mire of political campaigning, compromise and manoeuvre: those who stake their lives on the proposition that the party label is a badge of honour.

A century later Benjamin Disraeli put the same case with a moral tone rare in his way of thinking. 'Above all,' he said, *above all* 'maintain the line of demarcation between parties, for it is only by maintaining the independence of party that you can maintain the integrity of public men, and the power and influence of Parliament itself.' Disraeli had a special interest in hating any idea of a Coalition of parties, and for claiming that England hated them too. Much of his parliamentary life was devoted to fighting Coalitions of Whigs, Liberals, Peelites and Radicals who kept his purified Tory Party out of office for two decades or more.

And doubtless one of the particular combinations he had in mind was the Fox–North Coalition of the early 1790s in which, at least to the satisfaction of some of our most eminent historians no less than his contemporaries, Charles James Fox destroyed his reputation for political integrity; had he not, like all the others, been seduced by the sweets of office, and, to enjoy the feast, had he not stooped to join the basest companions? The relish with which hard-headed, Right-wing realists marked the debasement of Fox is both unmistakable and repellent. Every man had his price after all, as the old clear-eyed corruptionist, Sir Robert Walpole, had insisted, and the point could not be overlooked that even the immaculate Edmund Burke had been prepared to stoop too. But, in this sense, both Disraeli and Burke were voices crying in the wilderness. Together, despite the interest which each would serve in his own way, their common judgement should help to dismiss the crude depreciation of 'party politics'.

Here, in our own century, the Burke–Disraeli doctrine has become more rigidly applied than they had ever imagined possible. Party organisation, both inside and outside Parliament, has become incomparably more powerful; party mandates and manifestos shape the public argument; party rivalries and disputes, external and internal, dominate the political scene. The loyalists have become more essential to the successful conduct of our 'party politics' than ever, but they are seldom allowed even the thinnest of theoretical draperies to cover their nakedness, their schemings, their sordid, self-interested manoeuvres. It is time justice was done.

The loyalists are not always right. No Socialist who was a member of the Labour Party in the age of Aneurin Bevan would ever dare make so preposterous an assertion; but he, for all his splendid individuality and poetic imagination, was no loner. He was born and bred a member of the Labour movement, and could not think of politics except in that context. For a more precise definition of the word *loner*, by the way, I refer the reader to page 186 in the essay on Enoch Powell. There have been a few great loners in British history and a few, maybe, in modern times, and a much larger assortment of most reputable cross-breeds. Indeed, most politicians must be included in this category. A few real loners eventually expose themselves, and it is not always a pleasant revelation, although even here the point could be pressed too crudely, as is indicated by the Prime Ministers listed in these pages. Of the four I have written about, only one, Baldwin, was a full-scale, fully-committed party loyalist, and he guided his party and the nation to the edge of disaster; whereas the three others, Lloyd George, Churchill and MacDonald, could never be accused of rating loyalty to their parties, or even their closest friends, among the highest virtues.

Some of these pieces have appeared before as book reviews, but almost all of these, as explained in the text, have, for one reason or another been elaborated. Naturally, for me, the 'loyalty' question emerges most strongly in those entitled to take their place in the Labour Party gallery. I have mentioned the choice of Prime Ministers; all of them I saw in action. All the selected cross-breeds are, or were, personal friends, and I trust may remain so. The true prophets, as befits this high calling, are all dead. They form, I know, a strange, assorted list, but if they were alive, I believe they would all share one distinction. They would all wish, if they were eligible to be on the electoral register, to be members of the present-day Labour Party, led by Neil Kinnock.

# A Labour Party
# Gallery

# Jennie Lee

———◦◉◦———

I believe in the fireside. I believe in the democracy
of home. I believe in the republicanism of the
family. I believe in liberty, equality and love.

> Robert Ingersoll
> *The Liberty of Man, Woman and Child*

Jennie Lee's book *Tomorrow is A New Day*, first
published in 1939, is now out of print, but the same
volume, with some additions, was published in
1963 under the title *This Great Journey*. Her latest
book *My Life with Nye* was published by Jonathan
Cape in 1980.

On the first day of January 1985, Jennie Lee, just eighty years old, suddenly found herself transferred to Charing Cross Hospital, Fulham, for an operation on her eye next day. One reason for the suddenness was her insistence that no National Health Service rule should ever be bent, much less broken, for her benefit; she more than anyone else knew what a battle there had been to establish the principle of one service for all. But a by-product of the sudden move was that she arrived there without any books, and when I got there next day, with some hastily assembled relief volumes under my arm, I found her in the grip of one of her splendid, ferocious passions against the inhumanity of man. Bereft of any other books, she had turned to the Bible on her bedside table, and she had read Psalm 137, a most famous one, as it happens, but who but Jennie in modern times, I wonder, had read to the end with such a seeing eye? 'By the rivers of Babylon, there we sat down, yea, we wept, when we remembered Zion.' Yes, famous indeed, and multitudes of men and women driven from their homes and homelands in this bitter century have recited some of the other verses hardly less fervently than the Jews themselves. 'How shall we sing the Lord's song in a strange land? If I forget thee, O Jerusalem, let my right hand forget her cunning.' There they are again, the most famous and prophetic words in the Jewish testament. But who remembers the final verses, the gospel of vengeance raised to the highest pitch? 'O daughter of Babylon, who art to be destroyed; happy shall he be that rewardeth thee as thou hast served us. Happy shall he be, that taketh and dasheth thy little ones against the stones.'

An idea, a doctrine, an Establishment which could contemplate such vengeance against innocent children was the kind of horror which Jennie had been fighting all her life, and, let me hasten to add, lest there might be any misunderstanding whatever, her fury was not in any sense directed against the Jews or their religion. Jennie has always been passionately pro-Jewish, more especially it may be said, since the foundation of the State of Israel. Like Aneurin Bevan, she was one of Israel's earliest supporters and defenders. But those horrific verses, which she read with fresh eyes, jolted her back to her childhood when she learnt a quite different creed at her father's knee.

The story of that childhood is lovingly, proudly, almost arrogantly told in Jennie's own book *Tomorrow is A New Day*. The first time I read it I thought it worthy to take its place on any shelf of Socialist classics, and I thought so again when her Charing Cross Hospital imprecations against those who would hurl little children against the stones sent me back to it. I underline the arrogance, since Jennie often mentions it to me. 'I was taught to be arrogant,' she says, and it is certainly one of the qualities she would like to see properly assimilated by the Labour movement, and one of the reasons why she loved Nye. She was never attracted by humble revolutionaries; they don't make revolutions for a start, and not much else to put in their place.

But in that book – and in her life – the arrogance is subordinate to other gifts, the love and the loyalty, the two interlocking. For the hero and the heroine of that book are her father and mother who taught her what to fight for, and how to fight, and helped to give her the means to be able to do it. For a short while, some real religion, if that is the right term, a God-fearing rather than a God-loving one which was the fashion in Scotland, captured her young fancy; but her gentle, instructive father, with the aid, maybe, of Robert Ingersoll's iconoclastic essays, soon knocked it out again, and had something else to put in its place. 'I didn't need any gods to guide me, I'd got him,' Jennie told me just the other day.

'Ma Lee' has been justly celebrated by many of those like myself who had the luck to know her in later years. 'Ma Lee, whom I shall love and remember always,' wrote Benn Levy, 'was everything she didn't know she was; in particular, a mighty influence.' We each had the idea that we were her favourite, when truly she was showing us what Socialist equality and comradeship could be around her blazing fireside. One of the reasons why Jennie could never cook was because her mother would not allow her into the kitchen. 'What was her phrase?' says Jennie. 'She didn't like us under her feet.' Ma Lee, I guess, knew what she was doing. She scraped and schemed and sacrificed to get Jennie off to Edinburgh University, properly equipped and dressed. But her father's influence was subtler and more persistent. By the time I knew him (in the late 1930s) his strength was fading a little, but the political assurance, tinged even with arrogance, was still there. He more than anyone else taught her what the Labour movement was and could be. 'Idealism, ancestor worship and a happy feeling that we were the people who would one day revolutionise the world so that "none shall slave and none shall slay" seemed to me just about everything in philosophy, religion and economics that anyone need bother about.' And central to everything, more important even than the love was the loyalty. Loyalty to her family, loyalty to her Scottish home, loyalty later to Nye (even and especially on the rare occasions when she didn't agree with him), loyalty above all to the Labour movement. Jennie, it often seemed to me, understood loyalty better than anyone, although it was never an easy choice for her, since her individualism, her ego, was vibrant and demanding too.

1926, the year of the general strike, was just the first momentous occasion which, for her, put these competing strains to the test. As it happens, I had frequent opportunities to mark her reactions during the whole period of another miners' strike, in 1984 and 1985. She could share the emotions of that time better than anyone; she knew how the hearts of men and women, in their communities and homes, could be torn so that the rents would take years to heal. She knew how good was the miners' case, how necessary it was for them to be supported, how piteous it was when sometimes their leaders traded on such matchless loyalty, not recognising sufficiently how precious a quality it was, and how tragic it would be if the generalship of the people at the top did not match the magnificence of the army they led. She had seen many great miners' leaders in action from Alexander Macdonald and A. J. Cook to her own favourite, Bob Smillie. She understood how agonising the new choices could be, like the old ones. 'Solidarity for ever, was our song,' she would say, at the most poignant moments of a crisis when two rights seemed to clash, the necessity for action and the equal necessity to avoid measures which would wreck the cause.

Jennie was sitting for the finals for her MA in Edinburgh in June 1926. She longed to get home. Once she was back in Fifeshire in the remaining months of that year, and the even sadder and more terrifying one that followed, she saw naked, ruthless class war in action, as her Marxist tutors, her father among the foremost, had taught her. 'Miners, it seemed, when they set out to improve their wages and conditions, had to reckon with the physical forces of the state as well as with the money and influence of the coalowners . . . Lies, batons, broken promises, soldiers' bayonets, all these we were familiar with in the coalfields.' When she came to this chapter, her whole story darkened; the poverty cut deep down to the bone. Some of the most courageous defenders of their class were driven into exile. Whole communities were strangled.

Yet, in Jennie's burning pages, something even worse happened in 1926. 'One evening in June an unofficial conference took place around our fireside between my father and two other firemen from the same pit. What were they to do? Blacklegs were being allowed to work in their pit. If they continued acting as safety men, they would be keeping the pit safe for the blacklegs. If they left their jobs, they would be acting contrary to trade union decisions. I watched their serious faces.' They made the decision to come out, and one consequence was that the colliery where her father worked had no further use for him. He was victimised for years. And another consequence, even more hellish, was that, when they thought it suited them, some officials of the Communist Party in Scotland who were ranged against his political affiliation with the Independent Labour Party, tried to spread the tale that Jennie Lee's father had been a blackleg.

Momentarily, when the chance came, Jennie, like the Labour movement itself, turned from the industrial to the political battle-field. She tub-thumped her way around the Scottish coalfields and made a sensational appearance at an ILP Conference in 1927. Fenner Brockway, who was old enough to be her uncle, described the scene: 'A young, dark girl took the rostrum, a puckish figure with a mop of thick black hair thrown impatiently aside, brown eyes flashing, body and arms moving in rapid gestures, words pouring from her mouth in Scottish accent and vigorous phrases, sometimes with a sarcasm which equalled Shinwell's. It was Jennie Lee, making her first speech at an ILP conference. And what a speech it was. Shinwell was regarded as a Goliath in debate, but he met his match in this girl David.' The scene so excitedly recorded by Fenner caught the eye of the Labour movement in Scotland. Dour bureaucrats, whether in the official Labour Party or the Communist Party, were forced to take notice and make obeisance. Overnight she got an invitation to stand at a by-election in North Lanark, and in February 1929 she arrived at Westminster, the youngest woman ever to sit in the place, overflowing with abilities and vitality.

She had the world at her feet, and quite a range of individual applicants too. She could have provided the model for a new figure storming the Bastille to be painted by Delacroix, a red and black emblem of the revolution still to come, and doubtless he would have noted too the delicacy of her hands and feet, and every individual feature. Yet also – like Nye, as it happens, as she so soon detected – she had a savagery in her soul which derived from what she had seen in the coalfields in those terrible years, the strife between people with a common cause, something almost as evil as the infamies inflicted by the class enemy. Both she and Nye would subscribe at times to the William Blake maxim: 'The tigers of wrath are wiser than the horses of instruction.' In the 1929–31 Parliament, both of them had to apply their principles and their temperaments to a political crisis of truly formidable dimensions, the most serious in the history of the British Labour Party. It was for both of them a test of competing loyalties, and one measure of the agony is that at first they felt they must resolve it in different ways.

Jennie, it must not be forgotten, was in those years a better known political figure than he was. She had arrived at Westminster sooner, just before the 1929 general election. She had insisted on being introduced, not by the Party officials recommended by the Party, but by James Maxton and Bob Smillie. She was just twenty-four. She could always state her case with clarity and confidence and passion, and within that House of Commons, she already spoke for a group of others there beside herself: customarily a Commons advantage. The ILP had its own well-deserved reputation for parliamentary skills. James Maxton, John Wheatley and George Buchanan, in their contrasting styles, were three of the most powerful debaters in the place, and their most devoted followers contained a further range of talent. Had not MacDonald and Snowden, the Prime Minister and Chancellor, been bred in the ranks of the old ILP? Who could suppose that such a rich and authentic tradition within the Party would ever lose its vitality and indeed its capacity to seek out the next stage in the Socialist advance? Jennie already had some doubts about Maxton's wayward leadership; she was affronted in particular to discover that, in one of the major educational controversies of that Parliament, even some of the most principled leaders, Maxton included, would bow before the supposed requirements of the Catholic vote in Scotland. But her loyal heart was in the ILP and some mighty convulsions would be needed before it was ever moved elsewhere.

She like several others in that Parliament became quickly interested in the phenomenon from Ebbw Vale, but for her he had one immediate political appeal. The group of miners' MPs numbered nearly forty; all of them had been trained in hard political argument, but somehow Aneurin Bevan spoke in more subtle and riveting accents than the others. He too, like Jennie, had been scorched and moulded in the furnace of 1926; he had indeed, at one of the miners' national conferences, argued, more bravely than anyone else, how the miners should go back together when their power was at its peak, and even in his native Tredegar a few voices – some of them Communist Party voices – had been raised in criticism. Jennie knew how wounding those strident accusations might be. But she heard too how, in the interest of the miners, he would hurl everything into attack against the foremost figures in that Parliament, against Lloyd George even, whose hesitancies at such a moment might be even more deadly for the miners' cause than what might be done by their outright opponents. More and more he acted with the ILP even though he was not of their number. Once, in the summer of 1931 when the division bell rang and they hurried to register their votes, she said: 'You know, Nye, we could be brother and sister.' Back came his reply, with a mischievous grin. 'Yes, and with a tendency to incest.' Jennie and Nye, young and old, could always break the tensions with wit and laughter.

And the tensions of that Parliament rose to a terrifying climax, one in which the whole future of the Labour Party, the whole future of Socialism in Britain, seemed to be at stake. When the Labour Government was broken, when MacDonald and Snowden emerged at the head of a new so-called National Government, it was by no means clear what was the proper course for Socialists, in and out of Parliament, to follow; for the new leaders of the newly-aligned Party in the Commons had been supporting MacDonald and Snowden right up till the day before yesterday. No deep distinction could be drawn between the roles of the two sets of leaders. That was the judgement of Maxton and the ILP; but how effective had the rebels been? All through the Parliament Nye had attended several of the private meetings of the ILP leaders as a kind of unofficial but trusted observer; always he had advised caution in risking a full breach with the official Party, urging that the ILP must not destroy in advance the role it could play when MacDonaldism was exposed. He became haunted – not for the first or last time in his life – by the ease with which Left-wing Socialists could be tempted to reject all compromise, to save their immortal souls – and to condemn their cause to perdition. Once he became possessed by such a sure appreciation of the tactical choice, he could unloose his invective against friend or foe. On this occasion Jennie was the recipient of his courteous Celtic eloquence as he strode up and down her newly-acquired flat in Guilford Street: 'As for you, I tell you what the epitaph on you Scottish dissenters will be – pure but impotent. Yes, you will be pure all right. But remember, at the price of impotency. You will not influence the course of British politics by as much as a hair's-breadth. Why don't you get into a nunnery, and be done with it? Lock yourself up in a cell away from the world and its wicked-ness. My Salvation Army lassie. Poor little Casabianca! That was a hell of an intelligent performance, wasn't it? I tell you, it is the Labour Party or nothing. I know all its faults, all its dangers. But it is the Party that we have taught millions of working people to look to and regard as their own. We can't undo what we have done. And I am by no means convinced that something cannot yet be made of it.'

No portrait of Jennie would be complete without some remem-brance of that scene. It is clear that in the short time they had known each other, within three years, he had established over her an intellectual ascendancy – as he did over most others who came in contact with him. But, let us not forget, it is to Jennie, not to him, that we owe the report, and Jennie, too, who was willing to inscribe that taunt about the Salvation Army lassie. She knew, although she hated to have others point it out to her, that she could display an evangelical strain, to outdo even MacDonald. She knew how strong was Nye's argument, and she never forgot the devoted fury with which he had sought to persuade her. And yet, even more remark-able, an even stronger testimony to the excruciating nature of the choice is the fact that, for the moment, she chose the course which he derided with such rhetorical flourish but with such genuine fury too.

Jennie, like a multitude of other Labour candidates, went down to defeat in the 1931 debacle, despite all her campaigning zest and despite the special assistance given her by Nye. A newspaper photograph of the time showed her being sustained by an unknown 'sympathiser' whose features were not yet known in far away Scotland. But the aftermath was worse than the defeat itself. The new leaders of the Labour Party, in and out of Parliament, resolved, as one part of the remedy for what had happened, to devise and impose a stricter discipline within the Parliamentary Party or among those who aspired to join it.

The so-called Standing Orders of the Parliamentary Party must be made more exact and effective. Jennie, along with other would-be candidates who wished to be re-adopted, received notice of these proceedings, and they touched some of the rawest wounds left by the proceedings of that Parliament. Even at this interval it is possible to understand her anger: 'I did not want to leave the Labour Party. I wanted to take part in a political contest where the alignments were as energisingly simple as the one penny fairy-tale and comic cuts that had delighted my childhood. I wanted to slay all the dragons and set poor people free. I wanted it to be all of us *versus* the others.' But before any such possibility could be renewed, 'I found myself presented with an ultimatum. I was ordered to put my signature to a document in which I had to promise that I would never again "misbehave" in the future as I had done in the past. The "mis-behaviours" in question being that I had found out MacDonald before they did and had dared to oppose the policies that led us to disaster.' The North Lanark Divisional Labour Party wanted to keep her as their candidate, but here was the condition laid down by the central machine: 'I had to sign on the dotted line.' The letter which she wrote from her London flat was a cool, collected, classic statement of what she believed to be the rights and duties of a democratic Socialist elected to the British Parliament. And she could calculate exactly how painful for herself the severance would be. 'Once my letter was in the post,' she recorded, 'I felt very naked. The doorbell rang. When I saw Aneurin Bevan outside I had half a mind to pretend that I was not at home. But I had better get it over.' And she did. Their second bout was not quite so one-sided an affair as the first had been, according to Jennie's own account. She gave as good as she got. The outrage, of course, was that the Labour Party should ever have sought to enforce such an illiberal system of Parliamentary discipline on adult, elected representatives of the people. When eventually Aneurin Bevan and some of his allies had the power and the chance to remove it, it was removed, with the party bureaucrats still muttering their objections.

But we all had to wait for these modern amenities. The 1930s was not a distinguished period in Labour Party history for tolerance and the wisdom which derives from tolerance. A sign of those times was that the decade which began with the exclusion of Jennie Lee from the party ended with the expulsion of Aneurin Bevan. Although the details were so dissimilar, the offence was the same. Each of them found the Labour leadership in little England squalidly inadequate to deal with the challenge of the age; but each of them also turned to renew their Socialist inspiration, their unbreakable Socialist loyalty, from wider sources, and here it was Jennie who made the first explorations.

It was just about this time that I first met her myself. I climbed that staircase at Guilford Street, not knowing what molten lavas of Socialist invective had engulfed the whole place a few years before. Jennie was living next door to her friend Ellen Wilkinson, and I had been sent to talk to them both on the subject of the distressed areas. Jennie, years later, could not recall the meeting; I was more impressionable, indeed I would have been happy to have given Delacroix a few hints. Jennie and Ellen, equally passionate on the platform, shared the same kind of zest off it. Both of them were Socialist crusaders who would permit no besmirching of their faith, but neither of them was bound by any priggish conventions. Jennie has described in her own book her love for Frank Wise; she describes, too, his tragic death, and how some friends who would last her a lifetime, headed by Charles Trevelyan and Nye himself, rallied to her side. But she could always turn her tears to fresh exertions and diversions. 'Even the public school boys,' she would say, 'had their uses; they knew how to open doors,' and she meant that literally, not metaphorically.

For Jennie, international Socialism had already established its significance; it was a rich part of the ILP tradition, no less than the Marxist tradition. She went on her travels, partly to earn her living as a journalist and partly to test how strong was the international Socialist allegiance in Europe and across the Atlantic. She brought back reports from Brussels, from Paris, from Austria, from the Soviet Union and the United States, where Socialists talked a good deal more ambitiously than they did a few decades later. Most memorably, she saw working-class Vienna in its proud Socialist heyday before it was mowed down by the treacherous guns of the Dollfuss dictatorship, backed by Fascist regimes in Rome and Berlin and appeasing accomplices in London. Great companies of demo-cratic Socialists – the official historians rarely mention the matter – risked their lives to resist the onset of Fascism long before the rulers of Establishment Britain made up their minds: not that most of these, with a very few honourable exceptions, achieved the feat until the very last second of the twelfth hour.

For Jennie and Nye, who were happily if unconventionally married in 1934, the full synchronisation of their political loyalties came from Spain. They went on their honeymoon to Andalusia, and she marvelled at the ease with which Nye would shake off his inhibitions with a Celtic fervour to match his Spanish hosts. Then, barely a year later, came the outbreak of the civil war, the Fascist invasion, the test for international Socialism everywhere on Spanish battlefields. Neither Jennie nor Nye had a moment of doubt, and nor, to do them credit, had the vast overwhelming bulk of the British Labour movement, Labour Party members, the ILP, the Communists, everybody. Only some of the leaders held back, and quibbled and cavilled – among them a few of those later lauded as far-seeing opponents of Fascism, Ernest Bevin among the foremost. At the Edinburgh Conference of the Labour Party in the autumn of 1936, just at the hour when Labour's unequivocal support for the Spanish Republic could have been most helpful, the Labour leaders allowed themselves to be deceived by the British Government's support for the so-called 'Non-Intervention' policy towards the Spanish war: what this choice meant in practice was that the flow of arms to the Republic would be blocked while the invading Fascist armies received all the support they needed. It was an infamy indeed that Britain's good name should ever have been associated with such a calculated and disreputable piece of hypocrisy, and an infamy, too, that the leaders of British Labour should ever have backed such an idea, even if only for a few experimental months.

Jennie and Nye together shared the same sense of shame at that Edinburgh Conference, the same determination to seek some means of common action. For them, as for multitudes of European Socialists, the Second World War of 1939–45 started three years earlier on those Spanish battlefields, while Neville Chamberlain was still seeking pacts with the Fascist invader and while Winston Churchill's detestation of the Nazi horror was blinded for a while by his hatred of Socialism. And when at last the moment did come for full British participation in the world contest, and when the news came through that Britain and Nazi Germany were at war, Jennie and Nye celebrated the event by routing out to play on their gramophone an old Spanish Republican song which they had played so often before, to drown the reports from Barcelona and Madrid.

Thereafter, and until the day he died, they did become man and wife in a somewhat more orthodox manner. Jennie had once boasted to her mother that she wanted to match the exploits of the Suffragettes; her feminist instincts were strong, her natural ego even stronger, but throughout the war years, and even more consciously throughout the years that followed, she subdued her own life to assist his. She thought, with some excuse, that he was the most creative Socialist intelligence of his time, and she fought to assist him against all his foes, inside the Labour Party and out of it. Ma Lee had seen what Jennie would call 'the real inwardness' of the situation in those old tales of inter-Socialist quarrels even before she did; she exerted that hidden influence which Benn Levy had discerned. She demanded unity, was determined to have her demands met. 'It is quite clear,' Jennie was candid enough to write – in 1939 or even earlier – 'that the ILP could make no great headway so long as it had people like mother to grapple with. For her way of looking at things was typical of ninety-nine per cent of the men and women, who, actively or passively, take part in Labour politics.' Ma Lee was now truly a governing influence on both their lives, and that same influence radiated to many of the rest of us.

Jennie herself has given the sequel to *Tomorrow is A New Day* in *My Life with Nye*. Neither of the titles is a quite accurate guide to what follows; each volume is completely honest, although in some places reticent. If anyone has any doubts about reading them, I commend him especially to the review by Gwyn A. Williams in the *Guardian*, incomparably the most perceptive of any. But first he had an interest to declare. 'After my father,' he said, 'heard Jennie Lee speak on Dowlais Recreation Ground, he was in a trance for a week. My mother thought of citing the Labour Party as co-respondent.' Then later: 'Jennie Lee exists and existed in her own right, and in personal matters, her writing is hypnotic . . . I couldn't put it down, but I can't review it. It is simply not possible to separate her from her bright and blazing companion; it is not possible to separate either of them from the long bruised march of a generation.'

For twenty years of that march, Jennie and Nye shared every inch of the road, every victory, every defeat, every affront, every insult, every delight, and, governing everything else, the absolute loyalty to the Labour movement which over the years they had welded into the same common strand. To claim so much for this quality may at first sound pretentious. But it truly was like that. Each of them had an endless capacity for enjoyment, a fierce ego, a full dose of ambition, pride, and arrogance. Some of his opponents, particularly in his own party, were always ready with the charge that personal ambition was the real motive power. At one time or another the charge was made in terms intended to be destructive by Churchill, Bevin, Morrison, Gaitskell, Dalton, and heaven knows how many more. It was a falsehood and always a falsehood. Jennie knew that best of all, but anyone who took the trouble could soon find out the truth for himself. The ruling passion with both of them was the way they could serve not the Party they had joined but the movement in which they were both born, their own flesh and bone. Here, for sure, they knew how to fortify one another.

The suppression of Jennie's ego – it is not too harsh a term – started in the war years when Nye in the House of Commons was challenging the Churchill Coalition, not single-handed but more intrepidly and farsightedly than anyone else. This was the period when sections of the Tory press, sensing that Aneurin Bevan and what he stood for was their most dangerous domestic enemy, started to look for ways to vilify and destroy him. Jennie in turn sensed the new need for her protection. She herself fought a by-election against the Coalition in bomb-blasted Bristol; indeed the place was so devastated that a real election was hardly possible, and even the most sharp-eyed Party bureaucrats averted their gaze and discipline from those Party members who went down there to support her. But this was a diversion; gradually she loosened her ties with the ILP and made her peace with the official party, won the nomination as the Labour candidate in the Staffordshire coalmining area of Cannock, and prepared for the 1945 Labour victory which Nye, more than any other figure on the political stage, foresaw and helped to win.

Then came the great days of the greatest Labour Government, the exultant hopes, the achievements, the victories which could not be denied or overturned, the setbacks, the disillusion which still – even in 1951 – did not withhold from the Labour Party the largest vote ever cast for a political party in British history. Nye had played his foremost part in all those events; the building of the National Health Service, the construction of the Welfare State, the establishment of full employment as a settled objective of national policy. Many outside observers, almost certainly a majority of Labour Party members, believed he was the natural successor for Clem Attlee as leader of the Labour Party and the next Labour Prime Minister. Then came the internal ruptures and explosions and all the mounting doubts of the cold war and the age of the H-bomb. Nye played his foremost part in all these events too, right until a few months before the day of his death. Once again, freshly barbed, came the charge that it was his personal ambition which destroyed his expectations. The Tory newspapers or many of them (with occasional assistance from those who should have known better such as the *Daily Mirror*) could always be relied upon to maul him afresh, whenever the Conservative Central Office gave the cue. And coupled with these direct campaigns of character-destruction came the attack on Jennie. She was supposed to be the ever-present, termagant, sectarian influence, blocking his own preference for the middle road. Somehow the Salvation Army lassie had been transformed into the witch of Endor, casting her spell and her blight at all the most fateful turns in his career.

How little did they know; how little were they interested in ever finding out. The stereotypes take over and become, in the public mind, the real man or woman and are never to be altered in any particular. This is not the work of the real caricaturists, it may be said. Usually, if they are to survive themselves, they must show more subtlety and some real power of observation. But the stereotypes of the Tory newspaper headlines, obsequiously followed by their posher imitators, came near to destroying altogether the man, the

Bevan

statesman later acclaimed, once he was safely in hospital or his grave. He had some provocation for calling the British press the most prostituted in the world, and Jennie certainly shared his judgement. And how wildly absurd and offensive was the picture presented of their relationship, the political aims which guided them, their way of life, the home, the fireside Ma Lee and Jennie had made. More and more Nye relished it, ached to return to it, hated to be torn away.

Some brilliant practitioners on the platform tend to become seduced by their art and their command over great audiences; the charge could never be properly levelled against Nye. No one who knew him off the platform would make so absurd a suggestion. Someone once remarked on the strange property of Gladstone's influence which was greatest with multitudes, less in society, least at home. Lord Acton, who made this observation, thought it was one reason why Gladstone founded no school and left no disciples. Nye's influence with multitudes who heard him directly was immense, but the charm and the magic did not evaporate as he moved into smaller companies; rather, it grew stronger and shone brighter. As for his ambition, he would never discuss that in personal terms. He did truly think first of his class, his country, his cause. It was no pose when he always discussed political problems in this way with his friend Archie Lush in Tredegar back in the early 1920s. It was no pose when he did the same with Jennie, from that 1929 Parliament right till the end.

And when that end came, her heart burst. When he died, the personal tragedy mixed with the political tragedy, and she had no power to keep them apart. She felt that he had been murdered – by his enemies but also by his friends. And this mood was no mere passing affliction. She could still feel it, without any abatement whatever, five years later. In those first days after his death, we had agreed that I should try to write Nye's life, and she gave me every possible encouragement and assistance. But five years later – on 17 October 1965, to be exact – she wrote me an amazing letter, parts of which appeared in her own book, but parts of which she censored, in kindness to me, I imagine. Here it is reprinted in full (with her permission):

Dear Michael

I primed myself with two strong martinis before coming to talk to you because I have not got over the impulse to run away from the very mention of Ni's name. Strangers, all kinds of people, come up to me to say kind, admiring things and I am at best abrupt with them instead of taking their remarks in the spirit they are offered. Afterwards I am displeased with myself for being so self-indulgent. Explanation? So far as I understand myself, it is unbearable pain, resentment and wrath when I recall much that Ni had to suffer. He had a great capacity for suffering, for self-torment as well as for taking both intellectual and sensual delight in being alive.

In my bitter moments, I have said to myself a thousand times, he did not die. He was murdered. When Ma died it was a gentle grief. Relief to see her saved from the torments of extreme age, the knowledge that if she could not go on working for those she loved, life had no meaning for her. Grief for Ma is selfish, inward-looking, the missing of a comfort and companionship such as she gave to all around her.

With Ni it is different. That great frame and brilliant mind would have carried him through another ten years in top form, maybe longer if the tensions imposed on him had not been more than any sensitive, responsive human being could possibly stand. It was, in the last phase, a complicated kind of martyrdom. He was beset, misjudged, maligned, on every side. He was caught in an impasse from which there was no way out. Working under Gaitskell for one of Ni's intellectual arrogance and proud spirit, was plain hell. Refusal to do so was once more splitting the movement at a time when, rightly or wrongly, Ni deeply believed mankind was again and again within a hair's-breadth of nuclear war. He had sufficient confidence in his party, and in himself, as to believe it was urgently necessary to get the Tories out. As Foreign Secretary, with Gaitskell as PM he would have had a monstrous burden to carry. But he was willing to face up to this. That is, intellectually he was, rationally he was, but the emotional undercurrents were tearing his very guts to pieces.

Then, although he never said this to me explicitly, in so many words, he was wounded to the very depths of his being by the refusal of so many of those in the party with whom and for whom he had worked, to give him their trust. No blank cheque for Ni. No room to manoeuvre. He got everything the hard way. That is, everything in public life. I tried to restore the balance in private all I could and with my father and mother to help me made that side of his life just about all he ever wanted. When I said last night that I had had an easy, indeed spoiled time by comparison, I was thinking of the good food, warmth, peace of my parents' home, the privilege of my university years, journeys twice with Frank through Russia, the second time over the Caucasian Mountains, then on to Persia, now called Iran. I suffered in 1926 because I was totally identified with my family and neighbours in Lochgelly.

But compare all this with an abnormally sensitive child *not even fourteen*, sent underground to work, a weak father (whom he loved), a dominating mother (whom he admired but fought), a stammer caused by the impact of his home environment in his youngest years, a horrible sadistic teacher at school. Ni the dunce, Ni the figure of fun. Can you imagine it? He had to find his solace, the outlet for the fine taste that was always so great a part of him, by climbing above the squalor of Tredegar's tips and bins and side streets into the mountains. By digging with bare hands into the rich mines of learning. Books – that was all he had but he went after them, devoured them, assimilated them and could even now have been alive and using so much that most of us learn parrot-wise at college and forget soon afterwards.

There is, of course, an entirely different way of looking at all this. Could Ni not have been more tactful, handled those he disagreed with in his own party more skilfully, used his wit and charm more, the sledge hammer less? He himself, often said to me, 'I am a misfit in public life. I should have been a don. You are much better suited to it.' That last is irrelevant so far as it is true. I had in the course of the years more and more accepted that to help sustain Ni's creative intelligence was much more important than aiming at the dizzy heights of maybe being a second Alice Bacon. But could he have been more tactful? Instead of resigning in 1951, for instance, should he have bowed his head and waited his time? There can be no absolute answer to that kind of conundrum but Ni gave the answer in part when he repeated on different difficult occasions: 'In public life, those who would change things must shout to be heard.' You have heard him often on that theme.

Being Ni, that combination of temperament, gifts and circumstances, he could [do] no other. In *In Place of Fear* Ni writes that all truth is earth-bound and time-bound. Again he writes that it is only after we have lived through an experience we can see what it was and that often what we do leads to ends other than those we had envisaged. All this is his strong sense of the passing of time, of the relativity of all things and values. Do you recall that one interview he gave to the press when he thought he was beginning to get his strength back at Asheridge? What he said about biography and autobiography, about those still active in public life writing about themselves and their contemporaries? His mind then was still brilliantly clear.

Yet he did not know he was mortally ill. He guessed it sometimes. He questioned and cross-questioned his doctors, John Buchan, me, but we managed to deceive him and I am proud of that and take what comfort I can from it. It was because he was essentially so simple and trusting that I could do it. He was spared at least the final sorrow of knowing that he would never complete his job, that he was beaten by illness, that I would somehow have to go on without him. He was more optimistic then than before his illness. He enjoyed the praise and love that flowed into him, he was ready to start all over again. If I had to go through that nightmare period again I would do exactly as I did. Now I have a feeling of total unreality, total irresponsibility. No life of my own, just wandering in and out of other people's lives. But that last is irrelevant, unimportant, except as a clue to my behaviour at times.

I am just sane enough to know that where Ni is concerned I am not quite sane. I have refused every offer, however seemingly profitable and worthwhile, to talk or write about him. The truth might seem like the ranting of a hysterical half-wit. It is so much easier to write about faults than virtues, cruelties, insensitivities rather than humour, kindness and the rest. But Ni's faults were on the outside. The closer anyone was to him, the more a kind of Rabelaisian Jesus Christ quality came out. How he would be irritated by that kind of expression. But I am thinking of his attitude when Desmond Donnelly attacked him – by arrangement and for cash. Ni was sorry for him. He sent Hugh Delargy to see if he was all right. Then when I was blazing mad with you (and Howard and Jack Hylton and others were ready to withdraw support from *Tribune*), it was Ni who would have none of it. I apologise for mentioning you in the same breath almost as Donnelly but you know what I mean. In different contexts, relationships, Ni simply could not act small or spiteful. He could curse and shout to get his own way – you remember that lunch at the Café Royal – but he would not act meanly.

Sorry, Michael, about my typing but it is the lesser evil. My writing is worse. If these free association notes are any use, I shall write again later. Believe me I know the difficulty of the job you are doing. You too are a bit too close to Ni. But if only the bone structure of fact can be accurately and unchallengeably set down – this in itself is a great deal.

Jennie

Note the date when that letter was written: October 1965. The Jennie Lee who wrote it had been for just about a year a middle-ranking Minister in Harold Wilson's Labour Government of 1964. She understood the horses of instruction as well as the tiger's wrath. She was the first Minister of the Arts in British history, and she had the not exactly easy assignment of performing this novel role, first under the umbrella of the Ministry of Public Works and later under the Ministry of Education. A separate Ministry would not have been easy to carve out of two or three others, and, on the other hand, the subordinate position within other Ministries and under other Ministers had its drawbacks too. But Jennie quickly proved herself an excellent administrator, a good negotiator, a skilled operator of the Whitehall machine. One of the Ministers under whom she served was Tony Crosland and a hint of their relationship is given in a conversation he had with his wife Susan, recorded in her book on him – '. . . she [Jennie] thinks that everything in the entire Department should be subservient to the arts. To tell the truth, I'm not frightfully interested in the arts at this moment.' Of course she exploited her special relationship with the Prime Minister who had appointed her, but that needed to be done with tact and drive and diplomatic skill. Jennie proved that, when she wanted something, she had plenty of all three qualities. Not only was she the first real Minister for the Arts; the widely held view is that she is still the best we have had. She set the standard for her successors, and made it impossible for any subsequent government to revert to the old ways. A Minister for the Arts had become a necessary part of any civilised government in London, as it had long been in Paris.

When Harold Wilson made the appointment and when Jennie accepted it, a principal aim which they had in mind was that she should take the lead in the establishment of the Open University. Harold Wilson could justly claim to be the original enthusiast for the project; he had spoken of the idea of a University of the Air, using to the full for educational purposes for the first time the facilities of television. Commitment to the project was included in the Labour Party Manifesto of 1954, and the commitment of the Prime Minister in the newly elected Government was of paramount importance. But it was by no means the case that this combination of factors made her task simple. She had to face stubborn opposition or at least a sullen lack of enthusiasm in several quarters. The

Treasury had no eagerness to supply the necessary resources; other educational institutions had entrenched prejudices and interests of their own; and some of those who were Junior Ministers of Education in the same Government wished to allocate their limited resources to other priorities. No mention whatever of the Open University appears in Susan Crosland's happy conversations with her husband. Without Jennie's determination, the whole idea could have been killed. More probably, without her influence, the likelihood would have been that the conception would have been transformed into something much less ambitious and far-reaching. This was the constant threat, and time and again Jennie could recall the same kind of pressures which had been mounted against Nye when he was seeking to proceed with his plan for the establishment of the National Health Service on 5 July 1948. It was Jennie who insisted that the highest academic standards must apply right from the start, that there must be no departure of principle from the long-term vision. But she herself insists: without the support of the Prime Minister and of Arnold Goodman who was persuaded to become Secretary General of the Arts Council, it would have been impossible for a Junior Minister to overcome Treasury hostility and the indifference or plain hostility of other Ministers, most of all (as Jennie also insists) Anthony Crosland's resentment that she had been pushed into his department.

The Open University received its Royal Charter in 1969; the first students were admitted in 1971; the declared aim was to make university education available to all adults, regardless of status or previous academic qualifications. Soon a full-time staff of 2000 or 5000 part-time tutors and counsellors were recruited. By 1984, it was Britain's largest university with more than 100,000 students and had awarded 62,000 degrees with over 5000 being added to the total each year. It was an achievement which can be mentioned in the same breath as the establishment of the National Health Service: a political achievement, but like other political achievements one with a never-ending human aspect too. Here I select one letter which Jennie received in July 1985.

Dear Madam,
    You may remember a letter I sent some time ago telling you how valuable the Open University was to me. Since writing to you I have

graduated BA April 1984 and I now plan to work for honours, music and art at third level. After graduating, I decided to offer my help to my own age group (I am 73 years old) at the local pensioners' day-centre. This week four of the candidates I presented for the O Level English Literature examination have received very good news. Six ladies (ages ranging from 70–77 years) sat the examination, but one was really physically unfit, the weekly meeting was the 'highlight' and only outing she had, although I knew from the beginning that only a miracle could bring her scholastic success; the psychological effect has been therapeutic. There is further demand for the 'English class' and also for a pensioners' magazine, in which I hope to include some of the wonderful real-life short stories submitted for homework during the past 18 months. I wonder what your dear late husband would have thought could he have foreseen the fruits of his unique and brilliant scheme to help the less fortunate. This week I have returned from Cardiff University where I attended the Music Summer School in connection with this year's course. What an uplifting experience and in such perfect surroundings – Beautiful Wales.

Jennie had naturally watched with pride the development of the Open University, and she has other comforts too; a home and hearth, like the one her mother made, to which she can always return. She, like Nye, had fought for her own privacy and she treasured it as the most priceless of riches. But for her also politics has always meant the politics of the democratic Socialist revolution. She never wavered in that conception and allegiance, and the miners' strike of 1984 stirred her memories of 1926 more sharply than for decades past.

The truest poet of those times – he spoke for the Scots no less than the Welsh – was Idris Davies from Rhymney, the neighbouring valley to Sirhowy which sheltered Nye's own Tredegar. Nye always honoured the poets, and Idris among the foremost; like most people in Wales, he would never regard the poets as men apart. Their essential function was well understood by the Celts, if not always by 'the bovine Anglo-Saxons'. 'We shall remember 1926 until our blood is dry', so the characters in Idris's greatest poem, *The Angry Summer*, had vowed to one another. Jennie could sing with him:

> O valleys that gave me birth,
> And comradeship and song,
> Before I go back to the earth
> May my eyes see the end of this wrong.

But the wrong in Jennie's eyes, as also in the eyes of Idris Davies and Aneurin Bevan, was never just a sentiment about the past, nostalgia, a toleration of defeat. It was rather a call to action, effective action, against the common enemy. The most terrible wrong, in 1984, as in 1926, was when the strength and unity and incomparable courage of the miners was dissipated by their leaders.

> Dream no more on your mountains
> But face the savage truths
> That snarl and yell in your valleys
> Around your maids and youths,
> Down from your dreams in the mountains
> Back to your derelict mate,
> For the dreamers of dreams are traitors
> When wolves are at the gate.

Jennie and Nye and Idris Davies all had the same pride in their working-class roots. It was one of the reasons why they did not suffer too readily the instruction 'in practical politics' which the Attlees and the Gaitskells might sometimes affect to give them. Practical politics, as they had learnt them in the Welsh and Scottish coalfields, did mean that there was such a thing as a class war which the ruling Establishment, in the last extremity, would pursue without pity, and it was at those moments, above all others, when the Labour movement must invoke its capacity for passionate unity in action. Jennie, every time I saw her, could teach that lesson anew; it was her life.

# Barbara Castle

A little coquetry is perhaps inseparable from
female authorship as from female sovereignty;
and women are generally disposed to exact more
deference to their caprices than is reasonable in
cases which have nothing to do with gallantry.

William Hazlitt

Barbara Castle's first batch of diaries, covering the
period of 1974–6, were published by Weidenfeld
and Nicolson in September 1980 and the second
batch covering the period 1964–70 in September
1984. I had two bites, not exactly at the cherry, but
at as rich a political dish as was ever set before
the modern political public.

Blessed are the diarists; for they shall inherit the earth. At least they have a better chance than the meek, the discreet, the diffident, and all those who allow themselves to be distracted by other preoccupations. It is the Pepysian view of the reign of Charles II which prevails, and it is the inspired tittle-tattle of the Duc de Saint-Simon which describes what posterity truly wants to believe about the Versailles of Louis XIV. And, coming to more modern and mundane times, it is predominantly the Hugh Dalton version of Labour history, and particularly Labour Cabinet or Shadow Cabinet history in the 1940s and 1950s, which holds the field against most revisionist assaults. He was the only one of that generation who kept a document worthy at all of the name of diary. Hugh Gaitskell, as we have learned much later, followed his example, and his diversion into this field has helped to bolster a formidable defensive biography. What would Aneurin Bevan have said if anyone had dared ask him if he was keeping a detailed, personal record of his life in a Labour Cabinet? Any such notion would have been dismissed as *obscene* – I can hear him saying it.

However, fashions or circumstances or tastes or personalities have altered, and three at least of the leading Socialists of more recent times have kept diaries which they never had any intention of hiding under a bushel. Dick Crossman unloosed his Cabinet diaries on the world, posthumously but none the less deliberately – and I write as one of his executors – as a major political act. He thought it was the most effective way in which he could tell the British people and the Labour movement how the British Establishment works, and he will doubtless be remembered more for his diaries and for the audacious political innovation which they represented than for any of his individual political achievements. Barbara Castle does not fail to make a no less principled defence of her conduct in following in Dick's footsteps.

How the Crossman version may compare with the Castle version in terms of historic accuracy is another fascinating question which must be left aside for the moment. The years covered by the Castle version do not yet overlap with the Crossman years, and we must await the late 1980s or the early 1990s, I suppose, for the comparison between the two to become the subject of learned theses undertaken by American university professors. And, please, don't let anyone in the meantime be misled by a few odd, overlapping extracts in the Sunday papers. They offer, compared with the complete diaries in the full massive volumes, ridiculous, misleading, infantile snippets, serving no reputable educational purpose whatever. Television, said Noel Coward, was for appearing on and not for watching. Much the same applies to the serial methods operated by the posh newspapers. They supply pensions for politicians and not much else. Barbara's diary, the whole of it, whatever else it is or is not, is a human document, hopelessly absorbing at least to her fellow participants in the affair, and one which mounts to a climax of passionate intensity – and which Sunday sensationalism has wretchedly dissipated.

But back to the third man, mentioned above, and let Barbara introduce him. Wedgie 'sits very pontifically these days, looking as though he has access to some secret and superior wisdom. He also scribbles copious notes and I am convinced he is keeping a detailed diary.' And so he was, most of us assumed, and why not? Wedgie, long before he became Tony Benn, was the most fervent and consistent champion of open government. Considering the venomous treatment which he has received from much of the press, he has some right to protect himself, and a diary offers one suit of armour. Moreover, he may be excused for imagining that he might require some protection from his fellow diarists. Will Tony have the last word on, say, the IMF Cabinet controversies of 1976, or the five per cent pay dispute of 1979? He has already had a few first words on these and kindred topics. However, in my view, old-fashioned though I know it to be, the debate should take the form of a good, rousing, polemical argument. The attempt to set diary against diary, or rather to allow the diary to be elevated to such a pedestal as the arbiter of final truth, is doomed to spread frustration and endless misapprehension. But let us take a few glances at the theme, citing Barbara's diary for the purpose.

Barbara Castle was a first-class Cabinet Minister and, over and above that – a much rarer bird – a first-class *Socialist* Cabinet

Minister. No one who sat in the Cabinet through the years covered by this book would ever question that judgement. She had diligence, persistence, resilience, courage, a grasp of Socialist principle, a determination to persuade and to succeed – yes, the infinite capacity for taking pains which perhaps in the modern political world more than any other arena does constitute something like genius. She knew what she wanted to achieve – what the party manifesto committed her to achieve in the vast fields of health and social security – and in two splendid, concentrated years, against the odds, she brought her plans to fulfilment or laid the foundations for their fulfilment. And the diary helps to illustrate, unforgettably, how she did it. She mobilised her department on her side; her fellow Ministers, her political advisers (no one ever had better ones), above all, the much-maligned civil servants. No nonsense from her, just as there was never any from Aneurin Bevan, about Civil Service sabotage! She knows and shows how the modern Civil Service can be made to work; how indeed it can be transformed into the most priceless asset for any reforming Socialist Minister; and how imbecile it would be if we ever allowed this essential instrument to be cast aside.

However, this review is not intended to be about Barbara the Minister; it is about Barbara the reporter, the observer, the diarist, indeed Barbara the Recording Angel who, in her mighty climax, pronounces death and damnation on Jim Callaghan and all his works and almost all his associates. Once Barbara withdraws her heroic finger from the dyke, the monetarist floods spread their devastation on every hand. Once Barbara departs from the scene, *Götterdammerung* descends. True, Tony Benn's contradictory claim, I guess, will be that the floods had swamped the land much earlier, and, indeed, his unheeded warnings often gave the impression that they were scarcely offered with the hope of persuading anyone; they were more there for the record from the start, which is another purpose diaries may serve. True also, I suspect again, when the Crossman and Castle periods of the earlier administration can be properly contrasted, they will expose sharply contesting judgements even about elementary facts and recollections. Both Dick and Barbara are honest reporters; the whole exercise would be utterly pointless otherwise. Barbara may seek to explain such discrepancies with the claim that she knew shorthand and Dick did not. But Dick had the more powerful, swift-moving mind; it ticked over like a Rolls Royce engine, and that factor might weigh in the balance against Barbara's incomparable assiduity. And Tony Benn's version, like theirs, will bear the stamp of his own ideas and idiosyncrasies. The more the comparisons are made, the more, I believe, it will be recognised that busy, over-worked, self-centred, ambitious Cabinet Ministers are not the most dependable observers. It is not their trade. Barbara's diary tells us much about Barbara, but nothing like so much as it pretentiously claims about the outside, objective world.

According to the diary, Barbara frequently appeared as the best Minister at Harold Wilson's disposal, sometimes as Joan of Arc facing (and confounding) her inquisitors, sometimes almost as a new Queen Elizabeth at Tilbury, rousing the troops and her countrymen as no one else could do. Of course, memory plays tricks, but my feeling is that it was not always quite like that, and, writing as one of her Cabinet colleagues who survives comparatively well beneath the deluge, it must be said that not only individual incidents but pretty well the whole picture is out of focus, thanks to the individual angle from which everything is necessarily seen. The great diarists must be snappers-up of unconsidered trifles; they must not in the next breath try and parade themselves as purveyors of the eternal verities. They must have some sense of their own insignificance, and Barbara's best friend never claimed she had that.

She tells, for example, in prodigious detail, the story of her own valiant struggle against all comers, headed by Harold Wilson, to secure the translation into law of the party's commitment about hospital pay-beds. Truly it was a magnificent, sustained exertion on Barbara's part; but she shows not the slightest inkling or imaginative recognition that many of her Cabinet colleagues were engaged in struggles no less valiant against vested interests no less resolute than the doctors. Indeed several of these campaigns were only brought to a conclusion – and this mere thought disrupts Barbara's demonology altogether – in the Callaghan era: for example, Eric Varley's fight against the shipbuilding employers, Shirley Williams's fight to execute the party's programme on comprehensive schools, the abolition of the tied cottage (quite an ancient Socialist aim), the enactment of Barbara's own child benefit scheme, the persistent, extensive exertion (more to be appreciated now perhaps than ever

To Jill—
my good feminist
friend—
Barbara Castle

before) to ward off and beat back the effects of the world recession on British industry and employment. All this, and much more, was done against odds quite as heavy as any Barbara had to contend with, and sometimes it was done with the connivance, at least, or even the open support, of the same Treasury which Barbara portrays as the root of all anti-Socialist evil. It was not quite like that either. Of course, on a whole series of occasions, both when Barbara was in the Cabinet no less than when she was out of it, more imaginative, more audacious, more Socialist initiatives should have been embarked upon. We may and must argue about what they should have been and could have been.

One such initiative and one such moment was in the winter of 1974, just after the electoral victory, when we had the chance, as we believed at the Department of Employment, to launch the only kind of incomes policy which could have worked: a much fairer, more egalitarian policy than anything subsequently attempted, starting at the top, and one which would have given us the chance to kill or at least contain the raging inflation which so nearly overwhelmed us then and returned to overwhelm us in the end. But Barbara, even though she was pretty well our best ally, had other distractions at that precise moment, as her diary indicates. (She even persuaded herself, for a moment, heaven save us, that the new lavish contract for the doctors which she was busy negotiating was a great stride forward on the Socialist road!)

The failure to seize the moment then was not due, as Left-wing mythology likes to suggest, to the fact that the mandarins at the Treasury had a settled policy which they had resolved to rivet on the necks of Labour Ministers; they were indeed, as far as I could see, as much baffled as anyone else by the world-wide slump and its terrifying consequences. It was much more that the policies which the party had devised were insufficiently apt and immediately applicable and in a sense, too, insufficiently far-reaching. So, for a while we hesitated and improvised; and yet the policies shaped by that semi-Socialist Government – devised, for example, to keep us acting in concert with the trade union movement – were much more attuned to the world situation and the nation's needs than anything we have seen since May 1979, and will become relevant again, no doubt in a drastically remodelled form, when next Labour Ministers enter Downing Street.

But Barbara's diary tells a different tale, points a different moral, offers a less subtle judgement. So much the worse for diaries, and not only Barbara's. They purport to tell all, and don't. They present supposedly considered verdicts, which in fact are perpetually dis-arranged by the obtruding ego. It is the rusted nail so near the compass which can wreck the argosy.

Perhaps Nye was right, as he so often was on these personal-cum-political questions. He had a passion for protecting his own privacy, and of course was no less eager to protect that of others. He believed that public men must have private thoughts and the means of moulding them in the company of their friends and comrades. The notion that serious politicians should be willing to expose to public gaze (and the gaze of the political enemy and the Tory press) all their interchanges between one another, every nuance of opinion, every tentative tactical consideration, would have been regarded by him, yes, as *obscene*. Of course, the public has the right to know what are the considered thoughts and propositions of their politicians, but politicians have the duty as well as the right to think, and to secure the circumstances which make that thought possible. The balance between the requirements of open government and the duty of individual thought is not so easy to establish as may be supposed.

Meantime, let us ponder the question: when a new set of Labour Ministers enter No 10, as I trust they soon will, are they all to keep diaries? It will add a new terror to political life. Or should they not leave this task to the historians who may be better qualified, especially if they possess the combined wisdom and scruple not to wrench from diaries the gossip which has already been wrenched from its original context. King Alfred – thanks to the power of the diaries or gossip-mongers – has had the misfortune never to be able to escape from the story of the burnt cakes. But, according to the marvellously popular tradition disinterred by modern scholarship, he was a real champion of the people, of incipient Anglo-Saxon democracy against the invading Norman tyrants. It is a much better story in the end.

Postscript:

Barbara Castle herself made no comment to me on this piece – not until some four years later when her next batch of diaries (*The*

*Castle Diaries 1964–70)* was just about to appear, in the autumn of 1984. The sequel was properly indicated, I trust, in this postscript to that first volume.

Barbara Castle urged me *not* to review this book: a strange request, it may be thought, since she and I are old political associates and personal friends, and I have never been reticent in expressing my admiration for her splendid Ministerial accomplishments. It is indeed fifty years ago since we first became acquainted and spent many happy hours together, reading from the works of Beatrice Webb or Karl Marx, and engaging in a whole gamut of even more joyous pursuits. I knew her better, I thought, I had certainly known her longer, than any of the others lucky enough to sit round the same Cabinet table. So why that waspish note of warning in her voice, which I also knew so well?

I recalled at once that I had written a review of an earlier volume of her diaries, covering the later years 1974–6, when we had in fact been members of the same Cabinet. It was during this second term of Barbara's membership of the Cabinet that I had witnessed at first hand how effective and formidable a Minister she could be. She truly did know how to use the Civil Service machine for Socialist purposes; a rare gift, alas.

During the first period of her Cabinet membership, covered by this volume, I had watched the scene only from a distance, from the back benches. So I was in a sense better qualified to review that earlier volume than this one. Yet she warned me off the course, in her most frigid tone.

Having already agreed to review this volume for the *Ham & High*, what was a scrupulous, incurable, indigent reviewer to do? I resolved to read it, or at any rate most of its monumental 817 pages, without even a glance back to my own seemingly offensive comments of a few years ago, and with only a few side-glances at other reviewers of the later volume who may be regarded as experts. I quote two, neither of whom were exactly Barbara Castle fans but each of whom pays a tribute of the highest quality to her as both diarist and politician. Roy Jenkins, who was a leading member of that Cabinet, gave her the fullest marks for accuracy and honesty, and specifically acquitted her of any charge of telling the story in a manner to protect herself or her friends. High praise indeed.

Hugo Young, writing in the *Guardian*, was, if possible, even more precise in his encomium. He, by the way, had some right to speak on such matters. When he was still employed by the *Sunday Times* (before the Murdoch massacres) he played a leading part in securing the publication of the Crossman diaries, without which the Castle diaries or large chunks of them would never have seen the light of day in this century. Hugo Young's verdict was: 'We should be glad Mrs Castle set this record down. It's the real stuff: funny, serious, hair-raising.' And, believe me, there was no hint of mockery intended here. By the real stuff, Hugo Young meant the real stuff of modern politics, helping also to fulfil a purpose which Barbara sets out in her own Preface: 'Eventually I hope,' she says, 'to produce an analysis of the Labour Party's role, its evolution and its future. I am firmly convinced that the starting-point must be to set down what actually happened during a period of Labour Government.' Barbara's considered judgement on the Party's past and future will, I would expect, be more worth reading than anybody else's. She has, after all, among Socialists in this country, had more modern experience as a practical politician, *retaining her Socialist faith*, than anyone else. The italics are justified. It is something no one – not even Jim Callaghan, the villain of this volume – could take from her.

So what about these diaries, on Barbara's own tests or claims? I read page after page with avidity, delight and instruction. Of course, I suppose those who know the characters (even if we were watching their antics from afar, as I was, in those years) may take a special interest in their feats and contortions, but anyone with an interest in Political Man or, more assuredly still, Political Woman, must be absorbed.

Put in your finger almost anywhere and you can pull out a plum. A minor row, it seems, blew up when some PPSs (Parliamentary Private Secretary; including Barbara's) voted against the Government: 'I said sweetly that I thought Ministers should be given clear guidance as to what PPSs could and could not do. When, as Stafford Cripps's PPS in 1945, I had voted against the Government on the American loan, he had merely looked a little sad and said of course he would not expect me to resign. When I had voted against the Government three times he had merely asked me not to make a habit of it. (Burke Trend smiled his wintry smile at this.) George [Brown] chipped in to say cheerily that when he had voted against the 1945 Labour Government several times and led a campaign to depose the Party Leader, he had been made a Minister. Harold was not amused and said things were very different then, with a hundred majority. PPSs are to be made to toe the line or get out.'

Yes, page after page I read, and often, as quoted above, the minor events crowd out the major ones. No harm in that either; such is the nature of all good diaries, scrupulous or unscrupulous. They must be practical-minded, concrete, illustrating the scene with sharp, minute detail. Barbara does that all right. She is truly a *very* good diarist. Not quite a Pepys or a Boswell or a Goncourt; but that's not her fault. Politics, for diary purposes, has nothing like the appeal of sex. Moreover, for some reason not immediately evident, distance lent to the view not only enchantment but an outward appearance of far greater authenticity and objectivity. Could that be true?

Yet, before I allow myself to be carried away completely, let me offer another glance of Barbara on holiday with another of the great Labour Cabinet diarists, Dick Crossman, just at the moment when Barbara was introducing her famous or infamous *In Place of Strife* document on the trade unions which provoked such a rumpus and so nearly wrecked that Wilson Government, even with its comfortable eighty or more odd majority. (How delicious, by the way, that majority does look to a later Labour Cabinet which had to make do with one or two or none at all. It does make a difference, and yet that later Cabinet had a much better Socialist record. But that's all by the way too.) I offer these few paragraphs, partly for the true taste they give of Barbara's most appetising, steaming dishes, but also with a malevolent purpose, hereafter to be revealed:

'Inevitably, we became aggressive and Dick and I were soon in a violent political argument. He was in one of his most *Götterdammerung* moods, foreseeing disaster facing the Party as a result of the IR Bill: the PLP in revolt and the Party smashed in the Election: another 1931 again. I told him the Party need not split. My own credibility was at stake but I could resign quietly, as could others like Roy [Jenkins] who were equally committed. Perhaps even Harold (though I carefully did *not* mention my conversation with him). "Then we really *are* in a 1931 situation," said Dick dramatically. "There will be two sets of candidates: one backed by the trade unions and Transport House and the other not. You and Harold have faced us with this without consulting us." (Only he doesn't speak coherently like this: it comes out in a rush and if he is challenged he interrupts after the first two or three words, then breaks off and charges off on an entirely different tack. For a so-called stimulator of argument, he is a great bludgeoner.) I retorted that Cabinet had been free to make up its own mind, and had done so: the only person who had been at risk was myself, for they had been free to repudiate me. And I reminded him that it was *he* who was responsible for our facing a crisis at this particular moment. *I* had never been in favour of rushing an interim Bill. And I taunted him. "Thank God I've kept a diary, Dick, so there will be someone to challenge the Crossman version of history. And, by heavens, I will!"'

Almost up to this point, as the honest reader will acknowledge, I had allowed myself to be swept along by Barbara's persuasive powers. *This is how it was. This is what did happen. This is the true history. Barbara's method is vindicated.* These were my semi-conscious conclusions, as others also may find.

And yet, what about Dick's version of history, so much derided by Barbara in these and other episodes? Is he to be pushed aside as a biased, interested, self-interested recorder of the scene? No one who knew him, including Barbara, would tolerate the charge for a moment. Dick Crossman's restless, reckless intellectual integrity was one of his most striking characteristics. He was always probing for new truths or new approaches to old ones. He would change his opinions of people and politics, in real life or his diary, seemingly with no regard whatever for the effect on his own reputation. Hence one explanation at least for the nickname, Dick Double-Crossman. In obedience to new discoveries he would change his chosen course so much quicker than his slow-footed, slow-witted comrades. It made for a lively life, and even livelier diaries. But, as Pontius Pilate is tediously alleged to have mentioned, what is truth? What really happened? We should all like to know, especially if, as both Barbara and Dick were so well qualified to do, the knowledge is to be used as the basis on which to write political treatises to guide us towards our future, Socialist or non-Socialist.

Diaries of different calibre offer varying degrees of delight and instruction, but even the best of them, those compiled with the most honest intentions, like Barbara Castle's and Dick Crossman's, must be treated with strict circumspection. It is still true: they purport to tell all, and don't, and can't. Some egos are larger than others; but that's not the main point. There's a case for politicians keeping diaries, *and a case against*, particularly if those diaries claim to probe into the real secret places where politicians make up their minds.

So I still believe that the Aneurin Bevan verdict on the diarists and their claims, explicit or implicit, to determine historical judgements is correct; but correct or incorrect, we have no assurance that so puritan a view will prevail. Some inscrutable Providence has bestowed his or her blessing on the diarists and no power whatsoever can alter the decree.

# Hugh Gaitskell

It was a battle between us for power; he [Bevan]
knew it, and so did I.

                              Hugh Gaitskell


Now in late 1962, as *The Times* political
correspondent put it, he was coming to terms with
the Labour Party . . .

                              Philip Williams


*Hugh Gaitskell*, by Philip M. Williams, published
by Jonathan Cape in October 1979, was the official
life.

Lloyd George said of Baldwin that he had a wonderful capacity to stumble on the truth and then pick himself up as if nothing had happened. It has been left to Philip Williams of Nuffield College, Oxford, in his magisterial and monumental biography of Hugh Gaitskell (both adjectives are needed if the proper sense of weight is to be purveyed) to raise this talent to the level of a new literary form. Bright, unexpected treasures are to be found everywhere in this vast, rich but still easily digestible pudding of a book. For instance, I pluck from page 368: 'Bowra's friend Mrs Ian Fleming drily supposed that "if we have to have a Labour Party it is as well that you should lead it".' Such flashes of recorded wit from a high Tory hostess cast rays of illumination before and after, but the biographer rarely stops to scrutinise these glowing subtleties.

However, before seeking to repair a few such omissions, let the tribute to the book itself be made in unqualified terms. Apart from offering a huge conglomeration of evidence freshly and meticulously presented, the biographer succeeds also in making his hero speak and live. The combined intelligence, honesty and courage of the man shine again; no one after this will ever be able to strip those qualities from him. Moreover, the means by which this end is achieved are themselves remarkable. Michelet said that, to appreciate the full drama of history, we must know not only what happened on Bastille Day, the first 14 July, but what happened too, all over Paris, on the night of 13 July.

Even on this high test, Mr Williams's book must be judged a success. It is in the months leading up to his major initiatives that the real Hugh Gaitskell must be revealed or unmasked. Mr Williams makes full use of the diaries of the time, some of them hitherto unpublished – Gaitskell's own surprisingly elaborate documents, but, even more notably, the Crossman diaries of the period. Without that last particular contribution, most copiously exploited, I doubt whether the author would have been able to meet the

Michelet requirement. And then, it must never be forgotten, one principal figure on this particular stage, indeed the leading villain, Aneurin Bevan, kept no diary, and would have thought it scandalous or demeaning to do so, and would have thrown back his head in furious disgust at many of the entries here recorded. But more of that in a moment.

First let me offer a few examples of the biographer's Baldwinesque proclivities; their significance is that they go far to justify the judgements which Aneurin Bevan himself or his followers were making at the time. For the charge against Gaitskell throughout the years of controversy was not that he lacked honesty or a fine intellect or courage; all his critics came to acknowledge those qualities, even if they did not appreciate the scale of them. The charge was that he lacked the imaginative sympathy to understand the Labour movement which he aspired to lead, and that he was constantly, almost congenitally, seeking to guide it into alien channels; and hence one potent cause of the Labour Party crises and convulsions which first pushed the Labour Government out of office in 1951 and helped to prevent any full recovery in the rest of Gaitskell's lifetime.

Take a glance, for example, at one sentence included in Mr Williams's verdict on that 1951 'Health Service' crisis which forced (quite unnecessarily, according to Mr Williams) Aneurin Bevan's resignation: 'Certainly Gaitskell was very stubborn about health charges, thinking them right and not just a sad necessity; his Treasury advisers would have been quite content to raise the money differently.' Indeed: here, as often in reading these pages, I advise what the film-makers call a double take – read it carefully again and consider the implications. If at the time some Bevanite journal, say *Tribune*, had published such an accusation, it would have been utterly condemned for attributing unworthy motives or spreading shameful lies. Now combine that admission with the reference to an explosion at the height of the crisis, by Gaitskell to Dalton: 'Nye's influence was very much exaggerated. If we didn't stand up to him, Nye would do to our party what L.G. had done to the Liberals. It would, he thought, do us good in the country to make a stand on this.' There (in a passage suppressed in Dalton's published diaries and not fully disinterred by Mr Williams) is a hint of what some suspected at the time: that Gaitskell had no inkling of what would be entailed in a breach with Bevan over the Labour Government's greatest achievement, the National Health Service.

Mr Williams immediately adds the words: 'But that intemperate mood soon passed.' Readers must judge for themselves whether that claim can be upheld. Certainly the intemperate judgement of Gaitskell on Bevan did not pass for several years. He could consign to his diary or unloose upon his coterie of the moment comparisons not only with Lloyd George, the party wrecker, but with a Hitler incapable of controlling his emotions. Sometimes Gaitskell refers self-mockingly to his immaculate Wykehamist manners; they did not prevent him from stooping, in the case of Nye, to judgements of ineffable imbecility.

Turn now to the denouement of another crisis, to the vain, inglorious effort of the Gaitskellites in 1954 to expel Nye from the party altogether. Here it is necessary to remind readers of the modern age (and Mr Williams himself, since he takes no account of it) that it was always leaders on the Right of the party who wanted to expel people on the Left, and never the other way round. That fact has always to be remembered in discussing Labour Party quarrels, if such words as 'liberal' and 'tolerant' are not to be misapplied.

*Tribune* and the Left were naturally critical of the way Gaitskell had acted and were much lambasted for saying so. How much more ferocious still their views might have been if they had had access to Gaitskell's own final diary entry on the affair: 'Most of my friends think I was very foolish to allow myself to be carried on by the "right wing", with the inevitable result that the Bevanites "framed" me as the "Chief Prosecutor" . . . I always find it difficult to behave in these matters in the subtle way which my own friends seem to expect. I don't see how one can have strong loyalties with people like George Brown (*sic*) and Alf Robens (*sic*), not to speak of the TU leaders, and continually refuse to do any of the dirty work for them and with them . . .' (*sic* again: all the *sics* are the reviewer's, not the diarist's or the biographer's).

The ramifications of this passage, for the whole postwar history of the Labour movement, are so wondrous and manifold that it would be tempting to devote a whole thesis to it, but here I just ask one question: how did these ultra-loyalists of the Right ever imagine they were entitled to practise unspecified dirty work against the

disloyal Left, and why should not a liberal, level-headed social-democratic academic probe a little more closely into the issues of principle involved? Gaitskell, he concurs, had used 'mistaken tactics in a vain effort to obtain a dubious objective'. True enough, but the conclusion is not sufficiently ambitious. If Gaitskell had succeeded in that particular exercise, Aneurin Bevan would have been driven out of the Labour Party and, maybe, out of politics altogether, and the whole Labour movement would have been shattered and shamed in the process. It was no small affair.

Gaitskell had learned his lesson; so Mr Williams implies. But had he? Nothing so ineffectual as the great expulsion fiasco was ever attempted again; but there were other episodes which revealed comparable failures in his imaginative faculty. Having established his leadership so brilliantly and bravely in the Suez crisis, having received from Aneurin Bevan a backing more magnanimous than anything he was entitled to expect, having been justly acclaimed in the election of 1959, despite the bitter defeat, how fatal must have been the infirmity in Gaitskell's political leadership which plunged him and the party, for no purpose whatever, into the Clause IV controversy? It was, indeed, as is now revealed, even more inexcusable than we suspected at the time. Most of his most devoted associates saw the fatuity of it: but pride and obstinacy and pedantry drove him (him *and* his party) on, almost over the edge of the precipice.

True, that same obstinacy changed to courage in the great nuclear weapons debate where the stakes were infinitely greater and his case incomparably stronger, but there, too, as both Frank Cousins and George Brown from different ends of the political spectrum could testify, the pedantry still played its part. A pedant is one who cannot tell the difference between small matters and large ones, small issues and great ones; its mark is a stunted imagination, and it was truly the gulf between them in this respect which made the sympathy between Gaitskell and Bevan so imperfect and unsustainable.

During the 1950s, when the careers and temperaments and outlooks of the two men clashed – mostly in the early years, but in effect through the whole decade – Gaitskell's supreme resolve was to fortify the Anglo–American alliance in the face of the suspected Soviet will to aggression, and Mr Williams has no difficulty in showing with what diligence and dedication he pursued his aim. Yet that purpose accorded with the current overwhelming, overpowering official wisdom on both sides of the Atlantic, in Washington and Whitehall, and in the first two years of the decade that took the form of predicting imminent, certain Soviet aggression in Europe. But Aneurin Bevan would never make obeisance before this orthodoxy, and both in government and out of it he insisted on delivering his own subtler, more imaginative and, as it proved, more valid set of prophecies. Mr Williams rarely does justice to this strand in Bevan's nature, and indeed at times seems to suggest that the full Cold War doctrine of the early 1950s must be upheld in the letter and the spirit and in every now-forgotten particular. No doubt that approach is necessary to vindicate the Gaitskellite attitudes of those years but historians, even biographers, writing so long after the death of their heroes, should assume a greater latitude.

But that is not Mr Williams's way; he is, first and foremost, a dealer in facts; facts, facts and still more facts. Nothing said here is intended to detract from the view expressed earlier about the calibre of this book, but it must be added that his own biographical method and perhaps that of the whole new modern trend in biographical writing – shall we call it the Nuffield school, in honour of the college and not its patron? – relies on the assembly of facts in a manner which may soon lead, if it has not led already, to palpable absurdity. Never, I would guess, in the whole field of biographical writing have so many facts been gathered together in one volume, at least never so many of those facts which may be denoted by quotation marks as extracts from diaries.

Look up where the extracts come from, however, among these vast networks of footnotes – readers are advised to brush up their Snakes and Ladders in advance and they will slip into the new game more simply – and it may be discovered that some vital fact derives from what Hugh Dalton allegedly whispered to another of the clique following a confidential message from Desmond Donnelly, the arch-informer of the Parliamentary Labour Party. Such is the raw material not of modern history but of modern historians; to what eternal mockery or infamy would, say, Gibbon or Macaulay have assigned these treacherous tittle-tattling tale-bearers? Nothing like enough is done by the scholars of the Nuffield school to discriminate between the diarists, and, indeed, between the differing suppositions of the same diarists.

And what must be the fate of the politicians who keep no diary at all? Aneurin Bevan was one, and in the hands of the Nuffield school his reputation is thereby irremediably damned. However, I recall that he himself left a prophylactic phrase to guide us. Not merely did he scorn politicians' diaries and the politicians who had time or patience to keep them; he was also magnificently scornful about those who believed in what he called the democracy of facts, those for whom all facts were equal. Mostly he had in mind politicians who relied too faithfully on the ever-equal facts supplied for speeches by their civil servants; but he would doubtless have been ready to embrace in the same category historians or biographers who allowed their trade to be similarly debased. The facts never are equal, and can never be made so, even by the most proficient of the Nuffield school as I can well believe Mr Williams to be.

# *Brother George* (I)

The most famous of all speeches ever made by any of your distinguished predecessors was that made by Speaker Lenthall on the most famous of occasions when the rights of the House were protected. All right hon and hon Members know the speech. Speaker Lenthall said: 'May it please Your Majesty, I have neither eyes to see, nor tongue to speak in this place, but as the House is pleased to direct me, whose servant I am here.'

That, I am sure, is what you, Mr Speaker, would have said on that occasion if you had been in charge. It is a good lesson for all susequent Speakers. I shall not press the comparison too strongly because Speaker Lenthall, despite his great service to the House and country on that occasion, was subsequently involved in financial dealings that led to an investigation. He wavered in his party allegiance, although I am not sure in which direction. He ended up in Oliver Cromwell's House of Lords. I do not know whether any such fate is to befall you, Mr Speaker.

My tribute to the retiring Speaker,
12 May 1983

*George Thomas, Mr Speaker*, The Memoirs of The Viscount Tonypandy, were published by Century Publications in February 1985.

When Viscount Tonypandy felt a sudden sense of relief from his shackles as Speaker of the House of Commons and let loose a series of attacks against ex-Premier James Callaghan and a few others, it was Jim, so much less famed for his Christian charity than George, who turned the other cheek. His letter to *The Times* of 26 February 1985, was a model of epistolary restraint and piety. He referred to a *Times* editorial which had been critical of the ex-Speaker, but he put behind him all temptation to join the counter-attack. 'Sir,' he wrote, 'Today's editorial, "Order! Order!", about Viscount Tonypandy's autobiography speaks of the "mutual antipathy" between him and me. This statement is untrue and I should be sorry if such an impression gained currency. When the House of Commons honoured Mr Speaker's retirement nearly two years ago I then spoke as "one old friend to another". That was my genuine feeling and until Lord Tonypandy's memoirs appeared last week I had every reason to believe that the feeling was mutual. I am deeply sorry to find it is not.'

Many Labour MPs, especially those from Wales, had long supposed that a slight strain of rivalry prevailed between the two members for the great city of Cardiff, who had entered Parliament together in 1945 and had been uniquely placed thereafter to note the development of each other's ambitions and methods of political operation. MPs from the same party who represent the same town or city and must have constant dealings with the same single municipal authority can never find it easy not to tread on each other's corns, not to trespass on each other's preserve. For such partnerships to work perfectly, both must be saints, and in the Cardiff case there was only one conceivable claimant for that title. Each was known to have different, preferred ways of performing their duties in Parliament, each attached himself, more or less firmly (and in each case, now one comes to think of it, the attachment was never firm in any sense whatever) to different sections of the Party. Of course, there were bound to be jolts and jars and imperfect sympathies between two such highly intelligent political animals strapped together to run a near-forty-year-old three-legged race. Some of us who represented the valley towns – as I did for about half the time span involved – had a special vantage-post for watching the Cardiff political scene. We knew about these mild personal sensibilities; we suspected nothing more.

Few can have been prepared for the sustained bilious explosion of personal feeling against Jim Callaghan which George Thomas let loose in his *George Thomas, Mr Speaker*, and in which Jim figured almost as prominently, as the index shows, as any other politician. Most of the references are hostile, right from the moment of their sharing of the common victory in 1945, when Jim is alleged to have revealed, much to George's disgust, his naked personal ambition, right up to a last entry when Jim – talking quite playfully, others might suppose – is accused of having depreciated the award of George's Viscountcy in the presence of a common Cardiff friend, Sir Julian Hodge. Most of these incidents are too petty and repellent (one or the other, and sometimes both together) even to be recalled. They are cited here to illustrate the nature of George's recollections and those he himself has selected as being especially noteworthy. However, there was one occasion which George does faithfully record and which, one would have thought, would have been sufficient by itself to expunge plenty of others, both before and after. When George was elected Speaker on Selwyn Lloyd's retirement from the office in February 1976, Jim left his seat on the Government front bench to sit alongside him. He said: 'We sat next to each other on our first day in this House. This is your last day on these benches so I will sit next to you again.' George adds the words: 'I was deeply touched by this gesture of friendship.' And truly touched he doubtless was at that emotional moment in his life. For the full repayment of the debt we had to wait for the memoirs in February 1985.

My own interest in *George Thomas, Mr Speaker* has no such sentimental origins or overtones. I first came across them when the *Sunday Times* published the first extracts in February 1985. I was so staggered by their contents that without any hestiation or consultation with anybody, Jim Callaghan or anyone else, I wrote immediately to George in the terms I shall soon record.

However, it is necessary first of all perhaps, in the light of the controversy which ensued, to explain why I was so shocked; indeed, more amazed even than offended. I did not believe that any Speaker of the House of Commons would do what George Thomas had done. I do not exactly add the words, *least of all George*: that would hardly be fair to other Speakers, but it certainly never crossed my mind that George, the immaculate upholder of convention and custom in all other aspects of the Speaker's duties, would be the first to break the most important convention of all.

The proper conduct of the Speaker's duties depends *above all*, it may be insisted, on the confidence which members of all parties have in his good faith. This proposition, I believe, applies more to the Speaker than to any other office-holder in the State, although, heaven knows, it applies to others too, from the Prime Minister and other Ministers downwards. Governments may fall or their strength is undermined when they are exposed as deceivers. ('A known liar,' wrote the great Lord Halifax, some three hundred years ago, 'should be outlawed in a well-ordered government.')

One of the virtues of the House of Commons is the way it has sought to sustain these standards over the generations. But good faith, the right of people to speak freely to one another without their confidences being broken, is one element in this proper conduct of affairs, and applies in the highest degree to the Speaker and his officials. Most MPs discover this truth soon after their arrival in the place; those who have been there longest should know it best.

Every week, every day almost, it might be said, the Speaker and his officials are engaged in confidential discussions with the leaders and spokesmen of the main parties and with individual MPs. Each individual MP soon discovers that his most indispensable friends or guides in the place are the well-versed, well-trained, utterly discreet officers of the House, all of them acting on behalf of the Speaker. He can approach them at almost any time; he can have his view conveyed to the Speaker; he can see the Speaker himself or in the company of those with whom he wishes to act. Of course much of this essential business is conducted through the so-called 'usual channels' of the Whips' Offices, and often the Mongolian hordes on the back benches may deride these necessary transactions, but they too can soon invent their own channels if they find the normal ones functioning inadequately. That channel if they wish can always lead to the Speaker himself. No Speaker in modern days would block them. And of course, I would hope now it hardly needs to be added: the whole of this elaborate structure depends on good faith, *above all*, yes, on the good faith of the Speaker. I was indeed astonished when George Thomas seemed to have broken this simple rule. So I wrote to him at once as follows:

> I am surprised to read, in the *Sunday Times*, extracts from a book of yours in which you report confidential conversations and exchanges which took place when you were Speaker. I cannot see how this can assist the present Speaker or future Speakers who may wish to have similar confidential conversations. It seems to me that their publication is a breach of trust and can only do injury to Parliament.
>
> I am surprised also – although this is a lesser matter – since, according to my recollections, some of your reports give a highly biased account of events. I shall naturally read the whole book before judging whether such a conclusion is justified. But, as far as I can see, nothing can justify your action which has led to my criticism in the first paragraph.

A few days later I got his reply:

> Thank you for your letter.
>
> The whole purpose of me writing this book is because, like you, I am a believer in open government. I believe that the nation has a right to know that the most difficult part of the Speaker's job is by no means sitting in the Chair presiding over debates, but rather the pressures to which he is subject behind the scenes.
>
> The intention of the book is to make life easier in this regard, both for my successor and for all subsequent Speakers.
>
> I hope that when you have read the book in its entirety that you will feel better, because I have endeavoured to write a truthful, but none the less benign book.
>
> You will know as well as anyone that I have left unsaid a great deal that I might well have included.

To which I replied in turn:

> I am sorry you have not attempted to deal with the main point of my letter – the breach of faith involved in reporting confidential conversations. I do not for a moment imagine that the present Speaker regards your precedent as an assistance to him: indeed, I imagine that he takes the exact opposite view.
>
> I will naturally read the whole of your book when it comes out. I

doubt very much whether it will change my view about the extracts which have already appeared and I will hold myself free to express my views in public when the book appears.

Even before the book was published, the controversy broke out, as it quite properly should, on a topic of such importance. *The Times* joined the rebukes to the Speaker, and he replied to *The Times*. Controversy was raging at that time about the way the Attorney-General had taken proceedings against Clive Ponting, a civil servant who had revealed not matters of security but other matters covered by the Official Secrets Act. I suggested to *The Times* Political Correspondent in the House of Commons that 'George might be covered by the Official Secrets Act. There's a better case against him than against Ponting. I am glad to see that the present Speaker is doing his best to restore the necessary confidential authority of his office.' This last was a reference to a reply given by the new Speaker, Mr Speaker Weatherill, to a questioner in the House of Commons. He had taken an early opportunity to make it clear that he was not writing any memoirs. So far from George's action having assisted his successors, it was evident that, if they followed his practice, the conduct of the Speaker's office would become impossible. Every MP with whom I spoke, every official or ex-official of the House, concurred with that view.

But the correspondence and the controversy rumbled on. I had added to my original letter of 4 March:

On the question of the conduct of the Speaker, not much more needs to be added. If the Speaker cannot have confidential conversations, he cannot do his job properly. I am glad to see that the present Speaker recognises this even if Viscount Tonypandy no longer does.

This is the question of major importance. However, perhaps you will permit me to add that page after page in Viscount Tonypandy's book is grotesquely misleading in the impression it seeks to give, and this is a view that has been expressed to me by several Members of Parliament who have now had a chance of reading the passages which refer to themselves.

I am accused by some of your correspondents of having attempted to 'bully' the Speaker. If I ever did so — and I deny the charge absolutely — it would have been for Viscount Tonypandy to remonstrate with me at the time. To my recollection, he never did so.

What he usually did was to accept without question the advice given him by his officials. He usually didn't seem to understand that these were matters of argument, and that there were other experts, including previous Clerks to the House of Commons, whose advice was just as good as that which he was always inclined to accept.

George himself replied a few days later:

> Mr Michael Foot's strident letter (4 March) with its unpleasant overtones is typical of the attitude with which I had to deal when I was Speaker. His implicit call for prosecution under the Official Secrets Act and his angry claim that I was too pliable in the hands of my advisers are unworthy of serious reply.
>
> With regard to Mr Foot's main complaint, I have nothing to add to the full rebuttal statement that I made at the Christina Foyle literary luncheon, and which was reported on the front page of your newspaper (28 February).
>
> If your readers really want to understand fully this correspondence, they should read the book as a whole and judge it then.

I replied again at once:

> I suppose it is some mark of progress that Viscount Tonypandy does not attempt to defend the indefensible. But he should still be required to answer the real questions:
>
> Does he think it necessary for the Speaker's job that he should be able to hold confidential conversations with Members of Parliament of all parties? What gives him the right to break those confidences? And why does he suppose that such breaches may not injure the work of present and future Speakers?
>
> He tells us to read his book, but readers will not find the answers there. What they will find is an unexpected streak of malice cutting through the cloying sentimentality. But I must not be tempted to stray from protection of the Speaker's office to book criticism.

And on that same day two others joined the controversy raising major questions of dispute, one Sir Charles Gordon, who had been Clerk to the House of Commons, 1979–83:

> Mr Michael Foot mars his letter on 4 March by its final paragraph.
>
> In the first place, Mr Speaker Thomas did not 'usually . . . accept without question the advice given him by his officials'; *experto crede.*
>
> Secondly, a retired Clerk of the House, not being in possession of all the facts behind a current procedural controversy, is in no position to give advice. I would never now presume to offer it unless asked to do

so either by the Chair or by my successor, in which case I should give it in private; indeed, I should consider it unprofessional to do otherwise.

The other letter was from Mr Richard Moore, Worcester College, Oxford:

I read Michael Foot's letter of 4 March concerning Viscount Tony-pandy's memoirs with a mounting sense of disbelief.

Is this really the same Michael Foot who acted as literary executor for the late Richard Crossman's diaries? A decade ago Michael Foot, and incidentally the *Sunday Times*, were to be heard upholding the right of a former Cabinet minister to reveal 'confidential conversations and exchanges' which had taken place in Cabinet. Are the disclosures by a former Speaker of what went on 'behind the chair' so very different?

Mr Foot argues that unless the confidential nature of the Speaker's business is preserved the latter 'cannot do his job properly'. He may recollect the Attorney-General's argument in the Crossman case that the revelation of Cabinet confidences would prevent the Cabinet from doing *its* job properly.

The *Sunday Times*, obviously, continues to reject this line of argument. Why does Michael Foot appear to have changed his tune?

I replied again, as I was certainly required to do, and I believe my final paragraph did carry widespread support in the House of Commons:

Permit me to reply to two of your correspondents. When Sir Charles Gordon, with all his experience, says that I am wrong to suggest that Mr Speaker Thomas usually accepted without question the advice given him by his officials, I naturally accept his statement. He is certainly an expert on that aspect of the subject.

However, he also adds, most intriguingly, that any later opinion he might form on these disputed topics would be conveyed only privately. I presume he might think that a similar discretion would be advisable for the Speaker himself.

A slightly different view was taken by a previous Clerk, Sir Barnett Cocks. At a moment when one of Mr Speaker Thomas's most contentious rulings was being discussed, he, with all his experience, described that ruling as 'a somewhat astonishing one'. That was what I felt at the time, even before Sir Barnett had ventured to give his views, and why I believed I was fully entitled to make representations, politely and privately, to Mr Speaker Thomas.

I doubt if I can help your other correspondent, Richard Moore, who says that he cannot see the difference between what a Cabinet Minister, fully engaged in party controversies, may properly reveal and what Mr Speaker, who has pledged himself to impartiality and independence, may reveal. I would have thought the distinction easy enough to make.

It is my view – and I believe it is widely shared in the House of Commons – that if Viscount Tonypandy's example of disclosure were to be followed, the independence and authority of the Chair would be undermined. I want to stop that happening.

I quote finally a letter I received from Sir Barnett Cocks, a previous Clerk of the House whose judgement confirmed my view of the matter rather than that of George Thomas:

I am most grateful to you for mentioning my name in your letter dated 8 March in today's *Times* about The Memoirs of Viscount Tony-pandy.

I remember the controversy over the Aircraft and Shipbuilding Industries Bill, in which the Speaker preferred to take his opinion from Robin Maxwell-Hyslop rather than from better informed authorities. It puzzles me that he now claims 'I had to keep to the rules of the House . . .' (pp 147–8 of the Memoirs).

I have in front of me as I write the books written by Lord Tonypandy's immediate predecessors, Lord Selwyn Lloyd and Lord Maybray-King. Neither of these former Speakers departed from the normal practice of respecting private representations by Members.

George Thomas was a very good Speaker. He had to deal with a House of Commons more narrowly poised between the parties than any of modern times, one where each division, each lurch in debate, could count for more than in most assemblies. He was thrown into these tumults at the deep end, yet he kept his head from the start. I tried to express this view properly on behalf of Labour members when we all paid tribute to him on his retirement on 12 May 1983. I spoke of his 'qualities of wit, humour, practical experience, Welsh courtesy and Welsh guile, all in their special quantities'. I made some mention of the way, thanks to the broadcasting of debates, a special flavour had been given to our proceedings, and how 'the bewitching and appeasing lilt of Tonypandy had been heard across the entire country and perhaps across the entire world . . .' And I referred also on that public occasion, I was slightly surprised to discover, to the relations between the two members from Cardiff, when one was Prime Minister and the other was Speaker. 'They gave me, as a naive politician from the valleys, an insight into the way in which Cardiff politics are conducted, which I have never forgotten and never betrayed.' Such was the mood in which most of us, certainly Jim Callaghan and myself, paid our farewell respects to our parliamentary colleague, Mr Speaker Thomas. Neither of us, I'm sure, had an inkling of the lash which Viscount Tonypandy was preparing to lay across our backs. (I use the word lash advisedly; George in his schoolmaster days could be a ferocious whacker; he was nicknamed 'the walking stick').

Here was a different George Thomas from the one most of us had known over the years, the one who loved to be loved and would do almost anything to secure it. *Sioni-bob-ochor*, they would call him in Welsh and in Wales: they knew the type so well. His good nature and comradeship were just a trifle too effusive and often seemingly overflowing in too many directions. That was indeed my experience all through the years when I had special dealings with him as Leader of the House or Leader of the Party. I could remember no occasion when he accused me of belligerence or ill manners towards him or his office. I did know that as Leader of the House I faced a longer period than any post-war Leader with only a majority of one or two or no majority at all. I thought he understood that well enough, and why it was so necessary, for the proper conduct of business and the survival of the government, for us to have prior knowledge of what decisions the Chair might intend to take. Nothing so severe as a critical word seemed to come to his lips naturally, and Jim Callaghan, it seems, during that same period had the same experience. All the more amazing were the charges of turpitude, moral and political, proclaimed in those memoirs.

Jim Callaghan was one chosen victim, but there were several others. I had not known until I read this volume how fierce was his hostility towards those who favoured almost any form of devolution for Wales and how some of this antagonism brushed off on Cledwyn Hughes,* at that time MP for Anglesey, when George was supposed to be serving him as Secretary of State for Wales. Considering how Cledwyn had assisted George, the personal hints here

* Later Lord Cledwyn of Penrhos

are a good deal less than generous. He discusses quite misleadingly the background to the devolution argument. He makes no mention of the utterly abortive plan of Welsh local government reform, modelled on an abortive English plan, giving most power to glorified County Councils which George himself favoured when he was at the Welsh Office and sought to thrust upon us. He even implied – quite monstrously – that Cledwyn showed less sympathy and understanding than George himself after the terrible Aberfan disaster.

The list of offenders is quite a long one. However, it would be false for me to pretend that part of my anger is not aroused by George's direct attacks. He claimed in the memoirs that all my representations, or all the ones that truly mattered, were misjudged or improper. Such belligerent attitudes were so offensive and persistent, so injurious to the conduct of the Speaker's Office, that they required a record or at least a recollection of them to be kept for later publication, as a protection for future Speakers.

Such is the George Thomas case, or rather the Viscount Tonypandy case, against myself. I doubt whether anyone will accept it, and, as I have said, I have no recollection of exchanges between us which would justify such constructions to be placed, nothing indeed which altered my general view of his term as Speaker. What we did discuss on almost all occasions – on the first early occasions concerning the Aircraft and Shipbuilding Bill and its alleged hybridity, but on many other occasions besides – were the fascinating real procedural arguments on which we, the Government, had one legitimate interest and the Opposition had another. On that particular one which provoked such furious scenes the issue was raised by the Opposition at a desperately late moment in the passage of the Bill and in a manner which designedly could have wrecked the Bill altogether. One Clerk of the House, Sir Richard Barlas, took one view. An earlier Clerk of the House, Sir Barnett Cocks, took a different one and a third Clerk, Sir Charles Gordon, took the view that Sir Barnett, having left the Clerkship, should not have given an opinion. So, it seems, there was something to argue about after all.

If the day should come when political leaders or individual MPs cease to believe they can present confidential arguments to the Speaker on such matters – if, to use George Thomas's quite false comparison about open government in other fields, the confidences of the Speaker and his officers may be broken – the office will have lost some of its authority and effectiveness. Some of the processes whereby the Speaker can be helped to reach the right decision will have been blocked. Happily, the Viscount Tonypandy disclosures have already been accepted in the place that matters most – that is, by the new Speaker – not as a pattern to be followed but as an example to deter.

Somewhat lopsidedly, this discussion of Viscount Tonypandy and his memoirs has concentrated on the peculiar controversy which his claims as Speaker provided. Yet the book could be studied as a revelation of the development of his political ideas. Most of us assumed that while his Methodism was certainly the strongest strand in his political character, his sympathies, deriving from his upbringing in the Welsh valleys, were certainly on the Left of the Party. At the outset, we thought he was a near-pacifist. During the Bevanite quarrels, we thought him a near-Bevanite. No one so far as I can recall ever questioned his Socialist allegiance.

However, the memoirs uncover deeper predelictions and animosities. All too often personal whims and pique seem to have played a larger part. The pacifist sympathies are allowed to run into the sand; even a fairly early and ostentatious support of the United Nations is not considered worthy of mention. The boast is made that 'in a way I helped to form' the Campaign for Nuclear Disarmament, but on the next page the suggestion is properly qualified. He is referring to the events of 1954 when the first protests against H-bomb detonations were led by Tony Greenwood, Donald Soper, Fenner Brockway and others, but he cannot recount the incident without casting a quite unworthy slur on Canon Collins – 'Even in the peace movement, there are people who think of themselves first.' As for Aneurin Bevan, almost every reference here is simmeringly resentful. At the time of Bevan's resignation in 1951 George had some exchanges with Jennie Lee which started to introduce him into the seamier side of politics – 'I was beginning to learn that the pursuit of power can be a very unpleasant business.' Jennie as the power-seeker makes this one brief appearance, and, considering the foremost part which Aneurin Bevan played in the politics of those times and the knowledge which any Welsh MP could have of his true mettle, the few scraps and sneers about him which figure in these memoirs leave a sour taste indeed.

However, George could always be gracious when he wished. Lengthy passages and even whole chapters are devoted to grander themes: 'To Wales with a Prince'; how the Queen herself came to Speaker's House to celebrate her Jubilee; how his last favourite, Margaret Thatcher, conducted the brilliant Falklands campaign when the demand came from 'the Opposition in increasingly shrill tones that Britain should return to the United Nations and talk'. A strange verdict indeed, since the official Opposition from beginning to the end insisted that if catastrophe was to be avoided the whole affair must be conducted within the rules and provisions of the Charter of the United Nations. 'Britain,' George concludes, 'would have lost all influence in international affairs if Mrs Thatcher had submitted to the pressures and gone back to the United Nations . . . The Falklands affair reinforced my belief that the British character has not really changed, despite all the troubles that we face with violence and sometimes appallingly selfish behaviour. We are still a tough little race, and now the world knows it.'

At this point, fortunately, the Viscount turns to discuss 'a question of religion' or his new political domicile: 'The continuation of a Second Chamber is essential for the maintenance of democracy in these islands.' But who could ever imagine democracy to be in peril with such a champion in its service?

# *Brother George* (II)

—◁•◯•▷—

He [Ernest Bevin] looked at me, said that he had
never really trusted me, and added, 'And now you
are acting as office boy for that bastard Dalton. I
don't want to see you again.'

From *In My Way*, George Brown's Memoirs,
published by Gollancz in 1970.

When Lord George Brown died at his Cornish home in June 1985 no comets were seen, but it is legitimate to suppose that some disturbance among the heavenly bodies must have occurred. For within a few days came a heavenly leakage or downpour, call it what you will, with the latest information, confirmed in colourful detail, that he had died a Catholic, that the local priest from Falmouth had been ready and prepared to perform the last rites.

None of us atheists or agnostics had any right to complain, for George had never concealed his strong religious convictions. But the Church of England, one might think, had some conceivable ground for irritation. For George had always taken pains to assert not only his strong Christian allegiance but also his Anglican upbringing and affinities. To desert them – just at the moment when it mattered most, or so some might think – and to take steps to ensure that full topical publicity would be accorded to the final conversion, when no decent opportunity for reply would be still available, was an act deserving critical comment. More than any other politician of his time, George Brown was shaped by three institutions: his trade union, his party and his church. He left all three, complaining, at least in the case of the first two, that all the blame rested with these institutions themselves or those in charge of them, and none whatsoever with himself.

Some voices may be raised at once to protest that these are not fitting topics for his fellow politicians to discuss, that George's body and soul should be left in peace. But a moment's thought should be sufficient to remove any such constraints. The manner in which the Roman Catholic Church negotiates with sinners about their admittance into or return to the bosom of their church has always been a matter of interest both to other churches and to mankind at large. A sensitive awareness of what men and women may feel at this moment in their lives is one of the ways in which the religious hold on humanity has been sustained, and it would be curious indeed if those who claim that these are the most important relationships between the church and individuals should complain about any independent investigation into them.

Anyhow, George himself could have no right to object; for he himself, quite gratuitously and offensively, presented a man's religious faith as the truest test of whether he deserved to be trusted as a Labour politician. The claim at first hearing may be thought too palpably absurd to be believed, but the evidence is offered not in what he may have said in the heat of some particular argument but in his own considered verdicts on some of his leading colleagues. (Father Walsh, who offered George spiritual help in those last months, also assures us that they discussed at length 'his relationship with others – with his fellow political brothers'. One wonders whether some of these judgements figured in the discussion.)

Here is George's chief, predominant judgement on Aneurin Bevan. He was, says George, 'a strange man. He had great ability and great ambition. He could do the most contrary things, but you could never call him insincere. He had a burning faith in whatever seemed good to him at the time, but, outside politics, had no personal faith at all.' At this point, or a sentence or two later, George slightly catches his breath as he recalls that his own hero, Ernest Bevin, 'grew up without religious faith'. He did indeed, and, so far as most of us know, never altered his view on these spiritual matters. But George in the very next sentence gracefully offers Ernie Bevin an absolution all his own; he was allowed to have 'acquired faith in such qualities as the dignity of man'. True enough, but that encomium would not have been sufficient to secure the administration of the last rite in Cornwall in 1985, and Ernie Bevin, I would guess, would protest that his acquisition of this faith was no last minute affair; he had had it from his youth. However, Ernest Bevin's faith gave him and his friends 'something they stood by all their lives' whereas, and here the indictment was driven home more finally than ever, 'Aneurin, and certainly his friends, seem to have grown up without faith in anything.'

Those of us who lived much of our whole political lives in the company of Aneurin Bevan and George Brown, and multitudes, I would guess, who watched or participated in these events from a distance, must find it well-nigh impossible to comprehend how an intelligent person like George Brown could reach such a conclusion.

Aneurin Bevan made no profession of any religious faith, but to leap from that proposition to the idea that he had no political faith, that he believed in nothing, is grotesque and, if it reveals anything, exposes in the mind of George Brown a strand of unconscionable intolerance; a religious intolerance, which can be the worst manifestation of the disease.

However, some part of the trouble may be traced to George Brown's general misapprehension about the character of the men and women with whom he had to deal. Some of his judgements were so topsy-turvy, so much in defiance of the common sense view, that the astonishing fact is how long his other qualities enabled him to survive at all. 'The contrast between Bevin and Bevan,' he wrote, just after he discerned to his own discomfort that their religious attitudes were not so dissimilar, 'was fascinating. Ernie always wanted to do things; he wasn't much interested in discussion, he wanted to get things done. Aneurin loved discussion, and except on one or two matters, I don't think he really much minded which way the vote went at the end. Ernie hated flattery – he would bawl your head off if you dared say a kindly word about him in his presence. Aneurin was the most flatterable of men.'

The contrasting portraits are false in every stroke. Of course, Aneurin Bevan loved discussion, but the notion that he cared little for the outcome in deed is a George Brown puerility of astonishing proportions. How did George, I wonder, ever imagine that the National Health Service was established? And the idea that he was easily 'flatterable' – by George Brown, of all people – is, to use again one of Aneurin's favourite words, *obscene*.

Such were a few of the irreverent thoughts which crossed my mind, as the news came through from Cornwall, and a few of them persisted as I read the obituary notices where no mention was made of those who had carried the burden along with him and others and been pushed aside off the road or out of the Party by George himself. Aneurin Bevan and Bertrand Russell were two such specimens, expelled with George's approval or direct incitement, and they presumably are still allocated to some political nether region. But what about Stafford Cripps, a fellow Christian, for sure, a fellow Anglican too, even on George's own acknowledgement, yet he was, in a sense, to change the metaphor, George's first scalp.

It was on a motion moved by George at the pre-1939 war Labour

Party Conference that Stafford Cripps was expelled from the Party, and George thereafter recorded that 'Cripps never spoke to me again. I've even stood in a toilet with him when we were both Ministers, and he still couldn't remember my name. He was a great Christian and certainly had faith and hope, but it never seemed to me he really got to the point about charity.' After which we may pause for a moment to recall that it was George who favoured the expulsion of Cripps and not the other way round. It was so often thus: George had a touch of persecution mania and never found it easy to forgive those upon whom he had inflicted some injury, whether trivial or severe. However, Cripps, Russell, Bevan and the rest were let off comparatively lightly: the longest sufferer surely was his rival and leader, Harold Wilson.

One of the cruel absurdities of British politics is that two men who hate each other's guts may be forced to stump the country handcuffed together as the leaders of the same party. Heretofore it has usually been necessary to wait until the real biographies or autobiographies are written to taste the full flavour of venom between such compulsive brothers-in-arms. But as in other industries, the pace of development in this one quickens beyond measure. Instant memoirs became the fashion, and in George Brown's it was possible to learn his verdict on Harold Wilson, who was still in party political business when he was not writing memoirs himself. Certainly the feud between the two dominated George's recollections, however much he might protest that nothing was further from his fraternal, Christian thoughts. Both the introduction and the postscript of his book contained fierce attacks on Wilson's leadership, and every clash between them recorded there somehow tended to underline the superior wisdom, foresight and brotherly virtue of – guess which.

We could read, for example, on page 83, George's view of the original electoral contest for the leadership after Gaitskell's death: 'I discouraged active campaigning on my behalf but that didn't prevent a bitter campaign from being waged against me.' Oh dear! The self-portrait of George as the aloof, almost aristocratic figure who would never stoop to intrigue or manoeuvre, and who, moreover, sternly instructed his hench or hatchetmen, such as the long-forgotten Gerry Reynolds, Desmond Donnelly, Frank Tomney *et al*, to be equally fastidious in never soiling their lilywhite hands, was sufficient to ensure for his book, as the main critical comment, a rousing horselaugh in the Parliamentary Labour Party. All the more so since it did also offer, after the last half-century of reputed splits and rebellions inside the Labour Party, the clinching proof of the one real putsch against the leadership which *did* actually happen – the one led against Clem Attlee in 1947 by those two ultra-loyalists, twin scourges of the rebellious Bevanites, Patrick Gordon Walker and George Brown himself: the one which drew from Ernest Bevin the reproof that he never wanted to see George again.

But perhaps the reader may protest that I am biased, and of course I am. The same George Brown who whispered at the top of his voice warnings against 'authoritarian' or 'Presidential' tendencies in the Labour Party, once got me expelled from it at a meeting called at three hours' notice, and at other much more significant moments did his best to drive out of our ranks a long list of noisy troublemakers headed, as we have seen, by Stafford Cripps, Bertrand Russell, and Aneurin Bevan.

George Brown, with a thumping majority at his back or a card vote in his pocket, could be a boorish bully, and part of the Brownite or Gaitskellite fury against Wilson, one suspects, was that he outmanoeuvred them at their own game of behind-the-scenes confabulations and contrivances. Certainly others, on social or diplomatic occasions, saw that George Brown in action, and the performance went far beyond the 'engaging rudeness' which he immodestly attributes to himself.

However, enraged as many readers of this book must be by George's patronage of better men than himself or his irrepressible, prancing egotism, let not the attempt here to rectify the balance be allowed to tip it too far. For, as friends and enemies will testify, there *was* another George, a man of good courage, zeal and willpower, and genuine streaks of imagination, the rarest of all political attributes. He needed all these qualities in his long fight against Treasury economics, what he calls 'their collective arrogance and incompetence'; in his arduous, often subtle exertion to secure a settled peace in the Middle East; in his devotion, however mistaken some may feel the objective to be, to the cause of so-called European unity.

George with his back to the wall could extort admiration from the bitterest opponents – as for example on that afternoon at Brighton in 1962 when, as he came near to alleging in his book, Gaitskell doublecrossed him on the Common Market, or that morning in June 1970 when he lost his seat at Belper and carried off the whole wretched calamity with a brave, good-natured shrug. Alas, it was not that George but the other one who wrote his autobiography. (Dismiss the talk of ghosts; you can hear the authentic voice.) Both together constituted the real man, and made him for years, along with Lord Hailsham, the most gifted, intrepid, scintillating schizophrenic in British public life.

Proper students of that volume might have been prepared for anything but I must confess I was a trifle surprised when he chose as his reason for leaving the Labour Party, on 2 March 1976, the Bill which I was at that moment introducing, to complete the repeal of the anti-trade union legislation placed on the statute book by the Conservative Government in 1971 and which included provisions about the operation of the closed shop. Some observers affected to believe that entirely new provisions were being incorporated, in that the closed shop was being established and protected from future assault in a way never envisaged before. That was never the case, as George could easily have discovered if he had troubled to ask me or those in charge of his old trade union, the Transport & General Workers. What the Bill did was to restore the pre-1971 legal position, the position which had prevailed throughout the whole of George Brown's adult life – with the single novel exception, as I am now jolted to recall, that there *was* a clause for protecting those who wished to invoke their religious views as their reason for not joining a trade union. But George never stopped to study what was in the Bill or out of it. He wanted plenty of commotion, as he left the Labour Party of his upbringing, and he secured it in full measure in the most bitter sections of the anti-Labour press.

I trust he left the Church to which he also owed so much with a trifle more dignity. A postcard from Cornwall to the Archbishop of Canterbury would have made a nice final touch.

# Ex-Brother David

———◁•◎•▷———

The impudence of a Bawd is Modesty, compared
with that of a Convert.

Lord Halifax

A politician who decides to kick away the ladder which has lifted him to eminence needs nerve and poise, and, for a while, the combination of attributes may be sufficient to rivet the attention of bystanders. But the time comes when the origin and purpose of the whole performance must be scrutinised more astringently, when later developments may seem to bear little relation to the first display of daring.

Such was one worthwhile comparison to be made in the case of Oswald Mosley. Despite, from the Labour movement's point of view, the oddity of his political upbringing, despite the swiftness of his elevation unwarranted at that time by any full proof of abilities, despite his arrogance and vanity and sheer insensitivity in personal dealings, his first major breach with his Labour Party colleagues had a most respectable intellectual basis. He was right to be impatient with them for their pusillanimity in tackling the great issue of mass unemployment. If ever a Socialist was justified in challenging the smug suffocations which seemed to encircle him, here was the correct issue. It was on these grounds that he broke with the Treasury-dominated Labour Cabinet of 1930; he was a planner before the real planners appeared on the scene. Only a few years later was his own ambition unmasked as the relentless, reckless streak in his character, the one which would dwarf all his other capacities, the wit, the eloquence, and the drive, and guide them all into the service of the most shameful of causes.

Those who dig deeply into the causes of David Owen's rupture with the Labour Party may be surprised, as I was, to discover that it was accompanied, with brilliant topicality, by the publication of a book. It was called *Face the Future* and it was published (by Jonathan Cape) in February 1981.* The so-called Limehouse declaration in which David Owen and a few others forecast their departure from the Labour Party was issued on 25 January of that

* The copy I've been reading was presented by him to the House of Commons Library on 10 February 1981 and catalogued by them on 25 February.

same year. So what could be more fortunate than the conjunction of these two events? Our saviours, the man and the book, were presented to the nation at the same unforgettable, immemorial moment, almost in the same breath. This new Moses did not fail to bring with him his tablets of stone. But, of course, it was not quite like that; even so excellent and efficient a publisher as Jonathan Cape could not contrive so exact a synchronisation.

In other words, the searcher after truth must acknowledge that the book was completed months before David Owen made his formal move to leave the Labour Party. While he was writing it, he was still in two minds – to give the lowest estimate – about which course might turn out to be the most profitable later on. Such ambiguity of purpose is inclined to play hell with literary styles less naturally opaque than Dr Owen's. Indeed, at one stage the reader might imagine that his whole idea was to erect 'fudge and mudge' into a new literary form or, rather, this reader was forced to recall a review by Malcolm Muggeridge of a book by Anthony Eden in which he complained how 'one had to fight one's way from sentence to sentence'.

However, we could all read the title, *Face the Future*, adapted from the famous Labour Party manifesto of 1945, and those who have had dealings with David Owen – I am sure David Steel or Roy Jenkins would confirm what I say – know how the Doctor has a special insight into, an obsession about, it might almost be called, an individual reversionary interest, in the future. He *knows* better than anyone else; he keeps that stony, ferocious eye fixed on the main chance.

I notice that these essential points were sharply recorded by Paul Barker, editor of *New Society*, when he reviewed *Face the Future* in the *Observer* in February 1981, and when he wrote: 'It has to be said, Dr Owen is no writer. You have to drive yourself through some of the chapters. And the book doesn't so much conclude as just stop – like a collection of *Guardian* leaders.' I interrupt the quotation at once to repudiate this slur on a fine body of men (and women, I trust); no *Guardian* leader writers, not even the under-cover ones later unmasked as lifelong social democrats, would serve up such offerings to their editor and survive. But I must let nothing deflect me from Paul Barker's final sentence: 'Tony Crosland,' he writes, 'once said that a social democrat was what you call someone who is about to join the Tory Party. I don't think Owen is. He sounds to me like a good liberal. Or even a Liberal. We'll see.'

Liberals, large and small, did show signs of demurring at the way crude, undiluted Owenism was shovelled at and over them, and if Paul Barker unwittingly started the deluge, they have a good grievance against him. And, of course, anyone who re-reads *Face the Future* today – or rather anyone who drives his way through it, according to Paul Barker's rules of motoring – will discover that its main theme is about something else altogether. It is a discussion – and a perfectly legitimate, if not very well-informed one – about the way democratic Socialists should not allow to be buried and forgotten one of their finest sources of inspiration and wisdom: the William Morris-G. D. H. Cole, anti-bureaucratic, anarchistic tradition. These two names are selected here, since they figure prominently in Dr Owen's recital. Each of them, along with his other gifts, had some taste in invective, and it is agreeable to imagine what they would have said about the purloining of their ideas to further Dr Owen's creed and career. Other less notable models contribute their quota to this modern Socialist encyclopaedia. The chapter on 'The Growth of Corporatism' reads like Tony Benn on an off-day at a Militant summer school, while the chapter on 'The Pursuit of Equality' opens with 'the howler' – as Paul Barker called it – that 'the Beveridge Report was published at the end of the Second World War'. But those were far-off days – 1981, I mean, not 1942 – before Beveridge too was to be recruited behind Dr Owen's banner.

The truth is truly startling; it needs no embroidery. The book so happily published just when Dr Owen was leaving the Labour Party was originally designed, whatever the final outcome, as a new Bible for Socialists about Socialism. He always likes to show how he knows better than anyone else; indeed thought of it first. It is as if the Apostle Paul, having just completed his journey from Damascus, were to express his readiness to re-write, say, the Book of Isaiah or, more appositely, as if Kim Philby would fly in from Moscow to lend a hand with the next Defence White Paper.

Some compunctions of this nature did afflict Dr Owen himself. He seemingly felt that it was not too late for something to be done about all those excessively elaborate sermons on the values of Socialism which figured so prominently in *Face the Future*. The future must be faced, but not quite yet. So, later that year, almost by sleight-of-hand, another edition of the same book or at least a similar book was published by the Oxford University Press, and the author himself explained the textual alterations, not expecting, I suspect, that too scholarly or sceptical an eye would ever be applied to compare the two works. The title of the first chapter was easily transmuted from 'The Values of Socialism' to 'Social Democratic Values', and a final chapter was added, in deference to Mr Paul Barker and any *Guardian* leader writers still smarting from the insult, called 'The Enabling State'. Several other alterations, too abstruse or tedious to investigate, were made in between, but the strangest addition was the large chunk in a brand new Preface devoted to the exciting revelation that Dr Owen's highly principled disillusionment with the Labour Party had really been developing much earlier. It could be traced, if devoted disciples wished to know, to a revolt which he and a few other rebellious spirits had initiated against the Labour Government of Harold Wilson in 1967. The seeds of the Social Democratic era were sown then when daredevil, far-seeing Dr Owen ranged himself against the Wilson Cabinet on three great issues of policy: against the deflationary course pursued by the Treasury, against the timidity in dealing with the Smith rebellion in Rhodesia, where Wilson himself was the worst offender, and, thirdly, against what Dr Owen called the incipient 'equivocations over race'.

Some of us recall those disputations vividly enough, since we took overt action to express our views in debates or in the voting lobbies. The accusation was true enough: the Wilson Cabinet did deserve criticism from democratic Socialists on all these three matters and a few more. But it is not so easy to recall how much support we received from Dr Owen, since he happily took the job in the Government offered him by a generous Harold Wilson in 1968, and his independent voice, whether democratic Socialist or Social Democratic, was not heard again for the rest of that decade. The sweets of office seemed to soften even the harsh Owenite accent. I presume, by the way, that his reference to the 'equivocations over race' must mean the Commonwealth Immigrants Bill, for dealing with Kenya Asians, rushed through by James Callaghan and the Wilson Cabinet in February 1968. True enough again: it did contain some racist overtones which some of us found so objectionable that we voted against the Bill. Dr Owen voted for it.

However, even these reminiscences, fascinating though some of them may appear, do not constitute the main point. If these historic episodes in our hero's own story took pride of place when he had left the Labour Party in the autumn of 1981, why had he thought they were not worth even so much as an oblique mention when he was completing the much larger survey of political faith in the year before? Maybe he still thought his future lay with the Labour Party, and – who knows? – another generous Labour leader might be offering him another office.

Enough has been said, however, to indicate the varying delights of the two editions of *Face the Future*. Dr Owen, the perfectionist, was still not satisfied. The rumour spread that all references to Socialism were to be excised from its pages. Something more than a rumour had it that the newly established social democrats were to set up a 'think tank' of their own, and that they proposed to call it the Tawney Society, taking the name from Professor R. H. Tawney. I was outraged to hear this suggestion, as were multitudes of other Socialists, and I took immediate steps to stamp on this preposterous insult to his memory. But first let me take a side-glance at Dr Owen's association with the idea.

Superficially, Professor Tawney might have been expected to have an especial appeal for Dr Owen, the earlier Dr Owen, that is, the would-be prophet of fundamental Socialist values. Tawney's Socialism – like Dr Owen's, it was alleged – derived from a Christian inspiration. Tawney's Socialism, thanks no doubt to his memories of the First World War, comprised a full-blooded defence of the way Britain must be physically defended – and Dr Owen was alleged to be interested in that tradition too. Tawney's Socialism was also inextricably soldered with his democratic faith; the two together so that no one could ever put them asunder. Tawney's Socialism could not be traced solely to William Morris (he knew much more about him than Owen was ever likely to know), but Morris's ideas and idealism were woven into the rich pattern of his political faith. Curiously or, rather, not so curiously it may be thought, in the light of later developments, Dr Owen's book contained only the most trivial references to Tawney. If a book was to be written to bring Socialist values up to date, it was an absurdity not to have considered Tawney's judgement on these same matters in his books *The Acquisitive Society* and *Equality* and indeed in his life and writings generally. No one but Dr Owen would ever have set out on such a mission without seeking Tawney's guidance. Yet the same Dr Owen who was not prepared to read his books was eager to steal his name.

The letter I wrote (to *The Times* on 3 February 1982) just a year after the Owen breakaway, it may be seen, was as follows, but I include thereafter two other letters provoked by the same controversy and which appeared in the *Guardian*. One of them – by Lena Jeger – requires to be re-read when anyone in any section of the Party is seeking to quote Tawney for his or her purpose. In his later years at least, she knew him better than anyone else.

> I read some months ago the acknowledgement by Roy Jenkins that he had not been accustomed for years to use the word Socialism. I read frequently, and most recently in your correspondence columns on Tuesday, that David Owen has removed from the latest edition of his book *Face the Future* all references to Socialism to be found in the original. I read also that the Social Democrat Party has chosen to call its 'think tank', the Tawney Society.
>
> Will the Society at its early meetings devote its labours to the removal of the word Socialism from the works of Professor Tawney? It would be a formidable task. And it would surely be more tasteful if · these new thinkers did not seek, for their own purposes, to debase the name of Tawney. Some of us can recall how proudly and passionately he pronounced the word Socialism, and scorned those who would not understand its true origin, meaning and glory.

> Sir,
>
> Your suggestion of a Tawney–Tawney ticket for the Labour leadership (Leader, 25 June) is attractively intriguing.
>
> The main problem, apart from Tawney's presence in Valhalla, is that if people read the whole books instead of making selective quotations, not many would vote for him. The fact that none of his books is still in print – except for *Equality* which sells about 1000 copies a year, including considerable exports – suggests that too many people here are only reading quotations from other people's quotations.
>
> The entrenched left cannot identify with Tawney in honesty for several reasons:
>
> The patriotic old wounded soldier from the Somme was always contemptuous of those of us who were in CND, and he strongly

supported Gaitskell's 'fight, fight and fight again' speech;

Tawney never accepted that conference decisions should overrule the judgment of the Parliamentary Labour Party or individual conscience;

He explained at one of our ward meetings in Kings Cross that, as conference decisions could change from year to year, it was grotesque and immoral that anybody should be expected to do ungraceful somersaults in obeisance to changing 'majority' decisions;

He did not accept majorities based on what he considered the total non-democracy of the block vote;

He also rejected decisions based on what he considered the monstrosities of illiterate 'composited' resolutions. He wrote: 'They sweep together great things and small; nationalise land, mines and banking in one sentence, and abolish fox-hunting in the next.'

The right would hesitate to vote for Tawney's ghost because of his commitment to Clause 4, to extensive public ownership, to his philosophical attack on the sanctity of private property. He wrote in 1934 that the Labour Party 'ought to tell its supporters that its business is to be the organ of a peaceful revolution, and that other interests must be subordinated to that primary duty'.

You are right. The ghost of Tawney, the whole Tawney, could shake them all. Shake them into a tolerant, rational attitude which respects disagreements; does not bully or threaten the dissidents from some invented orthodoxy; or produce a monolithic shopping list, deviation from one item of which means disgrace and darkness – and possibly non-reselection. Shake them away from the structured rigidities of formal groupings and pressure sects which threaten to balkanise the party.

Tawney was often in disagreement with Bevan. But he told me how much he agreed with Nye when he said: 'This is my truth. Now tell me yours.'

I will offend against my own strictures on the 'quoters' with one reminder: 'What men desire is not paragraphs in constitutions, but results in the form of arrangements which ensure them the essentials of a civilised existence, and show a proper respect for their dignity as human beings.'

Nobody is today's Tawney. And that is the sadness for the Labour Party. The alien cock-up of the 'electoral college' has nought to do with democracy; it only hands over control to half-a-dozen trade union bosses. This would not have been Tawney's way.

Lena Jeger

Sir

Evan Luard (Agenda Extra, 18 June) is wrong. A patched-up coalition between Labour, Liberal, and SDP – impractical in itself – would pose no threat to the Tories, and would be rejected with contempt by the electorate.

What is required is to rebuild the coalition *within* the Labour Party which smashed the Tory machine in four elections out of five in the period from 1963 to 1975, when the Liberals were irrelevant and the SDP consisted of Dick Taverne (Dick who?).

The mainstream of committed loyal Labour members and supporters – who still exist in their millions despite all the sociological psephology of the pundits – must set to work to build up again the coalition of shared ideals and common aims which has enabled Labour to provide the country with six highly effective governments since 1945.

The treachery of Owen and company damaged that coalition, but has not destroyed it. There will always be within the Labour movement differences of emphasis on policy, the instruments of government, and the feasibility and speed of implementing fundamental changes in our society and national economy; hence the perennial argument between left and right. Such differences will always be exploited by the corrupt evil malice of Fleet Street.

Nevertheless the ideals of equality, co-operative effort, the destruction of privilege bought by the purse, the harnessing of the immense skills and talents of the British people for the common good – not their exploitation by private corporations for the gigantic personal profit of a few individuals – the UK leading in world counsels for peace and fair shares, do appeal to men and women over a very wide spectrum indeed.

The Labour Party is the only political instrument with the remotest chance of carrying these ideals into practical effect, but to do it requires a renewal of the coalition *within* the party, a new emphasis on tolerance and loyalty, and a more powerful and sustained attack on the real enemy; the Tory Party.

Frank Hooley

Lena Jeger and Frank Hooley together show how Tawney can be enlisted for our modern instruction. His writings were read *and loved* – it is not too much to say – by one generation of Socialists after another. Hugh Gaitskell said at the memorial service for him at St Martin-in-the-Fields on 8 February 1962: 'I always think of him as *the* Democratic Socialist *par excellence*,' and those who might quarrel with Gaitskell about everything else would not dissent from that verdict. Ten years earlier – in June 1952 – Tawney himself had given, not his definitive definition, but a warning to all who would bowdlerise or debase the great tradition. 'The foundation of Socialism,' he said, at the beginning, 'is, in my view, a decision that certain types of life and society are fit for human beings and others not.' Then he continued, discussing both the theory of Socialism and its practical application in the post-1945 years: 'Nothing could be more remote from Socialist ideals than the competitive scramble of a society which pays lip-service to equality, but too often means by it merely equal opportunities of becoming unequal.' And then to the mighty climax: the real enemy to be fought, the one to whom Socialists must never surrender was 'the corrupting influence of a false standard of values, which perverts, not only education, but wide tracts of thought and life. It is this demon – the idolatry of money and success – with whom, not in one sphere alone but in all, including our own hearts and minds, Socialists have to grapple'.

Thus Professor Tawney had faced the challenge which Dr Owen purported to face. Tawney's life work, it might be said, was to face it. In one of his reflections on the subject (in his 'Religion and the Rise of Capitalism', the subject of a lecture in 1922) he would return to the presiding question of the purpose or purposes of economic activity: 'The question to what end the wheels revolve still remains: and on that question the naive and uncritical worship of economic power, which is the mood of unreason too often engendered in those whom that new Leviathan has hypnotised by its spell, throws no light.' But Dr Owen could not or would not try to see. He was happy to be hypnotised.

Maybe he was too busy erasing the word *Socialism* from *Face the Future* to pause to wonder what it might mean. No reissue of the book with the full erasures ever was published, but no repudiation of the charge that they had been attempted ever appeared either. But *Face the Future*, the first and second impressions, did have a sequel, published in September 1984, called *The Future That Will Work*, published by the Viking Press and Penguin, and now at last that future was to be faced without any of the old encumbrances. The offensive word *Socialism* appeared nowhere in the blurb, nor among the chapter headings nor, as far as I can see, except in a few sneering asides, anywhere in the actual text. Instead, the first chapter was boldly called 'The Social Market Approach', and the earliest available moment was used to dismiss 'Socialist revisionists' who had not shown the same aptitude as himself in discussing 'the mixed economy' or a few occasional derisive attacks upon 'the dwindling democratic Socialist wing within the Labour Party'. For the rest, readers must be warned, the style confirms and reinforces the old Paul Barker critique. 'Britain,' we are told at the end in a thunderous peroration, 'needs a fundamental change in attitudes; we need the background of understanding and shared interests that is inherent in the social market.' And if you're still left wondering what, in the name of heaven or purgatory, 'the social market' may be, I would refer you to another speech delivered soon after the 1983 election, at the Social Democratic conference at Salford, when Dr Owen thought the political wind was blowing so hard in the Thatcherite direction that he'd better move with it. This was the first airing of 'the social market' philosophy and it comprised an unqualified defence of the competitive society and its alleged conspicuous successes. A strange moment indeed, even for an ex-Socialist, to choose to trumpet so glowing and comprehensive a tribute. Unemployment was at record heights and still moving upwards; British manufacturing output was at its lowest depths for generations and still moving downwards; mass poverty was cutting deeper year by year by year, almost month by month; and the whole ramshackle economic recovery was protected only by the giant shield of North Sea oil. Where would the newly-discovered, matchlessly extolled social market be once that shield was removed?

However, this was truly the great new theme for public debate selected by Dr Owen himself in the post-1983 election period, and he quickly won applause in those circles, mostly ultra-Thatcherite in complexion, which already supported 'the competitive society' and didn't wish to be bothered with any new fancy names. And oh yes, there was another theme which began to emerge, more favoured by David Owen than David Steel but still backed by them both; the notion that they were somehow being unfairly treated by the television authorities, principally the BBC. Whole pages of *The Future That Will Work* were directed to this fresh cause of disgruntlement. Yet for most observers, surely, the idea of the two Davids being unfairly treated by the media was the most monstrous display of ingratitude since Goneril and Regan turned on their father.

Yet again, on second or third thoughts, is this really fair? Is the Owen style unmistakably still so inspissated? Is it not the case that the tone and temper alter, that they can rise almost to a screech? I cite a strange passage from *The Future That Will Work* which, I would have thought, others would have quoted before now, if only on psycho-analytical grounds. Maybe this is the surest proof that few readers of the book manage to get thus far.

Surveying those who have at one time or another stood across the path of his ambition – the top civil servants who scorned his methods and said so (he wants them pensioned off sooner, like redundant generals or admirals); the diplomats who would not learn the ways of business; the politicians who try to learn something about Parliament before despising the place; the chauffeurs (although he doesn't actually mention them himself) who wouldn't drive him again and submit to the same boorishness; the ruling élite, as he calls them, with more than a touch of paranoia – he concludes thus: 'There is no doubt that if there was the slightest chance of bringing it about, the quickest way of changing the total political configuration would be to make a change as radical as General de Gaulle did with the Fourth Republic – elect the Prime Minister directly, though retaining the monarch as head of state, while leaning further than France did towards the US system with its federal structure and explicit separation of power between the executive and legislature . . .' Indeed: quite an innovation, a cross between a French and an American President. And who, one is left wondering one split second, might he have in mind as the obvious first candidate likely to be elected Prime Minister under his brand-new system? And how thoughtful of him too, having destroyed any real Parliament, to leave the monarch in Buckingham Palace quite undisturbed!

But, again, we must be fair. The next sentence is supposed to take the curse off these fantasies. 'This is wishful, escapist thinking,' he himself insists, and then further adds, almost without noticing, 'Britain would have to be at or on the cliff edge of economic disaster before such a radical shift could have even a chance of implementation.' And then again a few paragraphs later he is writing of the radicalism which, if his words mean anything, would make credible his vaulting Gaullist ambition. 'Radicalism is a very easy word to use and objective to aspire to. It is in practice an extremely difficult political philosophy to live up to.' Such is Dr Owen in his most Delphic, graceful, epigrammatic mood. And what is the answer? No – or yes, if you prefer it. Radicalism is just another word – like Socialism, we may recall – which Dr Owen picks up and tosses aside without any clear grasp of its origin and potency. Like his servants and friends and fellow Labour Party members in his old Devonport constituency, they serve his purpose and are then discarded. It is not perhaps a minor matter that he uses words so sloppily and scurvily, and we are entitled to recall that if General de Gaulle had inflicted comparable wounds on the French language he would never have become the President of France.

However, it must not be thought that Dr Owen ends his new determination to face the future with a detailed prophecy of his own apotheosis. He is much too considerate of his latter-day allies, Roy Jenkins and David Steel. Like them, although in reverse order, he has become a convert to Proportional Representation. He knows well enough that that is the one absolute, irrefragable condition of the alliance with the Liberals, has been and always shall be. At one time, in the heady early days of 1981 when they talked of an imminent all-round Alliance victory, it was the only absolutely explicit condition. The first item on the agenda of two sections of the Alliance, according to their own most pressing patriotic declarations, in those far-off halcyon days, was that they would introduce a new electoral system designed to safeguard their own peculiar position for the future. It must have been the first time in modern British history in which public men came together on the basis of such a limited pre-eminent priority, and it recalled rather the spirit in which factions and sects might combine in the age of George III. Yet such a declaration had to be taken seriously. One of the few public measures on which the same group of public men have found agreement in the past was in their readiness to transfer essential controlling power over the British economy from Westminster to Brussels. They would not baulk at the next agreed step: to introduce some form of proportional representation both designed and equipped to ensure that all British governments until the end of the century and beyond would take on the character of some form of coalition. This was the Owenite theme already mooted in *Face the Future* and blazoned more boldly in *The Future That Will Work*.

Since the plank is so central to the Alliance strategy, it might be expected that he would argue the issue on its merits and explain why modern Liberals and their latter-day allies are so ready to destroy the single-member constituency which has for so long been the main support for the independence of individual Members of Parliament – once a good liberal, certainly a good democratic Socialist cause. But Dr Owen, with all the space in the world at his disposal, just does not bother.

In place of a grand theory, Dr Owen offers us some reminiscences from that blessed epoch in our history when he was Foreign Secretary. It was there, from the governments in European Community countries operating proportional systems that he learnt how, so far from producing weak governments, 'a proportional system breeds a different type of politics'. He explains further how West Germany had produced not 'the consensual politics, lacking real radicalism', but the Ostpolitik which did indeed change the prospect for Europe and replace with a new hope of détente the old cold-war dead-end. True enough, but Dr Owen might have added for the benefit of his less-informed readers that the first indispensable author of Ostpolitik was the Willy Brandt who refused to betray the independence of his truly Socialist Social Democratic Party, and who, along with the other Social Democratic leaders, was rewarded for skill and foresight and a long period of good government for Germany by the desertion at the most critical hour of the small band of German Owenites, the tiny rump which, according to the German proportional system (the best available, according to Dr Owen) wields inordinate power.

Of course there is a case for proportional representation, a case for permanent Coalition, a case for governments of different combinations, with Conservatives able to choose the large or small c exercising always the final dominance. And if the Social Democratic desertion from the Labour movement succeeds in its manoeuvre, this will be the consequence for British politics. One road only would be barred: the road to democratic Socialism. Or perhaps since Dr Owen maltreats words so mercilessly we should come to the rescue of another one. Any Radicalism worth the name would be barred too.

# Brother Frank

The wish for power was the key to Cousins'
action. Cousins was a demagogue and ambitious.
He was throwing his weight about so that he could
make his power felt.

> Hugh Gaitskell, in conversation
> with Alistair Hetherington,
> editor of the *Guardian*. July 1959

But Cousins was an honest man, and a proud one.
Contrary to Gaitskell's impression, he cared about
the substance of the issue, more than about getting
rid of the Party leader.

> Philip Williams, Gaitskell's
> biographer, discussing their
> relationship in 1965

Geoffrey Goodman's *The Awkward Warrior* was
published by Davis-Poynter just after the May 1979
electoral defeat for the Labour Party. Some of the
hopes for trade union advance which were still alive
then have suffered a crushing reversal; but it is good
to recall the real fight for democracy within the
trades union movement and who were some of its
initiators.

Can individual man or woman divert the course of history? Are we just the playthings of a blind or, according to the Marxist amendment, decipherable historical process? May heroes and heroines stamp their will on lesser mortals, in the manner once extolled by Thomas Carlyle?

All such variations on the old but still fascinating theme are posed in Geoffrey Goodman's *The Awkward Warrior*, and it is not surprising that he requires 600 pages of political background and personality skilfully blended with one another to tell the real story of Frank Cousins. He is not just a man: more a kind of man-mountain who could produce volcanic effects throughout the political world, seemingly all on his own. And before that claim is dismissed as an absurd exaggeration, consider what was the character and role of the Transport and General Workers' Union before Frank Cousins became its general secretary in May 1956. It was numerically, with over a million members, the strongest union in the country; even before the war, Ernest Bevin had seemed to fashion it in his own image, formidable and relentless and the single most powerful element in the trades union movement as a whole. But it had also become, as part of Bevin's legacy and under his successor, Arthur Deakin, the rock on which the Right-wing Labour Party leadership was built; increasingly that, first and foremost, and not much else besides. This was how the whole T & G apparatus looked to us on the Left of the Party: suffocating, insufferable but still unshiftable.

Then came the age of Frank Cousins. Within fourteen months of Arthur Deakin's death, a new man with new ideas, and yet a will and sense of dedication quite the equal of Deakin's or of Bevin's, sat in their chair at Transport House, and soon we were rubbing our eyes in amazement at the spectacle.

Of course the transformation did not happen overnight. Some of the best pages in this book describe what obstacles he had to overcome in the early years, within the T & G itself, against the entrenched Deakinite resistance movement, within the TUC general council against those who would have cut to pieces this overweening newcomer if they could, with the Tory government of the day which was obligingly eager to make available all facilities for the execution. Yes, Frank Cousins was almost destroyed in the once famous but now well-nigh forgotten bus strike of 1958: the story of why he had to fight, and the way he fought, and how the unloosing of democracy within the T & G, of all places, began to determine events, and how in the end something more precious than victory was snatched from the jaws of defeat, all this constitutes a classic tale of how that long-established British institution, the class struggle, was sustained in those far-off times.

Of course, it takes two, two sides at least, to wage a class war, and on this occasion the Tory campaign was conducted by a couple of engaging Highland chiefs, Iain Macleod, the real thing, and Harold Macmillan, the old crofter-poseur in person. 'I happen to believe in democracy,' said Frank, when he was being pilloried for his conduct of the strike. And then again, in another context: 'there is nothing dramatic about being democratic'. But he knew, none better, that from the general secretary of the T & G, and the leading, if still isolated, member of the general council, these were revolutionary utterances, and the fury which they goaded from his growing legion of critics, in the press and elsewhere, showed that he was touching the sorest spot.

It is indeed a marvellous paradox that the trades union leaders who were most furiously denounced by the millionaire-owned newspapers as would-be dictators were the very ones who, like Frank Cousins, risked so much of their own authority to help instil democratic habits into the trades union movement. Or, to put the same point the other way round; who ever heard, from Tory critics, that the trades union bosses were engaged in introducing elements of the corporate state when Arthur Deakin and Co. were doing precisely that and when it might be legitimately charged that the whole T & G was lumbering in that direction? The accusation only became fashionable long after Frank Cousins, Jack Jones and their supporters had staked their reputations and livelihoods on the task of making the trades union movement in general and the T & G in particular a much more truly democratic organisation. It was only done in the nick of time. Here we are shown how convulsive were the forces beneath the surface which, without the Cousins revolution, might have disrupted altogether the T & G as a cohesive body, and a multitude of events since have surely clinched the case. But the nature of the change owed much to the man himself.

The awkwardness of Frank Cousins, celebrated in the title of this book, was not just an ever-present wariness and prickliness: rather it was something splendid, granite-like, all of one piece, Promethean. It had an air about it of reckless allegiance to the causes in which he believed. But it was also associated with the vulnerable side of his character, and the instructive fact, properly stressed in these pages, is that it is impossible for anyone who knows him to imagine the phenomenon of Frank Cousins without Nance, his wonder of a wife. Hence, the essential man–woman hero–heroine formulation listed earlier. The New Year's Eve Co-operative dance in Doncaster in 1928 when he first met her and made up his mind to marry her on the way home that very same night was certainly what Geoffrey Goodman describes it, 'the decisive moment of Frank's life'.

She provided him with a fortress against the hostile or unsympathetic world, and thereby sent him out into it every morning with his inborn belligerence fortified. But she was also an indispensable contributor to his other great qualities, his charm, his independence of mind, his shining, unbending honesty. These too could win victories and victims; one for example, being George Woodcock, general secretary of the TUC, a most unlikely ally of the ever-suspicious, recalcitrant Cousins. Soon they were acting in the closest concert on the general council, and each deserves credit for his discrimination.

But were there not great failures too? For example, in his dealings with Hugh Gaitskell and the great H-bomb controversy, with Harold Wilson and the Labour Cabinet? Was not his journey from the union which he had re-modelled into the foreign territory of Whitehall and the House of Commons a political and personal tragedy? Nance had warned against the move, and his friends who had hoped to see him woo and subdue the Cabinet as he had succeeded against all the odds with the general council were naturally disappointed. And yet, after the early months when he was baited so unmercifully, with all the Tory curs yelping at his heels, he did begin to succeed in making the House of Commons understand what manner of man he was: his giant stature was beginning to be recognised afresh. He was also succeeding in the creation of a new essential Ministry out of nothing. There was indeed no failure here.

It was the clash with the rest of the Cabinet over incomes policy which made his resignation in 1966 inevitable, and who will say now that he was wrong? Dick Crossman (not necessarily to be appointed, unless I am seriously mistaken, the final arbiter on the Day of Judgement in these or other matters) concluded in his diaries two years later that Frank, maybe, had had it right all along. But, more significantly, Frank Cousins also had not doubts – that was never his style – but second, third and fourth thoughts. Once again back at the TUC in fruitful collaboration with George Woodcock, he helped to devise, not a cut-and-dried solution but a tentative, voluntary approach to the still towering, unsolved problem of incomes policy which might have saved a decade of agony thereafter. This part of the record has been submerged, although some of the propositions of 1968 were carried into legislative effect after 1974.

However, nothing hinted at here is designed to conceal the larger truth that Frank Cousins has had no great enthusiasm for the Lilliputian efforts of those who have followed him, whether in Labour Cabinets or the trades unions. He was never one to suffer his predecessors gladly, and the same catholic comprehensive question about human capacity was applied to his successors. His scorn remained magnificent and immaculate; not something prompted by egotism as his detractors were always so fatuously eager to infer but the same which inspired him in his utterly selfless dedication to the Campaign for Nuclear Disarmament.

Heaven knows, he had plenty of other battles to fight then; he could have spared himself that one. But it was his imaginative power which provided his driving force; once he was committed, he hurled the whole of his huge frame into the contest. His defeats on those other battlefields – as in the London bus strike – are not so important as the fact that the challenge was delivered, and the challengers lived to fight another day. A great stride forward in our democratic politics has been taken in the past quarter of a century, thanks in no small part to the growing strength of the trades union movement. Such a claim conflicts with the conventional wisdom or folly of the present hour, and bears no relation to the sophistries and shibboleths on which the 1979 and 1983 Conservative electoral victories were won. But we need not be detained by such transient delusions.

Anyone who wants to have a real taste of what life was like in Britain before this latest democratic advance, before the age of Frank Cousins, and how the change was made, and how he and the age reacted upon one another, can study it here, in a good book on a great theme, with a hero and heroine whom Carlyle himself would have been proud to place in his gallery.

# Brother Tony

Tony Benn's insistence on tape-recording every infernal interview is not for nothing: the tapes are to be saved for posterity by the Joseph Rowntree Social Service Trust which has just agreed to spend £20,000 transcribing them. The massive Benn archive lies in countless boxes in the basement of his Holland Park home in London . . .

*The Times* diary of 17 September 1985

Even careful or malicious students of modern British politics sometimes forget that Tony Benn was once an up-and-coming, middle-
of-the-road Labour MP with an excellent chance of becoming Prime
Minister. His fuller name at that time was Anthony Wedgwood
Benn – most of us who knew him at all called him 'Wedgie', and
couldn't easily get out of the habit. He had inherited and re-
fashioned for his own use a marvellous combination of wit, persuasive power, deep radical instincts, and a zest for politics. This was
the Wedgie Benn of the 1960s, the youngest Cabinet Minister of his
time, the youngest at least since Harold Wilson, in whose footsteps
he seemed to be half-consciously treading. It was hard to see what –
or who – could ever stop him.

His own campaign to renounce his peerage as Lord Stansgate was
a model and a portent. He had an excellent democratic case but it
was chiefly by his own efforts that he won the essential support and
patience of his electors in Bristol, and the necessary wider audience.
Before he was victorious, most observers thought he could never
win; after it was over, they wondered what the fight had been about.
Without his own personal, single-minded determination, the good
deed could never have been done. So the Wedgie Benn of those times
possessed, along with his other gifts, a practical sense about how to
get things done. He was sometimes dismissed as just 'a whizz kid',
fascinated by the latest political or technological craze. But that was
always an error. He had a serious, almost a religious bent to his
mind and a preference for thinking and acting on his own insights.

If personal ambition had been the sole driving force in his nature,
he might have continued to step forward and upward with some
ease and confidence. The place in the Labour Party spectrum which
he chose to occupy was central or just left of centre, much as Clem
Attlee had done or his other mentor, Harold Wilson although, in
Tony's case, he seemed to pick his way with less deliberation. When
Frank Cousins resigned from the Wilson Cabinet in 1966 as Minister of Technology, Tony stepped into his office and his shoes: not

the act of a man making gestures to the Labour rank-and-file in the country at large. Indeed, in the attitudes he adopted on questions of policy, there were not so much as a list towards Left-wing demagogy. He gave every impression of being a good administrator and was always an effective defender of his department in the House of Commons. He was a strong supporter of Britain's entry into the Common Market. He backed Barbara Castle in her proposed trade union legislation contained in the document *In Place of Strife*. He was not notable for protesting against the Wilson Government's support for the American war in Vietnam. On all these issues which caused so much ferment on the Labour back benches and in the constituencies outside, Tony showed few signs of wishing to join the argument more openly and assertively. He was doing his job as a good member of the Labour Government, and, after 1960, as a member of the Labour Party's National Executive. He was always ready to help his colleagues in the arts he did know more about than most of them: how to use radio and television. No observer in his senses ever doubted his power to persuade, and his power to persuade himself first and foremost.

He was not an eager joiner of groups in the Party: a weakness, some thought, but maybe rather a source of strength. He had never been a member of the *Tribune* group or the Keep Left group or the Victory for Socialism group or the other groups on the Left which were formed and disbanded in the 1950s and the 1960s. He did play a leading part in founding the Movement for Colonial Freedom, and in organising the national appeal against the H-bomb in 1955, but he did not join the Campaign for Nuclear Disarmament started two years later. He never called himself a 'Bevanite' and he was not a 'Gaitskellite' either, although he did vote for Gaitskell in the 1955 leadership election. He had few enemies and few intimate friends in the Parliamentary Party. He had a few unexpected ones, as the biography of Tony Crosland subsequently revealed. He was quite accustomed to acting alone. And yet there was an exception which proved the rule; he had been for years a member of the Fabian Society and became for a while its chairman, but such a qualification counted neither as a virtue nor as a vice.

Such was the Tony Benn of 1970 or rather, still, the Anthony Wedgwood Benn; the conscious change in name and style did not happen until several years later. If Labour had won that 1970

election, as Harold Wilson and most other Labour leaders expected
to do, Wedgie would again have had a prominent post in the new
Cabinet, and the path to the Premiership would have been open
before him. However, during the decade of the 1970s he was
transformed – the word is too weak; *reincarnated* might be better –
into a different political animal altogether, still seeking the highest
post of leadership but by a quite different route. Before 1970, he
pursued the well-worn course of parliamentary advancement. After
1980, he was ready to win all his conquests by other means. 1980
was the year when he seemed to have touched the peak of his
influence and power within the Party – a peak, however, from
which he aspired or threatened to scale higher pinnacles still.

At the Party Conference in Blackpool that year he carried all or
almost all before him. Most of the delegates backed most of the
proposed changes in the Party constitution of which he had made
himself the leading advocate; they responded even more furiously to
the way he damned treachery in the past and projected safeguards
against a recurrence of the same evil in the future. He would name
no names; that was never his way; he abjured personalities and tried
to make a virtue of it. But no room for doubt was left about the
identity of the guilty party: it was the Parliamentary leadership
which had betrayed commitments enshrined in Party manifestos in
the past, and would do so again, if they were not bound hand and
foot by new constitutional bonds. Had they not, by the use of such
instruments as the Leader's 'veto' before the 1979 election, altered
the Party's policy on the House of Lords? So, one symbol of how
such machinations would be blocked in the future would be, in the
first weeks of a new Labour Government, the creation of a thousand
peers. This pronouncement, along with a series of other claims,
about Socialist measures 'vetoed' or 'ruled out' by the leadership,
was greeted with rapturous applause which swamped any concern
about how true the claims might be. Most of them were false, but,
for some of us, the most interesting feature of the affair was whether
Tony believed them himself. It was hard to believe he did, and
almost equally hard to believe he did not. Certainly his outburst was
not just the inspiration or lapse of the moment. Everything he said,
as usual, was written down in advance.

The detail of these events must be looked at a little more closely
later, but the clue to Tony Benn's politics and personality must be

sought here in this period. It so happens that this was also the period when I saw him at close quarters more intimately than I had ever done before and more amiably than I ever did afterwards.

So what *did* happen? Why did he change? There is a clear, indeed an obvious answer, and it is the one he himself elaborated over the years; it became his stock-in-trade, his motive power, the ruling passion which guided most of his actions. *It was his experience as a Labour Minister.* This was his message, and it certainly became one of formidable, sensational potency. However, several implications and subtleties in this seemingly obvious tale must be unravelled.

He was first elected to the National Executive of the Labour Party in 1959–60, and then after a short interval of his own choice, from 1962 onwards. No one in Labour Party history – not even Herbert Morrison in his heyday – applied his mind and energies more assiduously to the work of the Executive. He has witnessed huge changes in the way the Executive does its business and has been the guiding hand in achieving many of them. How far those changes have been beneficial for the Party's health is a chief part of our story, and the exact timetable is worth noting. It was at the beginning of the 1970s that he began to use his experience on the Executive to initiate the reforms. He became chairman of the Party in the autumn of 1970, a year of electoral defeat.

One of his first actions as chairman was to deliver a lecture – appositely, to the Fabian Society – on the theme of democracy within the Party and outside it, in which he gave his judgement on the performance of the 1964–70 Labour Government and drew deductions for the future. The whole tone was tentative and reflective; no one from any section of the Party could object. But he was setting out what he called in one section 'the need for popular democracy; a strategy of change from below', and yet, even while he did so, he showed that he was well aware of the kind of arguments which might prove especially sensitive or injurious to party unity. *Have we failed because Labour has been betrayed by its leaders?* This was one of the questions he deliberately posed from the outset, and the implicit, almost the explicit, answer was an inescapable No. Such an analysis would be quite defective, since it would imply that all that was needed for the remedy was 'a change at the top' and 'an endless search for new hero figures'. For good measure, at the end of the lecture, he underlined the peril of allowing wedges to be driven between different groups within the Parliamentary Party and between the Party in Parliament and the Party outside. Between these two reminders, which many might consider most salutary, he cited five specific examples of major policy questions on which the Labour Cabinet had found itself at odds with the Party outside, and on which, however, he took special pains to emphasise: 'I fully accept the collective responsibility that I personally shared, and still share with all my former ministerial colleagues for all the policies that I have described and am not seeking to escape from any part of that responsibility. What I am saying is that with benefit of hindsight it is likely that the movement had a surer instinct than the Cabinet.' Nothing could be fairer. And what were the five issues? A considerable list: (1) the 1964–6 deflation to preserve the value of the pound; (2) the failure to execute earlier the East of Suez withdrawal; (3) the Government's implied support for the American war in Vietnam; (4) the reimposition of prescription charges in the post-devaluation cuts; (5) the rupture of relations with the trades unions.

Yes, a formidable list indeed, and those of us who had sat on the backbenches or attended Party conferences throughout those years were hardly in a position to challenge his verdict. These were precisely the issues we had pressed, sometimes with effect and sometimes without. Yet, however fiercely we had made our protests and looked for new departures, we had never consolidated them all into a charge of general treachery. Had we done so, all the Ministers would have had to be arraigned as traitors, including Tony Benn himself. Had that final indictment been pressed, the Party would have torn itself to tatters in the early 1970s and no early recovery, no early return to power, would have been conceivable.

Moreover, as no one knew better than Tony Benn, there was another issue even more potentially destructive for the Party than the five he had tabulated or all of them rolled into one. The prospect of entry into the Common Market presented the hard, immovable reef on which great parties could wreck themselves entirely or exclude themselves from office for generations. Such, for the Tories in the 1840s, was the repeal of the Corn Laws, and such could have been the result for the Labour Party in the 1970s of the Common Market votes, both before and after entry. No issue in British post-war politics had posed for us so dangerous a choice, since both sides, with justice, regarded the question as one of first principle. To Tony Benn's credit, it was the device of the referendum which he more than anyone else favoured that had offered a way out of the impasse, a truly democratic way out. Without it, before the 1974 election, the Party might have been tempted to resort to the old method of Party discipline; a considerable segment of the Party would have been driven out altogether. Without it after 1974, and without the subsequent agreement to differ inside the Labour Cabinet, the fatal split would have come then. As it was, the Party was preserved on the honourable foundation of a new tolerance. But all of us knew how near to the rocks we had sailed.

Even without this special peril, our hold, the Labour Party's hold, on events, was shaky enough. We won the first election of 1974, but had no overall majority. We looked out for the first opportunity of winning a new election, as Harold Wilson had done before in 1966. We won the second election of 1974, but with nothing like the 1966 majority. We had at the outset, after the second 1974 election, a majority of three but by 1977 it was eroded, and we could sustain ourselves from month to month, from week to week, only with the votes of the minority parties or one or two of them.

So was this the experience of government which Tony Benn found so shattering and convulsive, such an affront to his Socialist ideals? It could hardly be so; he was there and could see for himself. He could see that both in the period when Harold Wilson was Prime Minister up to 1976 and in the period when James Callaghan took over up to 1979, we carried through, sometimes only by one or two votes, a series of Socialist measures, manifesto commitments, more ambitious and consistent than anything the previous Labour Government (with its majority of 100 and Tony Benn in the Cabinet) had attempted. Moreover, the programme executed with such determination covered a whole range of policies – industrial relations, public ownership, the rescue of many industries large and small, the extension of social services and the fulfilment of long-standing promises on such items as child benefit, comprehensive education, the abolition of the tied cottage. Almost for the first time, a real concerted advance was made in extending women's rights: apart from the child benefit paid to the mother, new maternity rights were introduced, a Sex Discrimination Act was placed on the

Statute Book, and the Equal Pay Act was brought into operation, despite all the other obstacles in the arena of pay policy. Even during the last period of the Lib–Lab Pact when we were prohibited from proceeding with larger Socialist measures, we still continued to carry through several of considerable importance in our pro- gramme – measures on devolution to which the whole Party was pledged, a new Merchant Shipping Act, long desired by the National Union of Seamen, a co-operative Development Agency Act, long desired by our friends in the Co-operative movement, and many more. No post-1945 government, except that Labour Gov- ernment of 1945 itself, ever carried through a more substantial series of reforms – which is one reason why the subsequent Thatch- er Government has spent so much of its time abrogating them. One of my jobs during that latter period was to see the legislative programme placed on the Statute Book. No one could question the zeal of the individual Ministers. Tony could have seen that too, if he had wished to look.

But wait: what about general economic policy? What about the moment when the International Monetary Fund was invited in, and that Labour Government agreed or was forced to inflict a whole range of cuts on the very services we wished to improve? Surely this was the decisive event in the whole record of that Labour Govern- ment, and has it not been quite legitimate for all commentators ever since to make the most of it – whether Tony Benn himself or Tory propagandists who use the same cry for their own quite different purposes? And of course, the moment was significant; there was a real debate. A range of cuts was imposed, and Tony Benn played his part in opposing them. So did several others, some more notably than Tony himself. Peter Shore, for example, put the case best of all; he wanted to win the argument there and then, if he could. Thanks to his advocacy and that of others, to the scepticism of one of the Ministers at the Treasury, Harold Lever, to the pressures from outside, thanks to Denis Healey's own realism, the original IMF propositions were at least mitigated, and the Labour Government retained the chance of seeking a new advance later. We were not prepared, any of us, to risk the alternative: opening the gates to the Tory enemy, through resignations and the destruction of the Gov- ernment. And the discussion round the Cabinet table, conducted in intelligent terms among Ministers who recognised their obligations to both the country and the Labour movement and who knew the nature of the Tory enemy, was an evenly balanced argument, never a clash between loyalty and treason.

Furthermore, one test of the course we should adopt concerned employment policy: how we should stop the rise in unemployment, how we should adopt and follow through a whole range of measures to turn the rising figures back the other way: how our aim must be to restore full employment. No major Cabinet meeting of those times discussed the general economic situation without also discussing in particular these employment and unemployment prospects. And truly we were faced, in those early years, with a steep, a hideous rise in unemployment. But we did not just watch the phenomenon, mesmerised and complacent. We took a series of measures to check the flood and turn it back the other way. Some of those measures were concerned with short-term training schemes; some were concerned with keeping in being small firms which would otherwise have been swept away by the slump; some were directed to the larger industries, steel, the motor industry, shipbuilding, machine tools and many more. Without this programme of Government investment and support, great tracts of British industry would have been wiped off the map altogether. So the rise in unemployment *was* checked, and turned the other way. As it happens, 1978–79 was the period when the numbers in employment were higher than ever before in the whole of British history – before and more especially since. And such was another part of the background to the debate in the Callaghan Cabinet about economic policy.

Considering how fierce and far-reaching was the world slump which hit us in 1974, considering how slender or non-existent was our majority, taking the economic record of the Wilson–Callaghan Cabinets from 1974–9 altogether, here was a situation which a democratic Socialist could honourably defend. Of course, many individual decisions were taken which each of us might have preferred to see resolved differently: such choices, such arguments face all Cabinets, especially Socialist Cabinets, I suspect. But no policy was thrust upon us either by circumstances or our fellow Ministers so deeply offensive to Socialist thinking as, say, the exchange policy of 1964–6, or the pro-American policy in Vietnam, or the departure by the previous Labour Government from its

understandings with the trade unions. And in the 1974–9 Government the fresh undertakings on industrial policy renewed in more
emphatic terms, thanks precisely to the experience in the late 1960s,
were executed faithfully in the letter and the spirit, and constantly
renewed. Even during the so-called 'winter of discontent' in 1978–
9, the lines of communication with the unions were never broken,
and the concordat agreed after it was a fresh, intelligent way of
seeking a solution to common problems, especially for the lower
paid workers whose discontent had been so real.

At some stage during the proceedings of that Cabinet, Tony Benn
lost interest in the present, in the sense of seeking to influence
immediate decisions, and turned his brilliantly agile, inventive
faculties to the future. It was more, I believe, a psycho-analytical
than a political problem. I do not say that the transformation
happened overnight during the IMF crisis; rather, signs of it
appeared much earlier. Even before the 1974 election, chiefly owing
to the proposals for extending public ownership in industry with
which he had been associated, he had been elevated by the most
vicious sections of the Tory press to the honourable post of Socialist
bogeyman Number One. He was vilified and harried in the most
unconscionable manner by such newspapers as the *Daily Mail* and
the *Daily Express*, and such campaigns can produce a sense of
claustrophobia in the victim. Soon after that election he found
himself embroiled in an argument about his plans for compulsory
planning agreements with Harold Wilson, and this quarrel he
represented later as a flagrant and deliberate effort to tear up
manifesto commitments. Even before the second election of 1974 he
would sometimes talk in fantasies about the way some of his
colleagues, headed by Jim Callaghan, were preparing for a Coalition. Sometimes he would enlarge on this theme with a truly
scintillating satirical talent, and sometimes he was boringly in
earnest.

Several of such moods and moments of sudden, new departures,
indeed of the mixed motives which may govern us all, are recorded
in Barbara Castle's diary. For example, in June 1974 – as early as
that – she describes a quite minor manoeuvre designed to ensure
good publicity for himself which Wedgie had executed: 'We agreed
to have a row in the Cabinet about Jim's lack of consultation. I then
had a bit of a row with Wedgie, whom I love but whose unctuous-

ness about "open government" irritates me, perhaps because I sense the ambition that motivates it.' Then she describes how Wedgie had contrived a calculated leak for his own advantage, how Harold Wilson had had to face awkward questions in the House on account of it, how Wedgie had 'told us loftily that he believed in taking people into his confidence', and how she had gone 'into a great passionate diatribe on my old theme: collective responsibility'.

The clash compressed here was repeated on numerous occasions, and indicates one of the profound reasons why Tony fell out with his colleagues in almost every group he ever worked with. He did believe in open government; no doubt whatever, and he could conceivably claim that he had believed in it longer than anyone else. But he did also once believe in collective responsibility, particularly for the Cabinet – witness his long-forgotten lecture in 1971 in which he had stated it in terms with which even the righteous Barbara (and she certainly was on this topic), a truly passionate believer, would have approved. But gradually his belief frayed; gradually his other loyalties elbowed out this allegiance; gradually, from the point of view of his Cabinet colleagues, or even his smaller group of associates, he became – literally, it is hard to avoid the term – not to be trusted. This was the practical conclusion to which many who worked with him were forced. As Barbara shows, he would often seek to conceal such moments with an unctuous avoidance of the real argument. Tony in his pulpit preaching his often newly-discovered revelations to his congregation of Socialist sinners was never an appealing figure. But then, to be fair, we must add a few sentences in the same diary entry: 'Wedgie disarmed me when he suddenly said, completely naturally "But you are able to do things, Barbara. I am in a department where, at present at any rate, I can do nothing but talk." I clutched his hand sympathetically. When he is honest like this I will back him to the hilt.' I heard Tony talk in those terms, too. He did think he was especially circumscribed by Harold Wilson in the way he was able to operate at the Department of Industry, and he was even more outraged when he was shifted from it. He could be a brilliant Minister with technical detail more at his fingertips than most others, and then he could throw it all away in a spasm of frustration. But sometimes, and more frequently, those spasms came to be calculated too.

Every few months he would act on his own, usually in a way

which defied collective Cabinet responsibility, and then the rest of us, Barbara, myself and a few others according to circumstances, would spend anxious hours trying to help solder the Cabinet together again. At some moments of personal crisis he would suddenly upbraid one or other of us for not recognising his claims properly, but these outbursts, some excusable, were rare indeed. Much more often he was his cool, controlled self, content to apply his talents elsewhere, at great public meetings in the country or directing the Home Policy of the Party's National Executive; more and more that was his base. The meetings outside certainly played their part. Gladstone, said one of his biographers, learnt his glimmerings of democracy at the great mass meetings of the Midlothian campaign, and the huge audiences addressed by Tony affected him maybe even more than he affected them. Even in the testing, strained years of the 1974–9 Cabinet, he did not lose his high spirits, his effervescence. Yet all the while he was adding another strand to his personal strategy: to cut loose from present dilemmas, and prepare for a later day.

Somewhere in Tony's own mountainous stacks of recorded events the exact timing of this choice may be set down, although I doubt whether the full reality will be uncovered. During my first two years in the Wilson Cabinet of 1974 I sat next to him at the Cabinet table, and these proximities have some interest. He would, as others have noticed, be writing non-stop, either making notes for what he would say himself or tabulating events for his diary. I see that Barbara records, quite early on, 4 January 1974, to be precise, before the 1974 election, how she thought he was keeping a detailed diary. She should know the signs. However, I doubt whether he will reveal much about himself, except unconsciously. My guess is that the Tony Benn revelations when they come will recall, recite and endlessly elaborate the series of serious political initiatives which he presented to his colleagues, and which the insensible company refused to heed, including even those who might have been expected to be most sympathetic. On countless occasions when he told us of wrongful decisions being taken in his own department or elsewhere, we would urge him to take the issue to the Cabinet; all too often he rejected the advice, and would bring instead some half-baked, but grandiose proposition which had no chance whatever of acceptance, but might look good on the records or recapitulated at some packed meeting of party supporters. Often then and later, he reminded me of Stafford Cripps, and of course the young Stafford of the 1930s who had just discovered Marx, and not his statesmanlike post-1945 successor who picked out instead the path of Puritan rectitude and austerity. Stafford would talk of his new discovery like a child, but he could never hold his own on the sacred subject with, say, Aneurin Bevan or Noel Brailsford, who knew the doctrine in all its magnificence and subtlety. Marxism *is* a thrilling creed, and one which can open our eyes and ears to the excitement and glory of working-class history. Tony was touched by it during this decade, even if, as with Stafford, he seemed to assimilate it too crudely. Moreover, Tony managed to wed, without too much difficulty, his Marxism with the Christian tradition. Others, with more delicate philosophical skills than himself, have attempted the task, but with Tony the marriage, like some other of his manoeuvres, looked like one of convenience.

Whatever the accumulation of impulses and inspirations, Tony Benn approached the crisis of the Callaghan Government, both the defeat and the sequel, in a very different mood from all his fellow Cabinet colleagues. The moment he had expected and prepared for had come. An observer has recorded that when the Cabinet of 1914 met to face the terrible news of the outbreak of war, one of their number greeted the moment differently than all the others: Winston Churchill was ready and cheerful. So was Tony Benn in 1979 and 1980. Few of us were surprised when he did not turn up at the post-election dinner we had sought to arrange on the Sunday afterwards. He had his own plans and his own new body of close associates. He moved with rapidity and skill. Nothing was to be left to chance this time; no leisurely, reflective lectures for the Fabian Society.

According to the version of history which Tony himself would devise later, what followed the 1979 defeat was a widespread, spontaneous revolt throughout the movement against the betrayals of the Labour Government and a resolve to produce the remedies which would forbid any repetition. Of course, the discontent was deep; the defeat was a heavy one, in some parts of the country quite unexpectedly so; and a genuine, full-scale inquest was required. But some other features of the situation were worth noting, and are now quite forgotten. First, Jim Callaghan himself, whatever his failings, had kept his hold on the public. He was a considerably more popular figure than Mrs Thatcher; he had his own effective way of communicating with the British people, and without him our defeat might have been even more serious. Moreover, soon after the election, we had the chance of showing how the Party kept its hold. Labour came within a hair's-breadth of winning a by-election at Southend. The Party was not quite in such disarray as subsequent history or re-written history might indicate.

However, a special kind of post-defeat operation was being organised by Tony Benn and his closest associates, and the place he was principally able to use for the purpose was the National Executive of the Party itself. And the instrument he was able to wield was the caucus. No doubt similar caucus meetings of like-minded members of the Executive concerting action together before individual committee meetings or the full meetings of the Executive itself had often been a feature of Executive proceedings. Some of the trades union representatives had worked such a system in the far-off Bevanite–Gaitskellite years, and sometimes the Bevanites had felt they were entitled to retaliate by instituting comparable meetings of their own. But under Tony Benn's guidance and drive, the system became more regular and efficient and demonstrably effective than ever before. More than ever, the caucus meetings and the decisions taken there about the way the later votes should be cast, under-mined the chance of real open debate in the Executive. All through this post-election period, he could count on a good majority in the Executive, and a little later (after 1980) the caucus meetings system was combined with a special Bennite provision – all in the name of open government – for the recording of voting lists at the Executive. Not only did this arrangement add considerably to the length and tedium of Executive meetings. Voting lists were widely dissemi-nated throughout the movement, and their dissemination would influence future patterns of Executive voting. The case for this innovation was, of course, presented on democratic grounds. The effect, and no doubt the purpose, was to consolidate the particular majority which already existed.

Month after month – in the aftermath of the 1979 defeat – fresh Bennite or Benn-backed propositions were published or presented. One, a pamphlet about the Prime Minister's so-called dictatorship, purported to describe how the power of a Labour Prime Minister had grown so inordinately that it undermined the protections of Labour's own constitution. Another proposal, mooted first at the fag-end of an Executive sub-committee but soon acquiring the status of a fully-Executive backed resolution for Conference, was that the so-called Clause 5 meeting between the Executive and the Parliamentary leadership at which the leader was alleged to exercise his veto should lose its authority. The final decision-making power should be transferred to the Executive, thus depriving the Parliamentary Party and its representatives of a power which it had held since 1918. I remember voicing my objection to Tony at that first sub-committee, pleading at least that the matter should be discussed with the Parliamentary Party before it was raised, much less pressed to its conclusion. The most elementary requirements of consultation, of common respect for the democratic process, made that desirable; but he would have none of it. The mood for the kind of change he wanted was there, and he would do nothing to soften it.

Throughout those years he became the foremost advocate of the three constitutional changes required, as he claimed, to remedy the ills from which Labour governments had suffered: first, the mandatory re-selection of MPs; second, a new system of electing the leader, replacing the Parliamentary Party with a larger college outside; and, third, the transfer of the final authority for making the manifesto to the National Executive. For each of these changes there was a plausible case to be made, and sometimes a good one. Proposals along these lines had come from other quarters. But in the manner in which they were now combined, and in the context in which Tony Benn himself presented them, this was the charge-sheet of betrayal, against the leadership in particular and the Parliamentary Party in general.

Tony himself would still take unctuous pride, to use Barbara's word, in his refusal to engage in personalities. But – especially in the light of what he himself had said after the 1970 defeat in that rarely-quoted Fabian lecture – it is impossible to suppose that he did not know what he was doing. He was accusing the leadership of treachery in the precise terms which he had specified as so intolerable in 1970. He was driving ever deeper the gulf between the Party inside Parliament and the Party outside. More and more he ceased to make regular appearances in the Parliamentary Party and would never speak a word in defence of MPs who might be under attack in the constituencies from the very elements he had sought to arouse, MPs in some instances with much longer Left-wing credentials than his own. Challenged on such matters, he used the protective gesture which some of us had come to know so well. He would turn aside, almost as if he had never heard the awkward question, and talk of something else.

At the 1979 Conference the mood was set; most of the fire was directed against serried ranks of the Parliamentary Party. At the 1980 Conference, as we have seen, Tony delivered his major onslaught against the previous Party leadership, and after considerable commotion and confusion, carried two out of the three constitutional changes. One night at that Conference Jim Callaghan told me he would be resigning. Events there had not forced his hand; he had always intended to go soon. I strongly urged him to stay, and renewed the plea when we came back to London. For I strongly believed that he and I acting together would have the best chance of avoiding a year at least of bruising internal battles.

1981 could and should have been the year in which the Labour movement applied all its energies to concert united vengeance for the wounds inflicted upon our people and to destroy the Tory Government. Instead, we turned it into a period of futility and shame, and the responsibility for transmuting every controversy of the time into an internal Labour Party dispute rested directly with Tony Benn. One of the first steps which the National Executive took at the beginning of the year, with my full support, was to organise a series of demonstrations against the most obvious scourge and the source of almost every other social ill, the rising flood of mass unemployment. Sometimes in past periods, it had been true that the national leadership of the Party had failed to act promptly on these greatest issues. No one could say the same now. The lead was given, and every section of the movement showed its eagerness to respond. The first great demonstration was staged at Liverpool, and it was a mammoth and unmitigated success: it showed what could be done by unity in the right cause. The second demonstration was at Cardiff, and was well-nigh wrecked by a sectarian mob (mostly imported from outside Wales) on the side, screaming applause for Tony Benn and execrations on Denis Healey. The third in Birmingham was wrecked absolutely by even wilder and more indiscriminate scenes of sectarian shrieking. Perhaps they were encouraged by the fact that Tony had characterised the Cardiff display as nothing more than part of the old British tradition of heckling at public meetings. Birmingham, and Cardiff before it, were truly something quite different from that; these were open displays by the sectarian groups which had no real connection with the Labour movement except to batten on it. Actual financial loss for the Party at Birmingham could be reckoned in several thousands of pounds; the appalling political loss conveyed far and wide across the country on the television screens by courtesy of the Labour Party itself was incalculable.

All other political events within the Labour Party for the scavenger Tory press and the vulturous television cameras had been overtaken by the decision of Tony Benn to challenge Denis Healey for the deputy-leadership of the Party under the new electoral college system. He had embarked upon the contest despite pleadings from almost every quarter, mine amongst the foremost. A last-minute touch of typical tomfoolery – or Bennfoolery – was provided by his decision to go ahead with his candidature before the *Tribune* Group in Parliament could present to him their appeal to stop it. A few months after having joined the *Tribune* group for the first time, he had succeeded in splitting them down the middle; they were not quite so used to his methods as those of us who had seen him operate elsewhere. And truly, no skill in prediction was needed to see what would happen. The Cardiff and Birmingham fiascos were only the most spectacular. A whole hot, ugly summer followed. Week by week, the areas of dispute were enlarged, the gulf cut deeper, while our Tory opponents watched in gleeful disbelief and gratitude. Gradually or not so gradually, the charge of bad faith against the Labour Cabinet was turned into one of bad faith against the Shadow Cabinet. And frequently insult was added to the injury, in the most precise terms. Those who protested against this particular election were berated for opposing the electoral process itself. Some of us denounced the wisdom of his standing and he said we were interfering with his rights. Tony Benn in such a mood could belittle democracy itself and reduce the affairs of the Labour Party to the politics of the kindergarten.

This deputy-leadership election surely was no 'healing process', as he described it. He was out to win, whatever happened, and as we came nearer to the end, he and his closest backers thought they were winning, right up to the Saturday night of 27 September, before the result was declared. Throughout the day, at the pre-Conference meeting of the Executive, he used his majority there to push through one proposition after another he favoured, often overturning the advice of the Party officials who warned against the folly of accepting commitments which had never been costed. Nothing else counted. He thought the next day would mark the climax of all his exertions over those years. Not the absolute climax, of course; that would come when he would be able to stand and win the next full leadership fight – no doubt after yet another 'healing process'.

He was a bad loser on that occasion – not, I must acknowledge, his customary reaction to setbacks. Normally, he would recover with a will to fight again. 'Wedgie never gives up,' Barbara had written in her diary; that is how he is made. But perhaps he recognised at Brighton the measure and permanence of his own defeat. Right from the moment when the figures were known, I thought I did my best to renew the possibilities of common action. After all, he did represent a big following in the party; reconciliation was imperative. But he would make no response there and then, and back in London, fresh overtures brought the same reaction. Soon we found ourselves embroiled in yet another argument on that old, hoary theme of collective responsibility – this time, as it applied to the Shadow Cabinet – and one consequence of our dispute was that he was not re-elected to it. 'I have paid the price,' he said, 'for taking a stand on principle. I would like to be in, but one thing I have to make clear is that I am not prepared to accept that if you are in the Shadow Cabinet you should be asked to abandon the policies of the Labour Party.' It was slightly galling, although not at all unexpected, that he should climb back onto his pulpit of high principle just at that moment. For, of course, the doctrine of Shadow Cabinet collective responsibility, a looser copy of the full-dress Cabinet cloak, is not some old, musty constitutional suit of armour. It is much more concerned with commonsense, good faith and comradeship among those who must act together in Parliament, if they are to give effective leadership to the Labour movement in the country. No substitute for that good faith exists; Tony Benn has not discovered one.

I had a further reason for my feelings at that time, and maybe he shared it. I suppose, in the interests of open government or open shadow government, it may now be revealed. One of our talks in my Shadow Cabinet office finished ahead of schedule when I urged upon him that one contribution he could make, to assist the National Executive and the Party at large to function effectively, would be to call off the pre-Executive meetings caucus, or at least, to mitigate its operation, to stop the rigid pre-arranged votes which prohibited real discussion, to give us a renewed chance to let the Executive perform its proper function: to prepare to fight the Tory enemy. He shook his head as if to deny that any such effective caucus existed, and when I persisted with the charge, he persisted with the denial. So I called him a liar, and he got up and left.

How this scene will be recorded in his memoirs, I cannot tell. It will be there somewhere, and there somewhere I suppose, suitably 'shredded', if that's the right word, will be the record of what was decided at the secret meetings which he implied never took place.

And this is the trouble, or one of the troubles, as Barbara so well understood in her well-tabulated Cabinet collective responsibility arguments. Men and women in charge of political affairs of some importance will require places where they can discuss matters and offer tentative arguments before they reach their conclusions. They ought to be able to do that on the National Executive of the Labour Party: the sooner, the better, in the interests of democratic Socialism.

# Brother John

An intellectual is someone whose mind watches itself.

Albert Camus

John Strachey had a gift of clarity surpassing that of any other Socialist publicist of his time. He could make plain the most complicated themes: Marxism, for example, in all its modern connections. Yet his biographer could not explain all his contortions, and he himself seemed quite content with a liberal creed of the most modest pretensions.

One of the sillier quarrels which breaks out periodically in the Labour Party is that between the so-called intellectuals, the rootless, too-clever-by-half, brain specialists (Stafford Cripps, Dick Crossman, Anthony Wedgwood Benn, etc.), and the hard-headed, down to earth sons of toil (Ernest Bevin, George Brown, Ray Gunter, etc.), who usually know what's what, and how to substitute this ill-defined substance for outlandish ideas of Socialism. Or rather this was the picture drawn for their own comfort by Labour's opponents before so many applecarts were upset by the arrival on the scene of leaders like Frank Cousins, Jack Jones or Hugh Scanlon. How could they be slotted into the old contest between middle-class revolutionaries and solid, tame trades unionists?

But maybe the pattern never existed, and a classic figure steps forward to prove that thesis, the subject of a biography by Hugh Thomas, *John Strachey* published by Eyre Methuen in 1973. For Strachey was the super-intellectual of all time. Rarely in our political history can there have been a man who so steadfastly sought to resolve every problem by the pure light of reason, and rarely has a practising politician been gifted with superior powers of lucid exposition. He surveyed every shifting scene in the political drama which passed before him with what so many of his friends saw as his cold intellectual eye. 'He won't have a heart for years yet, I expect. It is almost terrifying to realise how cold he is,' wrote his sister to his first lover. He was then in his early twenties. Forty years later, the same recognisable Strachey was analysing the possibilities of worldwide nuclear destruction with the same piercing, freezing remorselessness and intellectual courage.

Yet the irony, or the comedy or the tragedy, is that the power of his logic had been used to justify and expound one contradictory position after another. At various stages he took his stand at every point from the extreme Left to extreme Right, and in his latter years he became truly the best intellectual defender the stodgy, orthodox Party leadership had ever had. True, in this final appearance, he never quite recaptured the panache and the assurance which was his in the 1930s as the all-conquering Marxist theoretician. But no one who listened to or, better still, read what he had to say could question what a formidable arguer he was, how he could sweep all before him – until the final moment of practical political decision actually arrived. Then he would waver or turn aside, distrusting his supreme intelligence at the supreme hour, or searching for guidance from his adopted father-figure of the period.

Many of us who had witnessed these agonising crises in Strachey's political performance, from far or near, came to believe that he was chronically unfitted to be a man of action at all, and it is fascinating to see that he himself, when he first stood for Parliament in 1924, shared the presentiment. 'So there I am, *launched* on a political life,' he wrote to the same first love who had been the confidante of sister Amabel. 'No one knows better than yourself how deeply unsuitable I am to it. But still it is Life, and I really find I care for little else.' Appropriately, his biographer looks for psychoanalytical explanations of Strachey's politics. He was one of the first Marxists who dared to attempt to incorporate Freud in his system of thinking; this formed part of his intellectual ambition to embrace the whole range of modern knowledge. He was quite capable of out-analysing his own analyst, and when he married a second time, much more wisely and happily than on the first occasion, he and his wife went to their separate analysts on their wedding afternoon.

However, it is the long parade of father-figures which is properly elevated to the major role, starting with the real one, followed by an assortment which included Professor Joad, Oswald Mosley, the Communist Party and the Royal Air Force, and finishing up with his filial adoration divided between Herman Kahn and the Hudson (nuclear war games) Institute, and the one and only George Brown, later Lord George-Brown.

It would be possible to tell the tale comically, pathetically, savagely. Hugh Thomas avoided all those temptations while writing, apparently, with absolute candour, and the feat is the more remarkable since, presumably, he had little political sympathy with the Strachey of the 1930s when, as Thomas rightly says, he had a spark never fully rekindled thereafter. Perhaps the absence of a larger background of those years in the book robs some of the performers, Strachey in particular, of their best vindication.

For those of us who knew Strachey only in his outward political manifestation, the book is absorbing, it should be hastily added, in the whole spectacle of the clash between such a brain and such an age, and the comments upon it of those who were his companions in the struggle. Here, for example, is the Aneurin Bevan of 1930 on that old theme of the role of the Stracheys in the Labour Party: 'It is the besetting sin of intellectuals to be too much influenced by the drive of their own minds. They are too reluctant to submit themselves to the pressure of events. In intellectuals, there is a tendency to want to dominate and shape things arbitrarily. They can influence these events only by being moulded by them.' That was the Marxist Bevan pragmatically instructing the ex-Mosleyite Strachey in his pro-Marxist period in pre-Hitler days, and the tumult of argument sounds as fresh as the newest branch of the New Left.

John Strachey himself wrote brilliantly on his fellow intellectuals, and one such volume was *The Strangled Cry*, published by Bodley Head in 1961.

The strangled cry of that title is the protest embodied in the present-day literature of reaction against the values of Communism. Strachey dissected with splendid insight and clarity, not excelled in any of his writings, five books – Arthur Koestler's *Darkness at Noon*, George Orwell's *Animal Farm* and *Nineteen Eighty-Four*, Whitaker Chambers's *Witness* and Boris Pasternak's *Dr Zhivago*. But his counter-attack was not confined to these authors and these books. He claimed to be criticising a whole range of literature which 'has by now so formed the intellectual climate of the West that many people may regard the subject as closed'.

His accusation, in his opening paragraphs, is not muffled. For his quarrel is that these writers represent a reaction, not merely against the doctrines, dogmas and crimes of Communism, but against 'five hundred years of rationalism and empiricism; against, in short, the enlightenment. That is its scandal, and its power.' His conclusion, in his final paragraphs, is that this branch of literature has more than served its purpose; in several of its manifestations it has become a positive influence to 'dissuade us from even attempting to apply reason to society'. Those responsible 'have deserted, whether they know it or intend it, or whether their inner motive be weariness, class-prejudice, or simply despair, to *the enemies of civilised life*'.

The italics are mine. Strachey in his Communist days could not have used harsher language.

In this sense, this book is a magnificent, brave, liberal manifesto – liberal, of course, in the use of the word which embraces democratic Socialism; brave, because Strachey is challenging the current orthodoxies of those with whom his own furious disillusionment with Communism might be expected to place him in close sympathy; and magnificent, because the argument is raised to the highest level. He cherishes, respects and honours all his chosen opponents; tackles them in the fortress of their strongest ideas; and wastes no space on secondary skirmishes.

Yet once all this much is admitted, criticisms abound. For some reason which this review may not succeed in explaining, no Socialist surely can read the book without a flat feeling of inadequacy at the end. Almost the only firm conclusions which Strachey reaches comprise a condemnation of 'the anti-politicism' of his selected authors, chiefly Pasternak, and a reassertion, in satisfactorily extreme terms, of the right of dissent and the paramount need for any civilised society to protect that right. No libertarian Socialist could question these limited verdicts, and yet, however much we may rejoice to see them so passionately vindicated, they do not satisfy. This is too thin a gruel for Socialists to feed upon.

Liberalism is not enough; precisely for that reason Marxism was born and flourished. Liberal economics proved self-defeating, and will surely do so again. The same failure is likely to occur even more certainly in other fields. To insist on everyone's right to say what he thinks freely as the cardinal item in the proper creed for our times and for decades to come, and then to have precious little to say – this, almost, is the new Stracheyism, and it will not prove sufficient to protect the liberal idea itself any more than it was when people like John Stuart Mill and Lord Macaulay reached similar conclusions a century or so ago. (Mill, as it happens, at last acknowledged the deficiency and became a Socialist in the process.)

Ex-Communists may find this diet sufficiently luscious; for them the newly discovered fruit of liberty must taste all the sweeter. Yet, for Socialists, essential political vitamins are lacking. Men must *do* and *act* as well as *think*, and *talk* and *argue*. And if men who believe in freedom do not act effectively, others who despise freedom will act in their place. This was what happened before. This was the way the road was left open for Fascism or that quite different phenomenon, Communism. Strachey apparently believed that nothing of the sort would happen again, chiefly because of his combined assumption (a) that Western societies, thanks to Keynes, democratic pressures and mild doses of Socialism, have it in their power to solve their economic problems and conjure the class war out of existence; and (b) that Soviet society has achieved nothing but the large-scale industrialisation which could have been achieved by other means.

Altogether, there was a profound complacency in the Strachey creed, however much his eloquence might succeed in masking it. Because the revolutionary ideal ended in the distortions and horrors of Stalinite Communism, he appeared to accept that it need never be invoked again in different shapes and for different purposes. He seemed to forecast that his liberal semi-Socialism could broaden down from precedent to precedent in a pleasantly cool atmosphere.

Who could believe it? What could all Strachey's former students in Asia and Africa make of such comfortable caution? Would caste and privilege and power abdicate so gracefully? Or what will happen here? Will ICI or the upholders of our public schools and the whole Establishment yield and be subdued without a struggle? Possibly the only reason why they look so tame now is because no one is threatening them. The rudest power-maniacs can be courteous to suppliants. Strachey's whole tone, if it is approved, must exacerbate the chronic disease of social democracy – its lack of daring, dignity and resolution. Both in the main essay included in this book and in some of the others, he seemed to suggest that the post-Keynesian revolution in Western societies had gone much further than it has gone and that future tasks look trivial compared with the simple need to restore the prestige of reason and liberal methods against both the Communists and the reactors against Communism.

And, in applying this theme elsewhere, could it really be that his mild potions would cure the unimaginably vast perils of the nuclear age? May it not be true after all that diseases desperate grown by desperate appliance are relieved or not at all? Reason could point to that conclusion as readily as to any other. To take a specific example, how could Strachey remark so casually that no one in Britain was frightened of America? The thought of the enormous power assembled in the hands of some of the least liberal elements in the United States should surely stir men and women to sentiments more revolutionary than the bland hope that nothing more is required than the free exchange of opinion. (Not that the American military scientists even think of permitting that. Their offences against the liberal tradition may be as monstrous and even more disastrous than those perpetrated by the Stalinites.) Thus the questions provoked by Strachey's book could be piled high one upon another. And doubts arise about his verdicts on the writers he analyses. George Orwell regarded Communism as a betrayal of rationalism; Whitaker Chambers saw one as the inexorable product of the other. The two men never deserved to be treated on the same scale. Moreover, Strachey's subtle apology for Chambers, 'the informer', provokes without settling a whole large debate about the relation between the true liberal and the State.

The criticism of Pasternak forms the most brilliant part of the book. Yet, unchallengeable as may be his greatness and certainly his courage, does Pasternak really come near to explaining what we most want to know? We must continue, says Strachey himself, 'to subject Communism to strict appraisal: for it fell from the highest pinnacles of human aspiration'.

Is it really true that that fall was doomed from the start, that it can all be traced to some fatal flaw implanted in the Marxist title deeds? This is a kind of apocalyptic conception in reverse. Surely it is much more probable that the worst results were due to a series of individual wrong turnings. If the original aspiration was so good (as it largely was), how did it become evil? The checks and balances required to protect freedom in Soviet society might have been retained (or rather inserted since they did not exist before) without casting aside the aspiration itself. More clues may be discovered from ransacking the writings of such people as Rosa Luxemburg, who had to grapple with the realities, even than in countering the doctrines of the 'anti-politicists', who do not even face the problem. And these, maybe, are the kind of disputations in which Soviet society will be increasingly engaged in the years ahead, to the advantage of many other countries besides themselves. Yet Strachey regards Soviet society as being utterly barren. Of the Soviet

Revolution's achievements he writes: 'the means were terrible, the results commonplace'. The verdict is too neat and arid.

Finally, it is necessary to descend from the heights of Strachey's argument to a more personal point. One of the oddest ironies was that Strachey, the ex-Communist theoretician, published his liberal, social democratic manifesto at the very hour when Bertrand Russell, the arch-liberal-social democrat who prophesied the horror of Stalinism fifty years before, was threatened with expulsion from the Labour Party, as a Communist dupe, by Strachey's own leaders. 'How *can* anyone,' asked Strachey in his liberal peroration, 'imagine that they know it all and have the right to suppress, by either the hard or the soft method, a contrary opinion? How *can* anyone any longer doubt the immense value of, precisely, dissent? For any real, genuine spontaneously held personal opinion *may*, for all we know, contain the grain of truth without which we are all doomed.'

How could Strachey, after that, fail to speak against the expulsion of Bertrand Russell? And let neither he nor anyone else demur with the quibble that expulsion from the Party involved no infringement of his liberal precepts. It was the suppression of freedom within the Party, as Rosa Luxemburg classically argued, which was the fatal choice which led to the Soviet tyranny. The empire of human freedom will never be enlarged by a party which fails to apply its principles within its own frontiers.

# Brother Fenner

Gerrard Winstanley, the Digger, wrote a pamphlet which was signed by himself and forty-four others 'for and on behalf of the poor oppressed people of England and the whole world'.

Christopher Hill in
*Puritanism and Revolution*

Fenner Brockway, in his nineties, could still talk about democratic Socialism with his old fire and force, but, even more remarkably, he could still write with ease and originality. Witness his book *Britain's First Socialists*, published by Quartet in 1980.

At the age of ninety-two and still going strong, Fenner Brockway retained undimmed at least two of the shining gifts which he started to bestow on British politics in general and the Labour movement in particular way back before the 1914 war – the sharp, clear style of a first-class journalist and the vision of a free, democratic Socialist society. But then there are many other attributes to be added in the same breath – the insight into some of the worst infamies of the century – imperialism, for example; the abiding allegiance to the ways of peace; the overflowing optimism about man's (and woman's) role on this planet; the capacity to turn every cause and institution with which he has been associated to some useful purpose – even the House of Lords.

It must be excusable in this instance to start with the author rather than the book; but the book deserves to makes its own way in the world. For one thing, it is beautifully printed and illustrated and presented, and, for another, it is a little masterpiece of vivid compression, the best brief introduction to what have been quite recent discoveries about the true history of the English people at one of their supreme moments of greatness.

No doubt Fenner Brockway, like British Socialism itself, may trace his inspiration back to the seventeenth-century revolutionaries, but if he had written this volume in his Edwardian youth, the materials would hardly have been available. He quotes (thanks to the researches of another unlikely lord, Leslie Hale) a few sentences from Carlyle on the executions in Burford churchyard:

> So die the Leveller Corporals, strong they are after a sort, for the Liberties of England; resolute to the very death. Misguided Corporals! But history . . . will not refuse these poor Corporals also her tributary sigh.

Many of his most eminent fellow-historians would not allow even that. Any notion of the depth and strength of the democratic revolution which so nearly took command of the Puritan revolution itself was removed from the history books as if by some invisible Stalinite hand. The Levellers, the true Levellers, the Agitators, the Diggers, the Seekers, the Quakers, the Ranters and the rest were dismissed as a bunch of sectarian cranks, irrelevant to the momentous struggle between King and Parliament, recorded by the great Whig historians, and by Clarendon for the Royalists and Carlyle, who achieved the necessary feat of resurrecting Cromwell from infamy.

Yet the Levellers did at last find a champion to match even these: twenty-two years ago H. N. Brailsford's classic volume was published and to it has been added the vast, rich treasure of Christopher Hill's historical learning and imagination. These two, with a few assistants, have restored the dimension of English history so nearly lost. Fenner pays eager tribute to his old ILP comrade-in-arms; the book is dedicated to Brailsford. It was he who showed that the poor Corporals needed no patronising sighs. They made themselves the driving force of the revolution. They and their Leveller colleagues – John Lilburne, Richard Overton, William Walwyn, Gerrard Winstanley, 'the father of British Socialism', as Fenner justly calls him, and the rest – take their place alongside the greatest figures in our history.

Indeed, even without Brailsford and Brockway, such men as these must eventually have found their modern audience through the very power of the words they spoke and wrote. Overnight almost, in the England of that tumultuous age, a time of 'teeming freedom' as someone called it, the new instrument of the printing press came into its own, and it promised or threatened to create a whole new society. Suddenly censorship collapsed and the English people talked to one another as never before; they helped to reshape their lovely Elizabethan language in a stronger idiom; one can hear the Ironsides in Cromwell's prose and Milton's poetry and in William Walwyn's pamphlets – and he, more than anyone, could stop short, amid the battlecries, to preach a better cause still: 'It will be no satisfaction to God's justice to plead that you murdered men in obedience to your general.'

Out of the whole turmoil was born the idea of English democracy, or worldwide democracy, for that matter, since the idea was carried by English emissaries back and forth across the Atlantic. So little is it true that Socialism or democracy (and the two, as Fenner shows, are endlessly, inextricably intertwined) are imports from some foreign land. Long before anyone had heard of Karl Marx or Methodism or Margaret Thatcher's scholarly comments on such themes, English people discussed how the nation's wealth should be commonly owned and shared, and how the ballot box should be used to achieve these and other Leveller ambitions. Why, they even called their newspaper *The Moderate*, just to illustrate no doubt how the real extremists were the Norman conquerors and their marauding descendants who had stolen the people's land, the people's rights and the people's liberties.

# Four
# Prime Ministers

# David Lloyd George

Lloyd George was a bigger man than Churchill,
and one of the biggest things about Churchill was
that he knew it.

Aneurin Bevan

Here is what I trust I have a right to describe as a
family portrait of Lloyd George. The sources for it
are explained in the text, but an acknowledgement
is also due to the great biography of him by John
Grigg, the last volume of which, *From Peace to
War*, takes the story to 1916; and, above all, the
*Lloyd George Diary* by Frances Stevenson. Along
with other members of my family, and thanks to my
accidental friendships with two Lloyd George wor-
shippers – Frank Owen and Max Beaverbrook – I
had the chance to compare notes with her. It must
be added also that two leading historians, master
and pupil, A. J. P. Taylor and Kenneth O. Morgan,
have made a series of most notable contributions to
our knowledge of Lloyd George.

I was brought up in a home where the name of David Lloyd George was, above all others, the most accursed. The charge was that he had broken the once so-powerful Liberal Party; that he had thrown open the gates to triumphant, gloating Toryism; that the deed had been done in pursuit of raw, personal ambition: a heavy indictment for sure and one not easily refuted or forgotten. However, as the years passed, I, along with the rest of the family, came not to know him – that would be too strong a claim – but to see and hear him in a quite different light. My father's suspicions and my mother's scorn never subsided altogether, but somehow or other the Lloyd George sunshine – such a burning oracle as it is now difficult to conceive casting its rays across our political planet – penetrated the darkest corners, even in our far-away, West country, one-time Asquithian retreat.

My father fought and won a famous by-election as a 'Wee Free' follower of Asquith against the Lloyd George Coalition in the ominous year 1922; ominous, that is, for Lloyd George, for that was the year in which he was removed from the Premiership, never to return to high office again. No observer could suppose that so mighty a figure as Lloyd George, who had taken command of No 10 Downing Street in war and peace, was to stay excluded from office until his dying day, twenty-two years later. And, of course, my father's by-election victory, compared with the hammer-blows inflicted on Lloyd George from other quarters, was little more than a pinprick. Yet Lloyd George's skin, like that of the toughest political giants, could be sensitive. Moreover, my father in his brilliant campaign, knew all the weaknesses in the Lloyd George armour, and hit where it hurt – where Lloyd George, once the champion of great liberal and nonconformist causes, knew that he was vulnerable. My father unloosed his invective against the black-and-tan terrorism in Ireland, against the barren and vindictive terms of the Versailles Peace Treaty, against the smell of corruption which seemed to characterise the preferred Coalition method of doing business; altogether, against the surrender in almost every field to the raucous, bovine, flagwagging Tory majority in the House of Commons brought into being at the 1918 'Hang the Kaiser' election.

And who was the author of that crowning outrage against the liberal decencies? Never could Lloyd George wipe away the stains. It was his decision to exploit the moment of delirium, to act in collusion with the Conservative Party machine, to contrive in the process that the Liberal Party should be shattered at the polls and that he himself would emerge, with his shabby little band of sycophantic Liberal followers, not as the independent master of the new Parliament, but as the eventual sacrificial victim of the same evil forces which he had summoned from the depths.

Yes, that is what did happen. The Tories who had once hailed Lloyd George as the nation's saviour, the greatest since Chatham, kicked him into the gutter when it suited their party interest. Liberals, true liberals with a small or large L like my father, watched these events with an anguish which may be imagined; they could say to Lloyd George and his hangers-on: 'We told you so.' The admonition was both painful and true.

The mood of the early 1920s, which I have sought to describe, their judgement on Lloyd George, in many Liberal families and no less in most Labour families, derived predominantly from his conduct since 1918, the way in which all the promises of a new world of homes for heroes were debased and mocked. An old world of poverty and mass unemployment and social strife was restored, no less savage and unjust than the pre-1914 model. Lloyd George himself often struggled valiantly, either behind the scenes or even occasionally on the centre stage itself, to withstand these reactionary pressures. But mostly he was swept along with them or, in his periodic bouts of demagogy, had unloosed these demons himself. The true miracle was – as we shall see later – that, having been swept aside by such tempests, he could ever recover his radical foothold.

However, a new volume of John Grigg's biography of Lloyd George, taking the story from 1912 to 1916, when he started on his war Premiership, prompted another question about his near-destruction of the Liberal Party. Was not the 1916 overthrow of Asquith, and, even more precisely, the conspiratorial methods by which it was achieved, the real cause of the Liberal agony? Who could ever, would ever, trust Lloyd George again? Not the upright Asquithians, who would not soil their lily-white Liberal hands in such traffic; nor the Tory aristocrats who marked his methods with disdain; nor his temporary Tory allies, mostly from a lower drawer, who saw him at work at even closer quarters; nor even the seedy, second-class businessmen who used him to make money; nor the megalomaniac newspaper proprietors who took scoops from him at one moment and dished out insults the next; nor the up-and-coming, mostly idealistic Labour politicians who were, maybe, startled by the brazenness of his opportunism. All, or almost all, turned on him with one excuse or another in 1922, and many did cite 1916 as part of the indictment.

It is an oft-told tale, yet one that can constantly bear re-telling, and for obvious reasons. The 1914–18 Great War was, prior to 1940, the greatest crisis in British history – when our country faced military defeat; when the nation's manpower and womanpower were most prodigiously mobilised for the battlefields; when the slaughter, the bloodletting, was on a scale unknown in any previous conflict. It did appear, in 1916, that victory was beyond our grasp, that even if our armies survived on land, we could be strangled on the high seas. Yet two years later we were victorious on every front and ours was a most powerful voice at the peace table. The change from the Asquith Government to the Lloyd George Government was a momentous one. How it was done, and more especially so if the means to the end were dark and dirty and inscrutable, remains a topic of riveting fascination.

I recall, incidentally – not that I cite this as a matter of supreme historical significance – that my father had little to say on the subject. As he knew the rest of Lloyd George's misdemeanours by rote and was never afraid to recite them, I doubt whether he held 1916 against Lloyd George. I think he may have assumed, without maybe acknowledging the truth to himself, that there were excellent reasons – on the simple test of winning the war – for the displacement of Asquith by Lloyd George. I vividly recall how he would say – one world war later – that rogues were necessary to fight rogues, and that therefore he was content that the services of Leslie Hore-Belisha should be used to help fight Hitler. Many Liberals, many Labour people, who on other grounds would have preferred Asquith, were doubtless influenced by the vicious persistence of the anti-Asquith, anti-Liberal press. The First World War was indeed fought in an atmosphere of bitter, intolerant chauvinism and racism absent or almost absent from the Second. Lloyd George would and could appeal to that mood: Asquith hardly knew how. Good Asquithians, like my father, tolerated and upheld the Lloyd George of 1916 – as did Asquith himself.

So what did really happen in 1916, or, rather, how may it be said that John Grigg puts a new perspective on the record? The first person to tell the political story in detail was Beaverbrook, who understood that politics could be as exciting as war, and he published his version of 'the honest intrigue' in *Politicians and the War* in the early 1930s. It is staggering to see how much of it he got right so soon, how honest, in short, was his record of the honest intrigue.

But, of course, Beaverbrook was an interested party. He wrote to serve, not that frigid, unresponsive mistress, the Muse of History, but his own ambition, Bonar Law's ambition: above all, it may not be too much to say, Lloyd George's ambition. Lloyd George was Beaverbrook's real hero. More than most other observers, Beaverbrook saw, not only that the Asquithian style of government was perilous amid such times but that Lloyd George must be sustained in the highest national interest; that incompetent generals and an irresponsible War Office, shielded by the monarchy, must be brought under masterful civilian control.

John Grigg weaves together all the strands in the narrative in a manner which vindicates Lloyd George. He shows how Lloyd George held steadily before him, throughout the crisis, the legitimate objective of overhauling the conduct of the war; how imperative it was to achieve these objectives; and how, if Asquith had chosen to play his cards differently and, maybe, with less regard for his own amour propre, he could have kept the Premiership. Instead, he put himself at the mercy of anti-Lloyd George tale-bearers like McKenna, and overplayed his hand. However much Lloyd George may have contemplated seizing the highest place – and why not? He had all the talents – he showed more restraint and awareness of the realities in this particular crisis than Asquith. He was ready to act and to provoke others to act, but he was also ready to wait and see. In December 1916, it was Asquith who lost his patience and his nerve. All the more discreditable that he should have tried later to heap so much of the odium onto Lloyd George. (But none of these subtleties, I may be permitted to note, came through to our family home. None of us read *Politicians and the War*. It was not banned in our household – no books were ever banned. But no one remarked on the quality or appositeness of Beaverbrook's book. Indeed few people anywhere ever did until several decades later – in 1965, to be precise – when a sensational review by A. J. P. Taylor, comparing Beaverbrook with Tacitus, changed the literary fashion. For Wee Free Liberals, however, Beaverbrook always had the double deficiency of having worked for Lloyd George and the Tories. He proved that the feat of serving of two masters could be done – the Devil and Mammon. But all that is by the way.)

As in his previous volumes, John Grigg lets Lloyd George speak for himself. He will have no truck with the doctrine approved in some academic quarters which suggests that speeches in Parliament or on the platform must be relegated to a subordinate status. For Lloyd George, that would be Napoleon without the battles, and it is proper to be reminded how relevant these military or even revolutionary parallels might be. It is worth recalling, as Mr Grigg does, that in 1912 a leading Conservative described the Liberal Cabinet as 'a revolutionary committee' (yes, the Cabinet of Asquith and Grey and Haldane etc.) whose record was 'an example of destructive violence without parallel since the Long Parliament'.

Such was the political atmosphere in which Tory leaders and War Office generals had dallied with high treason in Ulster and in which Lloyd George was cast in the role of a revolutionary Cromwell. It was of course the Liberal action against the House of Lords which was alleged to have prompted such resort to extreme language. But the case had never been so clear. When Lloyd George went to Limehouse in July 1909 to defend his People's Budget, the charge was that he had used language 'calculated to set class against class and to inflame the passions of the working and lower orders against people who happened to be owners of property'. That was the verdict of King Edward VII, despatched from his royal yacht to his impenitent Chancellor of the Exchequer, and his tone doubtless reflected the feelings of many of his subjects. Balfour, the Tory leader, had spoken in the House of Commons, in the same sense. Asquith, the Prime Minister, was deeply alarmed lest middle-class voters (and there weren't so many others) would be offended. Lord Rosebery, the former Liberal leader, condemned the Budget tax proposals as 'the end of all, the negation of faith and family, of property, of Monarchy, of Empire'.

Yet an alternative view about who might be the real aggressor was held in some unexpected quarters. Margot Asquith, no friend of Lloyd George, suggested in one of her asides that it was 'the cool-blooded class hatred shown for some years in the corporate counsels of the House of Lords' which had unleashed the Lime-house invectives, while another most authoritative voice asserted bluntly that the Lords themselves, by throwing out the Budget, 'have started the class war, they had better be careful'. That was Winston Churchill, perorating to his neighbour at a London dinner party.

Most revealing was the response from Lloyd George himself. Prompted directly perhaps by the royal strictures, he had soon explained how 'a fully-equipped duke costs as much to keep as two Dreadnoughts', and a few months later again, to Margot's horror, how the British aristocracy was the ultimate issue of Norman plunder, Reformation pillage and royal indiscretion – 'I will give you our oldest and most ancient stock, and consequently our best, because aristocracy is like cheese. The older it is (A voice: "The more it stinks") the higher it becomes.'

Lloyd George's long training in the prosecution of class warfare – he never quite seemed to grow out of it and even so sure an authority as Lenin was paying his tribute years later – should never be forgotten or suppressed. He delighted in storms, real ones and political ones. He was the greatest natural orator in an age of great orators, and yet his driving passion was to act more than to speak, to put far-reaching reforming measures on the Statute Book, to root out the palpable injustices he saw all around him. He used Parliament for these high purposes, as few men have done before or since, and to succeed he needed to mobilise the forces of change outside Parliament as only very few – say, Cobden, Gladstone and Joseph Chamberlain – had done before. To Lloyd George, the appeal to class was part of the engine power of politics.

But to get things done, it was also necessary to argue behind the scenes, to conciliate, to compromise, to wheedle, to threaten, to manoeuvre, within his own party, with clashing interests inside the Cabinet, with the Prime Minister whose temperament so often jarred with his own. Usually, the only witnesses of these scenes are interested parties or egotistical diarists. But in Lloyd George's case – from 1913 onwards – he had at his side a unique witness: Frances Stevenson, for thirty years his secretary and mistress and eventually, as Countess Lloyd George, his wife in name as well. She was truly one of the great women of the century, but naturally her real stature can only be seen as the years unfold.

She made the choice of a lifetime, as a beautiful girl in her early twenties, in accordance with her own strong feminist beliefs but in defiance of all the traditions and pressures of her upbringing, and with her eyes wide open. Lloyd George told her, almost brutally, that he would never repeat the tragedy of Parnell and Kitty O'Shea, and she knew with what wrath she would have been consumed if he had been betrayed by a single indiscretion. She endured pitiful humiliation. She was at his side in his greatest days. And then she sustained and loved him all through the long, cruel aftermath when he was excluded from power by envious mediocrity. And time and again they talked about the Parnell–Kitty O'Shea story until it almost became part of their lives.

During most of those great days she kept a diary, a document without compare. Rarely can so great a man have been observed so lovingly yet so intelligently from such close quarters. This Josephine truly loved her Napoleon, and he never wearied of her, and somehow she had acquired a touch of Pepys as well. Certainly no one else ever knew Lloyd George as she did; and, as she reveals him, what a man to know! Once that diary was published, it became necessary to readjust the whole portrait.

Not so long ago, and for a variety of reasons, it even seemed possible that Lloyd George's 'womanising', to use the horrible word, would be allowed to deface his greatness and his glory. But Frances Stevenson proved his best protector. It is her diary – and her life – which may now rescue the story of his life from prurient exploitation: a gift unimaginable when both he and she – and maybe the rest of the family even more – sensed the torture of their situation.

But nothing stopped the diary. Consider this gleam upon their intimacy and the political intrigue of the day, and it is one of dozens equally good: ' "The reason that I like Lloyd George," said Carson, "is that he always put his cards on the table. Then you know exactly what he is playing." "That is all very well," was my remark when D

[Lloyd George] told me this: "You may put your cards on the table, but you take good care to keep one or two up your sleeve in case of emergency." D laughed. "You give me credit for a great deal more craft than I am capable of!" "I think you are a past master in craft," I replied, laughing. And D knows he is, too.'

Her diary came nearer than anyone else's observation to capture the quicksilver nature of his charm, the secret weapon he employed so mercilessly on men and women alike. She showed him wheedling, flattering, plotting, outflanking his enemies, deceiving, concealing his own physical cowardice, screwing his own moral courage to the sticking place, and manufacturing what someone called 'the brilliant hopefulness' he could spread all around them.

He needed that more than ever on the December night in 1916 when he finally attained the Premiership, when the lonely realist sat – so unlike the romantic Churchill – gloomily saying to himself, or rather to her: 'I wonder if I can do it.' Such scenes faithfully, lovingly, unchallengeably recorded – she could be critical too and she would still try to cling to her own feminism, her own radical upbringing – do transform the whole picture. Above all, they remove the impression that waywardness, opportunism, 'selfservice only', the fault he attributed to 'the cafeteria mind' of Lord Reading, for example, could be regarded as leading features of his nature.

He set his own objectives and preserved them. 'No one,' wrote Frances Stevenson, 'was ever able to persuade him to do something he did not want to do, or conversely, not to do anything he wanted to do. He had a will of granite.' She knew, better than anyone else. And one of the things he wanted was to keep her at his side for ever, against all the odds.

He did that too, while he was ousting Asquith and leading the British people in their most terrible war. Even those who might still argue about the rights and wrongs of that war (in Britain's interest or humanity's interest) could not withhold their acknowledgement of Lloyd George's greatness. By prodigious labours in which it was hard to know which to admire the more – the vision, the energy, the skill – he would extricate his country and himself from hopeless corners, and then suddenly, maybe, cast away the spoils and the laurels. So often he seemed to destroy the moment of triumph through some act of brutal impulse, some defect of character. 1918–22 was not the only period in which this pattern seemed to be repeated; it was the most spectacular, performed before a nation-wide, a world-wide audience. The fall of Lloyd George was a tremendous scene, like the stabbing of Caesar in the Capitol. Yet, for a while, few politicians rushed to save or succour him or defend his reputation. He had trampled too ruthlessly on the precious truths or shibboleths of others, the Liberals, the Socialists, the Tories by turns. Few could see what Frances Stevenson saw and she had to keep quiet.

And truly, there was a streak of hypocrisy in some of his most splendid achievements. He led his country to victory in the name of God and King, and yet had little respect for either. He did believe in himself and his people (the British people and, more especially, the Welsh) and he always found it easy to identify the one with the other, and perhaps here he was not so wide of the mark. The egotism of Lloyd George was rarely a self-centred passion, diverting his interest from the real world or real people. His zeal for discovering the truth, for discarding romantic illusions, never deserted him for long. Soon, after the ordeal of 1922, it reasserted itself afresh.

No observer of that scene, as we have said, could have imagined that he would be out of office for long. Maybe a dedicated few, such as Stanley Baldwin himself and a handful of the most vicious Asquithians, vowed to themselves that they would block his return, but they could hardly suppose that their sacred mission would prove successful. 'Never once did I imagine,' wrote Frances Stevenson (in the mid-1930s) 'that he would be in the wilderness for 13 years at least. When D said "Ten" in 1922 I laughed, and did not believe it or think that he meant it.' His own capacities were quite undiminished, and his ambitions as restless as ever. He and his band of followers, small though they were, occupied at least a sizeable portion of the middle ground in the political stage at a time when such territory looked especially enticing. He had often toyed with the idea of a Centre Party (even in the 'class war' atmosphere of 1910). Surely there must come opportunities for combination to the Left or the Right, and who could be better placed to exploit them than the Lloyd George who, despite all the accusations of untrustworthiness, kept several of his strange friendships in good repair – with Beaverbrook and Birkenhead, with Winston Churchill and J. M. Keynes and several more? Moreover, Lloyd George had money, the notorious Lloyd George Fund amassed by the sale of peerages, or even more unsavoury resorts. Money was all the more important, if elections were to be frequent. The general elections of 1922 and 1923 showed how even the shattered Liberal Party could still hold the balance and decide the day.

So Lloyd George turned all his energy and his imagination and his charm to the task. Reviving a dispirited near-moribund, deeply suspicious opposition was not so onerous a summons as the direction of the nation's central government in war and peace, but Lloyd George applied the same intellectual vigour, the same passion for politics. He set about wooing new friends or recovering old ones. He would calculate month by month, day by day almost, it might appear, how he could turn each changing condition to his advantage and, yet still, how he could lift the eyes of the political public to longer and larger visions; such had been the real source of his strength before 1914, and he knew he must recover it.

The Lloyd George of the 1920s did revive the Lloyd George of Limehouse and the People's Budget. There was no posing or posturing about it. Elder statesmanship seldom suited his style; he was more at ease as a class warrior. He launched a new land campaign; yes, God (even the one he didn't believe in) gave the land to the people. He was impatient to test new ideas; he was a Keynesian before Keynes and a New Dealer before Roosevelt. It was the new mass unemployment which moved, not so much his heart as his political imagination.

I was told what Lloyd George could be on the platform before I ever witnessed the phenomenon myself. I was told of his secret by an old Cornishman, Frank Trethewey, who later kept a boarding house on the fringes of Dartmoor where I went for holidays as a boy. Frank himself had been a farmer's boy, and one winter morning in January 1910, he got up early, long before daylight. He set out to go to Plymouth, twenty miles away. He walked to Torpoint and crossed the River Tamar by ferryboat. He had his lunch with him and his heart was on fire. He was going to hear Lloyd George. Some hours later he stood on tiptoe amid a heaving, breathless mass. Many of them had walked and waited too, but they were happy and eager and excited, as tense as the invaders from the North a few minutes before the kick-off at a Wembley Cup Final.

At last the moment comes. 'I am almost in despair,' Lloyd George says, 'with my weak voice of being able to make myself heard in this gigantic gathering . . .' The voice certainly starts slow and soft. It is like liquid silver deftly poured in sparing drops. But the vast assembly is silent. They wait for each drop as if the silver were champagne. Soon it will become a stream and a torrent.

'We raise very nearly nine millions for old age pensions,' he cries, 'and then there is the provision for including the pauper. Ah, I am sorry for him. Many an old man, who did his best to keep outside the workhouse gates, worked hard until he broke down hopelessly, and there he is looking from inside, hoping to see somebody unlocking the doors to let him out.' (Hear, hear. The silver voice is silent now and then suddenly it almost roars.) 'The moment you clear the Lords out of the way we will open the door.' (Cheers.)

'I hear that some of the Tories say in Devonshire, "We voted for including the paupers." Ah yes, the moment we brought in our Bill they voted for including everything.' (Laughter.) 'You see a ferry-boat crossing.' (They can see the old Torpoint ferry.) 'You consider how much cargo you can take on board safely. There is a man on the banks who does not want you to cross. He says, "Why don't you take this chap on? Why don't you take this other man on? And here's a third chap, why don't you take him?"' (Laughter.) 'He doesn't want to see them cross.' (Cheers.) 'He simply wants to swamp the boat.' (More cheers.) 'He does not want to see one of them safe; he wants them all to get drowned.' (Loud cheers.) 'Including the ferryman.' (Laughter and tumult.)

That was Lloyd George in 1909 and 1910. He went to Newcastle and told them of 'the great slump in dukes'. He went to Falmouth and complained of the ducal language, 'reeking of the stable'. He went to Limehouse and spoke of 'the very shabby rich men' who grudged pennies for the poor.

Lloyd George returned to the platform with all his old mastery and relish in the 1920s. He had never been away from it willingly for long; he could draw inspiration from great mass meetings, like the Gladstone he had heard as a boy. He never attuned himself to new-fangled instruments such as the radio, and he was even more at home himself on the platform than in the House of Commons. Always, as Frances Stevenson explained, he was nervous before he made any big speech, often he could become unbearable to his staff all around him in the hours or even days before its delivery. Sometimes, all too often when he was holding high office, he had not the time to prepare as he wished or, in particular, to learn by heart the passages which were best unloosed with that precaution. He hated having read a whole speech and, when forced to it, even he could stutter. Sometimes he would do – what I have never heard any other great speaker do – stop for what might seem a full sixty seconds or so, while he consulted his notes. Usually when he used this device, he might be searching for some especially recondite term of invective for some particular victim. Once he had resolved to destroy an opponent, no quarter was offered.

I first heard him on the platform in 1926. I had heard – from that same platform in the Reading Town Hall, where I was at school – Stanley Baldwin, the Prime Minister, who was ill at ease almost anywhere except the House of Commons; and Ramsay MacDonald on the 'Red Letter' election and all its assorted infamies. Ramsay swayed and turned and coiled and prophesied a new age in a voice of beauty and thundering echoes. He too could shake great assemblies to their depths, as, I imagine, Gladstone had done. But he had none of Lloyd George's humour nor his common humanity nor any such mastery of the language of the Bible and especially the great philippics of Jeremiah which Lloyd George had drunk in with his mother's milk. Such were the terms in which the moneychangers had been driven from the temple.

Lloyd George, in the months after the general strike of 1926 and in the years before the general election of 1929, set out in his 'We can conquer unemployment' campaign to recapture the radical vote which he had so bitterly alienated in the Coalition years. He showed his sympathy for the miners after 1926 just at the moment when some Labour leaders were afraid to do the same; he gave a magnificent fresh impetus to the attack on the new phenomenon of mass unemployment, and he schemed too, as he always would, to bolster the public attack with private or semi-private manipulation. An attempt was made, chiefly on Lloyd George initiative, to repair some of the old Liberal Party wounds. My father was one of those Asquithian nominees who went on a mission to Lloyd George's house at Churt, for this high purpose. After a weekend of negotiation, the compact was signed and on the Monday morning Lloyd George bade farewell to his guests with the cheerful appeal: 'Let our slogan be *Measures not Men*.' 'Edmund Burke,' replied my father, 'had something to say about that. I think you'll find it on page 530 of that beautiful Beaconsfield edition of Burke I saw on your shelves.' On his return home he looked up his own edition, slightly anxiously, and read of 'the cant of *Not Men but Measures*: the sort of charm by which many people get loose from every honourable engagement'.

Neither my father nor Lloyd George ever referred afresh to the tender topic of Edmund Burke. My father never took the risk of examining further whether Lloyd George's renewed geniality was due to tact or laziness or just the joyous resolve to face the future, which was one of his most notable qualities. Nothing for a while impaired the new association. Rather, in the immediate subsequent years, in the 1929–31 Parliament, in which the Liberal Party held the balance between the new Labour Government and the Tories – so long as the Liberal themselves held together – my father was one of Lloyd George's most devoted assistants. It was a House of Commons in which true radical spirits seemed to be unbared by events. John Simon, Walter Runciman and Leslie Hore-Belisha turned Rightwards into the arms of the Tories; my father and his friends, aiding and abetting Lloyd George's radicalism, moved Leftwards and would, maybe, have sustained the MacDonald Labour Government, if it had had the will to sustain itself. Lloyd George directed one of his fiercest philippics against the Simonites who sided with the Tories and left behind such 'a slime of hypocrisy'. Sir John Simon himself, an old survivor of the 1916 furies, was Lloyd George's prime target. 'How long,' said my father to Lloyd George's son, Gwilym, 'did your father take to prepare that speech,' 'Oh,' said Gwilym, 'he's been waiting thirty years to make that one.'

But when the 1931 crisis came, when the Labour Government was ousted, and Ramsay MacDonald's so-called National Government took its place, when indeed the subsequent general election was forced in the same Tory atmosphere from which Lloyd George had profiteered in 1918, he was out of action on a bed of sickness, aghast at what he took to be 'Liberal' timidity in the teeth of MacDonald's treachery and Tory blackmail. He who had toyed with the idea of many National governments of his own was not there when such a government was established, and even his closest friends were wiped off the political map in the process. Lloyd George said, according to Frances Stevenson, a few years later: 'We ran away at the last election, surrendering everything, and leaving all the bag and baggage behind': a verdict hard to contest. 1931 did prove to be one of the fateful elections in British history. Lloyd George had no part in it.

One night and one morning in the black years that followed he came to speak at Oxford and held one of his breakfast parties at the Randolph Hotel. I saw the electric excitement and the charm at close quarters for the first time. The conversation seemed to rise too high for his taste into political theory, and he brought it down with a bump and a twinkle in that reckless eye. He talked of Neville Chamberlain, the rising hope of the Tories at that moment. He called him 'a three-ton lorry', reminding us of the notice which appeared on some of them: capable of carrying three tons and no more. At that period, I suppose, he was more down and out than ever. The great exertions of the 'we can conquer unemployment' campaign, of the 1929–31 Parliament, had seemingly left him weaker and more friendless than ever. But Frances Stevenson's diary – for those years, alas more patchy than before – still indicates how active he was in mind and dreams and intrigues. Just before the 1935 election she noted: 'D has gone to Downing Street in a very truculent mood. If this state of things goes on much longer, he will burst – or someone else will.' And just after that same election, when the scattered Liberals were scattered afresh, she noted again, on 18 November 1935: 'He is already busy with plans for the future'. As one turns over those last loving pages, one is struck by the hideous waste of such towering political genius. Were we really so rich that we could afford to neglect his? 'I said,' says Frances on one occasion – it is almost her last entry – 'that the remarkable thing was that Baldwin and Chamberlain, both of whom have achieved fame in recent years, were regarded as duds in D's Ministry.'

The duds, having deluded themselves and a considerable part of the nation about the peaceful intentions and fine Christian principles of the Fascist enemy, took the British people into the Second World War, without proper allies, without proper arms and led us to the beaches of Dunkirk. However, before we reached that hour of supreme peril, Lloyd George had performed for the British people his final, unexpected, indispensable service.

The last time I heard him speak, the last time most others heard him too, was in the Norway debate, when Neville Chamberlain was overthrown. I watched every hour of it from the House of Commons gallery, and it was, without compare, a debate which shaped the nation's future. Not so long afterwards it came to be imagined that the defeat and removal of Chamberlain was inevitable. Nothing of the sort was ever true. Chamberlain still had a majority of eighty-one at the end of the debate. Theoretically, he could still have carried on.

The debate took place on a motion for the adjournment of the House, and there too was another theoretical ground for suggesting that the Government was not defeated. The official Labour Opposition had chosen to debate the issue on this motion, as they were entitled to do, precisely because they feared that a more severe and direct vote of censure might drive potential Conservative rebels back into the Chamberlain fold. So it was a wise preference – as events proved. But it might have been fatal too. It could have given the duds yet another reprieve, as they had seized so many in the preceding years. For in that House of Commons, the most ignominious in our history, be it not forgotten, the Tories had a majority of more than 200 over all other parties. Moreover, Winston Churchill, First Lord of the Admiralty, the man with the most direct responsibility for the Norwegian campaign, was to make the concluding speech. He was also, in a sense, the man whose war-making capacity was more respected than anyone else's. Might he not come to the rescue of the whole administration, even Chamberlain? Churchill was ruthless but he could also be gallant.

At the opening of the second day, the outcome was still in doubt and Lloyd George was not in his place. He was upstairs in another room, still debating with himself and a few others whether he should intervene at all. Suddenly the door of his room was thrown open. Had he heard the news? Chamberlain had shown a streak of temper when the Labour challenge was delivered. He had appealed for the support of 'his friends'.

With savage genius, Lloyd George saw his chance. An hour later he was on his feet, with the whole House gasping at the menace of his tone and features. He talked of the Norwegian campaign. He, too, had been thrilled by the story of the gallantry of our troops. 'All the more shame that we should have made fools of them.' Then his eye fixed on Churchill. It became almost benign. 'I do not think,' he said, 'that the First Lord was entirely responsible for what has happened.' Churchill jumped up at once. He would not allow his responsibility to be divided from that of his colleagues. He sat down amid cheers from the Chamberlain benches. But it was a fatal interruption. He had walked straight into Lloyd George's trap. For when the noise subsided Lloyd George had his answer ready. 'The Right Hon. Gentleman,' he said, 'must not allow himself to be converted into an air raid shelter to keep the splinters from hitting his colleagues.'

At that stroke half the effect of Churchill's concluding speech had been forfeited, and Lloyd George turned relentlessly to drive home his advantage. Chamberlain had talked of 'his friends', but this was an issue of the fate of the country. He had spoken of the example of sacrifice; but there is 'nothing which can contribute more to victory in this war than that he should surrender the seals of office'.

Few would deny now that his readiness to fight without quarter on that occasion served his country well. It was the humiliation of Chamberlain by Lloyd George which settled the issue. Partly his words determined the numbers, the thirty-three Conservatives who joined the Labour Party and the Liberals in the voting lobby and the sixty Conservatives who abstained. But maybe even these bare figures could have been borne. It was the piercing of Chamberlain's own pride which was decisive; it was Lloyd George who had done that.

This was the last great occasion when Lloyd George spoke to the nation. But some of us still had the luck to hear him in private; he kept open his lines to Beaverbrook, to Frank Owen, who had been his most faithful follower in 1931 and who still kept alight the Lloyd George torch as editor of the *Evening Standard*. Constantly we urged, partly on Beaverbrook's prompting, that he should be brought into the Churchill Cabinet: whether Churchill himself approved the proposition we were never quite clear. On one occasion I wrote an editorial in the *Evening Standard* comparing a Lloyd George return to the House of Commons with that of Chatham in 1761. So Frank and I went on a mission to Churt and were most courteously received by Frances Stevenson and Lloyd George himself.

He was still in control of his incomparable faculties; no doubt about that. But he was also, in his heart of hearts, defeatist. He did not see how we could win the war, and he did not see, in particular, how Churchill could lead us to the victory. He was deeply offended by a remark Churchill had made in a debate a few weeks earlier comparing one of his own sombre wartime speeches to the kind of speech with which Marshal Pétain might have sought to enliven one of the last French Cabinet meetings, before his surrender to Hitler. So when we talked of our mission, he brushed the suggestion aside with the inquiry: 'What, me? Old Papa Pétain?' And as he talked, he resorted to mimicry, and soon cheered himself and the company by the malicious impersonation of one political character after another.

He professed to be shocked by the subservience shown by members of Churchill's War Cabinet and the high-handed manner which Churchill displayed towards them. 'Now my War Cabinet was different,' he insisted. 'They were all big men. I was never able to treat *any* of my colleagues the way Churchill treats *all* of his.' Then the old man paused: 'Oh yes, there was one I treated that way – Curzon.'

Lloyd George was a marvellous mimic; he could have made another career as a music-hall comedian. Yet it was not this gift nor even his dark prophecies about the future by which we were most captivated on that memorable day. It was the spectacle of this Kitty O'Shea, still lovely in her gracefulness and good nature, in full command of her household, having outwitted all her defamers.

# Ramsay MacDonald

In November 1933, a two-line postcard with a
Swiss stamp arrived at Glen Cottage: 'With
kindest regards and old memories from Geneva,
JRM.' On it Katherine [Glasier] has written, with
a bitterness that the apostle of love and every loving
cause rarely allowed herself: '*See this tragedy!* I
don't know whether to weep or rage as at an
insult. What must he think of me – or better what
delusion still – holds him about what he has done
and *is* doing – poor, poor man.'

Katherine Bruce Glasier,
quoted in Laurence Thompson's
*The Enthusiasts*

By accident almost, I wrote a review of David
Marquand's biography of Ramsay MacDonald –
much the most important book on the subject –
while I too was a member of a Labour Cabinet
subjected to fierce and seemingly well-nigh uncontrollable financial pressure. I believed the moment
of writing added to the possibilities of insight.
Sometimes reviewers, or authors even, *should* write
under the pressure of events such as a politician
may endure.

By what ironic Providence was it decreed that David Marquand's long-maturing biography of Ramsay MacDonald should finally be pronounced ripe for publication in the year 1977 when were re-enacted, seemingly, so many scenes from MacDonald's most momentous or infamous year, 1931: a minority Labour Government, tenuously sustained in office by a Lib–Lab accommodation in the Commons, but confronted outside by a worldwide economic crisis far beyond its capacity to influence, much less master?

Or can it be that the excruciating topicality is due only to a publisher's stroke of luck or genius? Or, more plausibly, was it not always the intention of the moderation-loving biographer to rub home the moderate moral in his portrait of the Arch-Moderate? Is this the meaning of his final word: 'A radical party requires, not merely high ideals and skilful leadership, but intellectual coherence and a willingness to jettison cherished assumptions in the face of changing realities'?

These comparisons, however inevitable, are distracting; they are indeed unfair to book, author and hero (and even, let us add, to the modern performers on the stage; but who could care about fairness to them? At least, let's leave them to the last.). First and foremost, then, all such anachronistic verdicts misjudge MacDonald himself. David Marquand has valiantly sought to avoid hind-sighted stances, but he has not succeeded entirely. One of his major themes is MacDonald's consistency; he is always struggling to prove that the man who obeyed his innermost conviction in August 1931 was driven by the same sense of duty as the MacDonald who faced and refused to flinch from the trial of August 1914. Ironically again, however, this portrait is not so very different from, or rather not so much more valid than, that of the MacDonald of post-1931 Labour Party mythology: the man who supposedly had the seeds of treachery, along with the taste for duchesses, implanted in his bosom from the early years of the century when he would engage in Lib–Lab scheming behind the back of Keir Hardie, or the Party in the country. How fortunate – and discreditable – was this excuse for those who had followed him faithfully right to the door of the 1931 National Government, and how wretchedly it was invoked through the 1930s and thereafter to conceal later displays of pusillanimity. But David Marquand could not quite be expected to press home this line of assault. After all, the last-minute deserters of MacDonald in 1931 (Morrison, Dalton, Attlee, to name but three) became the champion Moderates a decade or so later.

The truth, I believe, is more favourable to both MacDonald and the Labour movement. MacDonald's temperament was temporising, calculating, cautious, gradualist to the fingertips. He understood the need for a political theory and had devised a kind of evolutionary sub-Marxism of his own (Marquand understands the significance of this attitude, but perhaps tells us too little of how MacDonald, a great reader and brooder, if ever there was one, acquired and developed his doctrine). He had enormous resources of diligence and patience and endurance. These qualities together made him the expert negotiator and party manager which he undoubtedly was, but by themselves they *would* help to explain how he surrendered in 1931, but would *not* explain so much that went before: why he had towered over other substantial figures like Henderson, Snowden, Bevin and the rest. For he also had great spasmodic gleams of imagination which enabled him to sweep aside the suffocating orthodoxies of the time and to make his own response to the rebellious instincts of the rising Labour movement. It would be misleading as well as churlish to neglect these periods; they helped in turn to shape the modern Labour Party.

The most memorable and sustained of these exertions was MacDonald's conduct during the 1914–18 war and the immediate aftermath. This was truly the period when the Labour Party remodelled the politics of twentieth-century Britain; and, supplanting the Liberals, made itself the second, and potentially the first, party in the state. Just prior to 1914, Labour had been led by MacDonald, the pragmatist, to a position of well-nigh permanent, contented subordination to the Liberal Government and the Liberal Party, and all the pressures of wartime could easily have pushed the whole Party, as it pushed most of its other leaders, still further in the same obsequious direction. But MacDonald, knowing all the perils for himself, as his own hesitations proved, still managed to resist the hysteria of wartime, and make a coherent (although, by the standards of the moment, a quite immoderate) stand against the prevailing storm.

He helped to save both the body and soul of the Labour movement. The body was held together by the manner in which both Henderson inside the wartime government and MacDonald outside it took meticulous care not to drive their divergencies to breaking point. And the soul-saving did not stop short of a denunciation of 'the class diplomacy' (MacDonald's own phrase) which had produced the war and the reckless militarist momentum which forbade a decent peace settlement in 1916 or 1917. Instead, after 1918, 'a peace to end peace' was forced upon the stricken, wartorn world. Lloyd George's 'knock-out blow' against Germany well-nigh knocked out with it any internationalist spirit within the Labour movement; but not quite.

Thanks to MacDonald among others, Labour embarked upon the post-1918 years not merely as an independent Party, but with an independent policy. Shamefully, the Party in Parliament failed to vote against the final punitive peace terms, and Labour's National Executive failed initially to oppose the intervention action against Soviet Russia. But nothing can rob MacDonald and the Labour movement as a whole of the stature which both attained through those tremendous years. The hour of the Russian Revolution and the first United States incursion into world affairs and the ending of the war in Europe was the age when a good peace, without victors and vanquished, should have been sought and might have been secured, to the incalculable benefit of Europe and the world. In Britain, only the Labour movement possessed that vision, and it was MacDonald who gave expression to 'the spring-tide of joy which had broken out all over Europe', and who strove to translate it into practical statesmanship.

No other comparable period can be cited – indeed no other comparable moment of opportunity presented and lost occurs in the century – but there were numerous occasions when MacDonald responded to the Labour movement's most deeply-felt impulses. For example, even if ours was not the age of *Daily Mail* forgeries (which age is not?) the Red Letter saga of 1924 and after will well repay examination. MacDonald may have fumbled some episodes in his first Premiership, notably the Campbell case (although he was surely not guilty of 'the bloody lie' attributed to him by the faithful Cabinet Secretary, Hankey). But once forced into the 1924 election, and once confronted, literally overnight, with the dilemmas involved in the truly bloody lie of the Zinoviev letter, he fought back with a spirit worthy of 'the Gladstone of Labour'. When MacDonald, most mildly and excusably, posed some doubts about the role of the Foreign Office in the whole affair, such journals as *The Times* and the *Daily Mail*, with their snouts in the same propagandist trough, sought to extract fresh advantage for the Conservative cause by pretending that the Prime Minister had unworthily questioned the good faith of his officials. Rather, even at this date we must marvel at his moderation (in the old, unadulterated sense of the term). Sir Eyre Crowe, head of the Foreign Office, offered no word of apology or excuse for a combined act of slipshod workmanship and sabotage against his political masters which must still leave the reader gasping some half a century later.

Time and again in these pages it is not MacDonald's delinquencies which strike home, but more the monstrous character of the enemy he fought, and this although David Marquand seems to have resolved not to stir the reader's emotions and anger. MacDonald, it has always been alleged on the Left with much justice, played a mean part in the general strike and its prelude and sequels, and it is true that his sympathy with the trades unions in 1926 or at any other period was far from perfect. But, as these pages reveal, at one of the most gruelling moments in that desperate summer and autumn, when the miners had been driven to the point of starvation, he did seek out Winston Churchill privately and they did shape together a tolerable compromise which would have spared the country the last lingering inhuman outrages in the drama. But the coalowners would have none of it, and the soft, appeasing Baldwin and the hard, upstanding Churchill joined forces afresh to humiliate the miners.

'For the first time for nearly two years,' writes the ineffably moderate Marquand just about this time, 'the Conservatives could be presented as the party of class war, and Labour as the party of reason and moderation.' It may be imagined what must have occurred to bring David Marquand's blood to the boil. MacDonald had reached that level more speedily. For all his own calculated moderation, he rarely lacked passion.

He more than any other leader, writes Marquand, could combine respectability with panache. But the compliment is too barbed. He was in some respects a highly gifted democratic leader, and if he had died, say, in 1928 just at the time when, after the industrial defeat of 1926, the Labour movement was mobilising afresh on the political battlefield, or in 1929 soon after the newly-gained victory at the polls, he would have been acknowledged as a worthy successor to Keir Hardie. All his weaknesses compared, say, with Lloyd George – the lack of wit, astringency and zeal for action – would have been placed in the proper perspective of his paramount achievement: the leading role he had played over thirty years in building a great new party. No doubt he could be vain, ultra-sensitive, self-pitying, ambiguous in word and action, and much too reliant on his taste for misty rhetoric. But if he had been lucky enough to leave the stage in 1929, no one would have sought to translate these flaws of character into veritable engines of history.

A paradox of his career – more revealing than any strained attempt to establish a false consistency – is that, in the last supreme crisis, his redeeming virtue deserted him. On so many previous occasions, at the eleventh hour or even later, he had renewed his strength and inspiration from the ranks of the Labour movement, often on the platform as Gladstone had done before him: so it was notably in 1914, 1922 and 1927. But in 1931 he did not know where to turn, and the lack of perception was certainly not his alone; it was shared by his entire Cabinet, and the bulk of the Parliamentary Party. He was surrounded by moderates but they had no notion even what to be moderate about, and in the absence of any other idea they were all content to become immoderate deflationists. Certainly the moderates of every shade offered no solution of the national crisis. It can be much more plausibly argued that the crying need of the hour was an extremist revolt against Treasury domination.

David Marquand does not seek to sidestep these questions. He insists that the intellectual salvation later supplied by Keynesianism was still only in the womb. That is incontestable; indeed, Keynes and his closest disciples were still offering confused and even contradictory counsel throughout 1931 and for several years afterwards; it required the upheaval of world war to enable Keynes himself at last to capture the ear of the Treasury, and MacDonald could not wait that long. More conceivably, he could have listened with great care to his old ILP mentor, J. A. Hobson, who, with his other ILP advisers, had more to offer in the idiom of the time than Keynes himself. But Hobson, it seems, was too diffident in pressing his arguments, and MacDonald, for all his creditable doubts, still in the end bowed before the prescriptions and pressures of Snowden and the Treasury as if they had just come down from Sinai. Of course, he could and should have turned to the trades union movement which at least was groping towards a wiser comprehension of the world deflationary crisis than most of the so-called experts, academic or otherwise. But MacDonald long since had persuaded himself that no good could come out of that Nazareth, and this surely was his gravest shortcoming as a Labour leader.

However, so limited and blurred was the advice which came from all these quarters that a Prime Minister faced with the necessity to make up his mind that night or the day after had some excuse for not prescribing a clear response. MacDonald havered and hesitated and prevaricated; but he did not consciously set out to betray. Nothing could have been wider of the mark than Harold Laski's bitter taunt that MacDonald positively welcomed the crisis as eagerly as he embraced the duchesses: 'Henceforth, he could live at ease in Zion . . . The ribbon is in his coat; and he will not live to read the verdict of history.' Rather, he was utterly crushed by the choice he had desperately made. No real ease was vouchsafed to him for the rest of his days, and the verdict of history pounded in his ears as stridently as the cry of outrage from the Labour Party at the time. After his own first outburst of spleen and fury against his erstwhile comrades, the self-doubts began to gnaw. A consistent MacDonald or an opportunist MacDonald would never have suffered the pitiful agonies which pursued him to his lonely grave.

1931 was a collective failure, not a personal failure.

> We'll hang Ramsay Mac on a sour apple tree,
> With Snowden and Thomas to keep him company,
> For that's the place where traitors ought to be.

That was the song we all sang in the Labour Party through the following years but there was always something squalid about the affair when Henderson and Co. and the other leaders joined the chorus as eagerly as most of them did. The scapegoat theory was an indecency as well as a falsehood, and insofar as David Marquand's conscientious recital of the facts re-discovers that truth, he is justified. But this is by no means the end of the story; it is not much more than the beginning. MacDonald cannot be condemned merely because he was baffled by the unknown features and unprecedented scale of the 1931 crisis; everyone else was baffled too, if not all in equal measure. But neither he nor the other leaders had a right to run away in their different directions, and thereby open the gates wide to the enemy. No theory, evolutionary or revolutionary, or moderate, could justify that.

And writing in June 1977, I may add that the moral still stands. Labour, both the MacDonaldites and the Hendersonites, all the moderates of every breed and hue, did 'run away' in 1931, according to the gibe of time. The hideous consequences both for the movement and the nation should help us at least to ensure that that precise piece of history is not repeated. It remains true that the 'National' Government of the subsequent decade was the worst in modern British history, and that the squalid pursuit of class interest which inspired so many of its leading members (the same old 'class diplomacy' which MacDonald had detected and condemned half a century before) helped to lead the British people to their moment of most deadly peril in a thousand years. It was part of MacDonald's torture that, even when he was half-blinded, physically and emotionally, he still could see, however, dimly, what was happening in Nazi Germany, in Dollfuss's Austria, in Franco's Spain, and how shameful and craven and unimaginative was the response of British Conservatism, wielding the well-nigh almighty power in the state which the 'run away' fiasco of 1931 had yielded into its hands.

# Winston Churchill

He cast himself in the role of the great advocate
who put the case of Britain to the world and the
destiny of Britain to the British. His name will
stand so long as war is remembered as a symbol of
what inspired words can do when there is a strong,
brave and devoted nation free and willing to back
them up with deeds.

Aneurin Bevan

When Winston Churchill died in July 1965, I wrote
an obituary for *Tribune* which I trust was neither
offensive nor sycophantic. Not quite twenty years
later, in July 1983, I had the chance of judging
afresh the Churchillian achievement of 1940. And I
came to Churchill's defence, when he was set upon
by his doctor.

Inevitably, the circumstances of Churchill's illness, his rich old age, the decline of rancours, the softening of so many of the controversies in which he was engaged (including one of the last, the Cold War) make it hard, almost churlish, to search for the truth about his fame. Most people will prefer the legend, even if they stop to recollect that a considerable part of it has been written in Churchill's own unmistakable hand. For years now the Annigonis have been at work (that was always the kind of art he preferred); even a few hasty sketches for a new Graham Sutherland may be considered in bad taste.

Moreover, seen from any angle, the scale of the figure on the vast canvas is stupendous. Not merely does Churchill bestride the century; not merely has he been a foremost performer in British and world politics for a longer period than almost any rival in ancient or modern times. The same giant lineaments are revealed when his particular faculties are examined. His vitality, his brainpower, his endurance, his wit, his eloquence, his industry, his application were superabundant, superhuman. The first and last impression left by the Colosseum concerns its size. So with Churchill: the man was huge.

Then, also, for the bulk of the British adult population, the moment which must stand out most proudly in their collective memory was 1940. More deliberately than at any other time in its history the nation united in a good cause. Men and women conducted themselves with intelligence, dignity and courage as members of a community with a freely recognised common purpose. That *was* their finest hour. Churchill was the prime organiser, the voice, the symbol and the historian of those great days.

In acknowledging his inspiration, it is not necessary to accept the vulgar libel on the British people that, without him, they would have surrendered to Hitler. Of course they would not. Many people in Britain had opposed Fascism long before and much more consistently than Churchill. His precise virtue then was that he *repre-*

*sented* his countrymen in that crisis better than at any other moment in his career. He exemplified, in word and deed – more, in every inflection and gesture – the untiring, resplendent courage which the hour demanded. Way back at the beginning of the First World War, A. G. Gardiner, in a well-known essay wrote of 'the Churchill audacity – that union of recklessness and calculation that snatches victory out of jaws of danger'. Rarely were the needs of a nation and the chief quality of its leader better matched than in 1940. Nothing can ever take that from him. No one in his senses will ever try.

Courage shines more brightly than any other feature in a politician; it is rare, magnetic, indispensable for the most splendid deeds. But there are other requirements, too, for those who are to be judged by the highest standards. Wisdom, prophetic foresight and insight, imaginative sympathy, an understanding of the forces moulding his own age and a persistent determination to further those working beneficently for the mass of mankind, a readiness to assist a new age thrusting to be born – these are the allied tests which in varying measure must be applied to the greatest men, to an Oliver Cromwell, to an Abraham Lincoln, to a Gandhi or a Lenin. And, judged thus, Churchill is deficient. This is not the place or time to debate the full issue. *Tribune* has stated its case over the years, and we see no cause to restate or retract it now. But the glorification of Churchill in recent years and doubtless in the days and weeks to come takes such an extreme form that it is necessary to offer some illustrations of its absurdity.

Churchill was not, as he is now portrayed, the gifted seer, the man of superior discernment brooding on the affairs of the planet and descrying before most others the course of man's development. Indeed, he was frequently the very opposite. He was always the opportunist, the buccaneer, searching for the enemy of the moment. That enemy was by turns the Liberals, the Tories, the Germans, the Russians, the British workers, the Indians, the Germans and the Russians again, and the Socialists at home. 'Brilliantly as he preaches,' wrote A. G. Gardiner, in that same essay quoted above, 'he is the man of action simply, the soldier of fortune, who lives for adventure, loves the fight more than the cause, more even than his ambition or his life. He has one purpose – to be in the firing line, in the battles either of war or peace.' Each word there still rings true fifty years later. Admittedly, the born fighter and leader spent some famous years out of office. It was then, in the 1930s, that he wrote his best books and delivered his imperishable philippics against Baldwin, Chamberlain, the Tory machine and the Municheers. But he was not in the wilderness by choice. Locusts and wild honey were never his idea of a nutritious diet.

And even then, when he could stand back and put his world in perspective, how slowly and awkwardly – over Abyssinia and Spain, for example – he came to see Britain's interest and shed his first myopic judgement of Hitler and Mussolini and the forces they represented. Churchill, the prophet, was still fighting the Russian civil war when Hitler was murdering Jews and Mussolini mobilising against Abyssinia. Once again A. G. Gardiner's essay hits upon the truth. 'He is always unconsciously playing a part – an heroic part. And he is himself his astonished spectator. He sees himself moving through the smoke of battle – triumphant, terrible, his brow clothed with thunder, his legions looking to him for victory, and not looking in vain. He thinks of Napoleon; he thinks of his great ancestor . . . Hence that tendency to exaggerate a situation which is so characteristic of him – the tendency that sent artillery down to Sidney Street and, during the railway strike despatched the military hither and thither as though Armageddon was upon us. "You've mistaken a coffee stall row for the social revolution," said one of his colleagues to him as he pored with knitted and portentous brows over a huge map of the country on which he was marking his military dispositions. His mind once seized with an idea works with enormous velocity round it, intensifies it, enlarges it, makes it shadow the whole sky. In the theatre of that mind it is always the hour of fate and the crack of doom.'

Who will dare deny the enduring perception in that portrait? How many times thereafter did Churchill mistake the significance of what happened beneath his nose? And who were the people who suffered for his grotesque misapprehensions? On so many occasions, much more was upset than the coffee stalls in Sidney Street. The mad war of intervention against Russia, the long agony of the miners after the return to the gold standard in 1926, the melodramatic scowls in the general strike itself, the cold, bitter, unending private war against the Indian people and their chosen leaders – these are some of the Churchillian escapades which still leave deep wounds and scars. Churchill's crimes, like his other feats, were on the grand scale. They were impulsive and romantic, but criminal no less. And this is the clue to the real Churchill, indicated by Gardiner and concealed by his sycophantic biographers. He saw most events through the same romantic haze which enveloped his perorations.

For him the world struggle could usually be reduced to a contest between cops and robbers, cowboys and Indians. In his anti-Soviet campaigns he frequently described his enemies as apes, gorillas, baboons. Rarely did he ever recognise an opponent as human. And nearer home he never had the foggiest notion how the British people lived, how they earned their bread, how society functioned, how it was being transformed before his eyes by forces he never even dimly discerned. He talked as if they all lived in 'cottage homes' and had the same chances of adventure and glittering advancement as the young Churchill in Edwardian England had seized with all the schoolboy intensity of his nature. He could be warm, humane, liberal, magnanimous. But the warmth rarely embraced the people except in his rhetoric, and the humanity could subside into tears and sentimentality. He was too much entranced by the game of politics, the game of wars, to let his heart bleed for the victims.

Philosophy, economics, industrial organisation, social realities, the struggle of classes, history itself as anything much more than a tale of blood and thunder were beyond his intellectual reach. History was a pageant in which noble knights guarded the sacred flame and in which, throughout most of this century, the same unmistakable King Arthur stepped forward as the hero. Thus, romantically misled or misleading, there were some times – in the 1920s when he led his one-man crusade against 'the foul baboonery of Bolshevism', in his praise of Mussolini, in the early 1930s when he attacked Gandhi as 'a naked fakir', in 1936 when he originally backed Franco, and in 1945 when he saw Clement Attlee as the harbinger of a British Gestapo – when he grasped the wrong end of the stick between his teeth so firmly that the miracle is he was not laughed off the stage altogether. But fortunately for all concerned, the nation's real enemies did actually coincide on occasions – above all, in 1940 – with the devils he had selected for extermination.

And on that note let us say our farewell to an old opponent whom *Tribune* has attacked more than any other newspaper in the country throughout the past thirty years and whom we would not insult now with mealy-mouthed insincerities. Often we were deafened by that roar, but we do not prefer the silence. Often the innocent were torn to pieces by those claws, but the guilty suffered too. Since his departure, the political scene has acquired a certain bleakness, for it is more creditable and exciting to hunt lions than rabbits.

*That was written in 1965, and I had the chance to revisit some of those scenes in 1983.*

### Finest Hour: Winston S. Churchill, 1939–41
Martin Gilbert. Heinemann.

Churchill's finest hour? No doubt whatever. Britain's finest hour? A good bid for sure, since the survival of freedom everywhere against the assault from the most infamous tyranny ever devised by man hinged upon Britain's resistance during those crucial months. Martin Gilbert's finest hour, too? Let us see.

Reviewers of books should not allow their judgements to be influenced by reading the reviews of other reviewers. But I must at once confess that I have grossly offended against the golden rule. After one of my oldest friends, Tosco Fyvel, invited me to review this latest volume for the *Jewish Chronicle*, other events intervened. I could not resist the temptation to read some of those other verdicts which happened to find their way under my nose and eyes. Mostly they acclaimed Martin Gilbert's achievement without qualification, and here surely is a wonderful story re-told with skill, scruple, elaboration and indeed fresh knowledge. Who could ask for more? The short and shoddy answer is Mr John Vincent, fresh from his triumphs in expounding the modern Conservative cause in the Murdoch press, *The Times* or the *Sun*, and who also, for some still inexplicable reason, has been invited to parade his prejudices in the *Standard*, once a great newspaper with a most discriminating book page. However, against the writer's intention perhaps, the Vincent review may serve a useful purpose. Having sought to damn the latest Gilbert volume as 'ponderous' and much else quite inappropriate, he seeks to intrude his own superior intelligence with the demand that many more interpretative judgements should have been offered.

Leave aside for a moment the obvious retort that Mr Gilbert's manner of selection – even in 1248 pages – is a form of interpreta-

tion: turn instead to the question posed by Mr Vincent which casts a
gleam of light over Conservatism past and present, both the brand
with which Churchill (and the rest of us) had to contend in the
1930s, and which, alas, has re-emerged to take command today.
'Above all' – yes, exactly, *above all* – Mr Vincent asks, 'we need to
know why we did not make peace in 1940 – and whether Churchill's assumptions in continuing the war were sensible.' And then,
in extending that question, defined as supreme, Mr Vincent describes how the making of such a peace could have been considered
excusable, feasible, honourable.

Not for years have I seen the old appeasement argument of the
1930s and 1940s so brazenly reopened, and the deed has an added
interest when it is done by a Conservative historian putting Churchill in his place and right off his pedestal – the Churchill of 1940,
mind you, and not the Churchill of earlier or later years whose feet
of clay are more excusably exposed. And, of course, there was an
argument. 'Churchill was a leader imposed on the Tories by the
nation,' writes Mr Vincent – quite true, and he might just have
added: by the nation, on the Labour Party's initiative, in the critical
House of Commons Norway debate, backed by a few others like
Lloyd George and the for-ever-to-be-honoured handful of Tory
rebels. Then Mr Vincent describes how sullenly the bulk of the
Tories in the Lords and Commons welcomed their new leader.
Right again. But then he re-states the tell-tale question: how far
were the Tory doubters right?

Yes, rub your eyes and read those words again. The Tory
doubters of 1940; how can history, Mr Vincent's kind of history, be
said to justify *them*? As Mr Gilbert explains, with 'ponderous' but
still startling accuracy, there were such Tory doubters not merely in
the months of the phoney war, prior to Churchill's appointment as
Premier, but in the critical weeks and months thereafter, *in the
period of our greatest national peril ever*. The most prominent of the
waverers was Lord Halifax, the Foreign Secretary still in Churchill's
Cabinet, and whom indeed George VI and the bulk of the Tories in
both Houses would have preferred instead of Churchill as Chamberlain's successor. Halifax wanted to use Mussolini as a mediator.
He believed some kind of settlement with Hitler might be attain-
able. He could not see how the war could be fought and won. And
the inescapable inference of Mr Vincent's question is that Halifax

was right. A fresh essay in appeasement was truly the most 'sensible' course for Britain to seek to follow.

So why did this sensible policy get such little support? It was Churchill, in the nearest Mr Vincent strays towards a coherent explanation, 'looking at the war through the rose-coloured spectacles of genius', who constructed his victory and our salvation on a splendid foundation of error. And indeed this much *is* true. Churchill was a romantic, and it was that quality more than any other which served him and us so well in 1940. A much more astute observer than Mr Vincent saw and said as much: 'Being a great artist,' wrote Aneurin Bevan, 'Churchill was not a great man of action. He always thought he was, but this was another of his characteristic illusions. How could he be? A man of action must be a realist. He may dream and have visions, but for him two and two must necessarily make four, and the facts of life must be the stuff with which he works ... Churchill's contribution was to fling a Union Jack over five tanks and get people to behave as though they had become fifteen.'

But back to 1940, and what saved us. It is all there, in Mr Gilbert's compilation, if only Mr Vincent, instead of flaunting his own second-rate paradoxes, had been a little more interested to learn. Most of us who were round about at the time understood. Tens of millions of our people understood. Churchill understood. It was the great source of his strength in 1940, the real measure of that genius. Churchill understood that by that time the British people were not going to give in to Hitler and Hitlerism, whatever happened. Any politician, himself included, who suggested yielding an inch would have been torn limb from limb. Churchill knew as much and said as much, as Mr Gilbert faithfully records. He does not attempt to surmise what would have happened if Halifax's fresh lapse into his pre-war postures had been made public, but it is interesting to recall how pardonable was the suspicion about the old Chamberlainite appeasers, expressed in such volumes as *Guilty Men*, published just about the time when Halifax was recommending Mr Vincent's 'sensible' course to Mr Vincent's self-deluded Churchill.

Churchill made many errors in the conduct of the war, and he had many strokes of luck, and sometimes the misjudgements and the good fortune combined together to enable him – and the rest of us –

to escape from some wretched predicament. The most notable example, also discussed although necessarily not exhausted in this volume, concerns his giant misapprehension about the capacity of the Russians to fight and survive. Churchill believed that the Soviet resistance would collapse, and yet, if it had collapsed, what would have been left of the Churchill strategy?

Churchill's would-be critics should concentrate on some of these issues; there is plentiful scope for investigation and reassessment, and most notably in this all-important field of Anglo–Soviet relationships. Some critics, notably Aneurin Bevan, conducted those scrutinies at the time, and it is fascinating to see how some awkward and risky exercises in wartime criticism are now vindicated. But let the new breed of Chamberlainites and Halifaxites lay off 1940. That was the year of years, the hour of hours, the moment when the British people much more surely than their leaders (on Churchill's own testimony) decided to expiate all the crimes and follies of those who had fed the Fascist monster. It was done magnificently and, more than ever before or after, Churchill's language fitted the time.

*The book by Churchill's doctor was published by Constable in 1966.*

Good books have been written by cads, crooks and offenders of every degree against every article in the Decalogue. So the question whether Lord Moran's already notorious memoirs, *Winston Churchill: The Struggle For Survival 1940–1965* are ethically defensible is one for some Medical Council, maybe, but not for me. Hippocratic oaths are neither here nor there.

Other awkward questions are posed only to be softly answered in Moran's own Preface. He tells how Brendan Bracken searched long for 'Winston's Boswell', and implies that Churchill's closest disciple went cheerfully to his grave, once he had persuaded Moran to take the burden on his capable shoulders. He describes how G. M. Trevelyan, after hearing the doctor's discourse for half-an-hour, insisted 'This is history; you must get it on paper.' Pretty cool, eh? But even before this sedative Preface, the Acknowledgements give evidence of Lord Moran's biographical bedside manner. 'When I put down my pen,' he writes, 'I wish to be sure that I have reported faithfully those who have talked to me about him. I trust that in checking those conversations I have forgotten no one.' Nothing could be clearer. With such a reassuring hand on his pulse, what feverish critic would not find his suspicions subsiding?

But wait. Could it ever have been true that – to take just one example – Lord Normanbrook approved the extensive comments on Cabinet proceedings attributed to him here? As Secretary of the Cabinet, he may once have been responsible for helping to ensure that Cabinet Ministers did not break *their* oaths, which are considerably more binding than anything handed down from Hippocrates. Could he ever have thought himself entitled to waive these niceties in favour of Churchill and Moran? I am not in the least surprised that he has written to *The Times* making it clear that he never did so.

Other doubts begin to stir. The author's vanity constantly obtrudes; he is a master of the self-congratulatory innuendo. He drops quiet hints to Admirals and Field-Marshals on how to conduct military operations, humbly offers suggestions to Churchill on the way to deal with Stalin, leaves a faint impression that he could put Graham Sutherland on the right lines about painting. Above all, the doctor–diarist prides himself on his piercing insight into character. Yet his glimpses of Beaverbrook or Cripps must astonish those who knew them, and which historical figure does he finally pick upon as the nearest likeness to his hero? You'll never guess. In the most grotesque passage in this book or most others, the born courtier's choice falls on, of all people – Queen Victoria!

And yet, despite these absurdities, prevarications and sly conceits, the book cannot be dismissed. Somehow, the calculating, self-conscious doctor does make a unique contribution to the story of Churchill and the Churchill epoch, and not by any means merely on the precise questions of the patient's health. Somehow 'Corkscrew Charlie' as Lord Moran is known to some of his intimates in the profession – he is hardly in a position to complain of any breach of confidence – does help to straighten things out.

Partly, and most obviously the achievement is due to the feast of Churchillisms spread before us.

*'I have made more bishops than anyone since Augustine.'*

*'I have lived seventy-eight years without hearing of bloody places like Cambodia.'*

*'Truth is so precious, it should be accompanied by an escort of lies.'* (Told to, and much appreciated by, Stalin at Teheran.)

*'Ha-ha, the FO make a bold gesture. They have told Tito that they are unable to understand the action of one of his officers. As if Tito cares a damn whether the FO understand!'*

*'There are always a lot of bloody rows in politics – that's what politics is for.'*

Just before his retirement: *'Circumstances may convince me of my indispensability.'* And just after: *'I am not thinking of a comeback. At least not yet.'*

There is spice on almost every page, but solid fare also. If Lord Moran rarely places his historical knowledge in a proper perspective, he does provide chronicles and clues for future historians which might have become irreparably lost. In particular here is essential information about Churchill's 1951–5 administration which his dear enemies in the Tory Party might be only too eager to suppress altogether.

What more moving and tragic and courageous story could there be than Churchill's lone effort, after Stalin's death in 1953, to seek a fresh accommodation with the Russians, despite his broken health and all the exertions of the Americans and the Foreign Office 'to bitch things up'. And what more hilarious episode in all our history has there ever been than the old man's brilliant and successful manoeuvre to stay in office when all his colleagues, headed by Eden, were so ready to bundle him out? This was his last stroke of revenge on the Tories, and was he not, after all, worth all the rest of the bunch rolled into one? Yes, but he was also a magnificent, romantic poseur, a master of grandiloquent words, but much too often also their deluded slave, the greatest ham-actor in English political history, the most colossal egotist since Napoleon. The biographer who puts all these indelible touches on the portrait must be accorded something of Boswell's art, after all.

And occasionally, too, he spills a whole basin of beans. For example, when in October 1954 Eden made the deal which settled the crisis about the immediate rearmament of Germany, but committed us to keep four divisions in Germany till the end of the century, Churchill said: 'It can be cancelled at any time. It does not mean anything. All words. Of course, I shall not say that. But what is all the fuss about?' Alas, the extravagant pledge still stands;

Britain's economy is still dogged by it. Churchill's cynicism has not saved us from the consequences of the post-war panic about the Soviet Union which he himself had done so much to inflame.

# Stanley Baldwin

A mean wine in a goblet of old gold. Here indeed
was the great past mimed by the ignoble present,
'History repeats itself,' said Marx, 'first as tragedy,
second as farce.' And here was farce. The pathetic
can never be epic, and here was bathos affecting to
speak in accents of the heroic. The Prime Minister,
who has a natural gift for the counterfeit,
surpassed himself.

Aneurin Bevan on Baldwin, 1937


There are three people, you know, who are
impossible to deal with – De Valera, Gandhi and
Beaverbrook.

Stanley Baldwin, 1933



The first official 'life' of *Stanley Baldwin* by G. M.
Young in 1952 was more like another case for the
prosecution. Then in 1969 came an even more
official 'life' by Keith Middlemas and John Barnes –
with some results hinted at here.

Were the Guilty Men truly guilty? The term, it may be recalled, first gained notoriety as the title of a popular pamphlet published in 1940. It soon entered general political parlance as a convenient way of identifying those who played the leading roles in guiding the nation towards the disaster of Dunkirk, the most dangerous moment in British history since 1066.

It won respectability, even at the loss of some precision, as what may be called the Churchillian view of modern times: the notion that the British people saved themselves in their finest hour from the shame and stupidity of the previous decade. And often the guilty men have seemed to offer evidence against themselves. None of the memoirs and apologies hitherto written on their behalf has done much to parry the indictment, and one of them, the 'official' biography of Guilty Man Number Two, Stanley Baldwin, (pride of place as Guilty Man Number One must surely always be allotted to Neville Chamberlain) sounded like another witness for the prosecution. But now comes a book of a quite different order. *Baldwin* (Weidenfield & Nicolson) by Keith Middlemas and John Barnes is more even than a well-documented defence and a fierce counter-attack: it is the boldest essay in rehabilitation since the Gospel according to St Luke.

No brief rebuttal, therefore, it may be understood, can do full justice to the book's claims. It provides, in 1100 closely printed pages, by far the most detailed account of Downing Street and Westminster politics during that epoch. It makes fuller use of recently released Cabinet secrets than any biographer has ever had at his disposal. It is scholarly and sensational by turns, and written with immense, persuasive skill and apparent moderation, and those who lived through those years will turn from page to page, as I did, mesmerised and almost bemused. But not quite, and not likely! For what do these indefatigable biographers tell us? Baldwin emerges as a saintly, not to say Christ-like figure; considerate, forgiving, selfless, guided by inner voices and possessing some unsuspected gift of prophecy. All that can be borne. By most accounts he was a nice chap; clearly he was never the lazy dolt sometimes portrayed; and the excessive tributes to his personal qualities may be excused, particularly in view of the lingering crucifixion he endured in his last years. Messrs Middlemas and Barnes persuade themselves that Baldwin's 1924–9 Government was one of the best in British history, that in the early 1930s he started to rearm the country as efficiently as circumstances would allow, that he faced the challenge of Hitlerism, that he was all the while educating the British democracy. Indeed: then how *did* a nation so well governed reach the extremity of Dunkirk?

Every now and again our biographers seem to realise they are proving too much; the thirteenth stroke of the clock casts suspicion on all the others. So one device they resort to is to unload an extra portion of guilt on other eligible heads; on Neville Chamberlain, who never possessed the Baldwin touch and deserves all he gets for his would-be 1930 treachery against the divine leader; on Samuel Hoare, whose deal with Laval over Abyssinia is exposed as even more scandalous than had been imagined; on Simon and the rest of the appalling crew. No one need protest too much on their account. But Baldwin, after all, held real power longer than anyone else. He combined – so we are ludicrously assured – several of the attributes of Abraham Lincoln, Disraeli and Walpole. Every student of British politics *must* read this book: it exposes as never before, except in Baldwin's own perorations, the excruciating self-righteousness of the Ruling Class Mind.

However, those who wish to know what actually happened in the 1930s, how the nation was so nearly led to its doom, had better stick to rough-and-ready guides like *Guilty Men*. And students of that work may be interested to learn that several of its wilder accusations are now unwittingly confirmed by the new scholarship. For instance: the story of how the Tory Premier Baldwin chatted with the Socialist leader MacDonald at Crewe Station for a few moments in the middle of the 1929 election and how one said to the other: 'Well, whatever happens, we shall keep out the Welshman' – meaning, of course, Lloyd George.

Detestation of Lloyd George was the driving force in Baldwin's political life, right from the moment when he helped break the Coalition in 1922. It played its part in the hitherto unexplained decisions to hold the 1923 election and to appoint Churchill Chancellor in 1924, and was indeed one of the reasons why Baldwin and MacDonald found their alliance, official and unofficial, so alluring and compatible. Here we have all the evidence needed of how mediocrity destroyed genius, the most baneful vendetta in British history.

# A Miscellany
of Cross-breeds

# Enoch Powell

All political lives, unless they are cut off in
midstream at a happy juncture, end in failure,
because that is the nature of politics and of human
affairs. The career of Joseph Chamberlain was not
an exception.

> Enoch Powell, in his
> *Joseph Chamberlain*
> (Thames & Hudson 1977)

Some of these reflections were first prompted by
Roy Lewis's book *Enoch Powell – Principle in
Politics*, published by Cassell in 1979, but avuncu-
lar sentiment and candour also make me recom-
mend *The Rise of Enoch Powell* by Paul Foot,
published by Penguin in 1969.

I was astonished to discover that the word 'loner' had not found its way into the *Oxford English Dictionary*, that final determinant of political fashion, until the very last edition published in 1982. I had thought that there had always been 'loners' at work in our political system, men and women who preferred to act alone in the last resort, who would always follow their own star or search out their own circuitous destiny, who, for whatever reason, would find the associations of party loyalty too insulting or irksome to bear. I never saw the definition, by the way, as one primarily of virtue or vice, but rather of temperament and character. Some men or women – say, General de Gaulle or Queen Elizabeth I – always made up their own minds on great questions in the end; others no less great or estimable had the gift of acting together with their closest companions, and since party is an indispensable element in the British democratic system, this for sure is a quality not to be spurned. However, even if the word is novel, the political species is not.

Enoch Powell, it seems to me, has always been a loner – no doubt his old leader and eternal enemy, Edward Heath, would concur – but at once the assertion prompts some complicated questionings. He is also the strong upholder of party ties and traditions, the sworn enemy of coalitions in any shape and contrivance. He is, further, as anyone who has ever had any personal dealings with him will testify, the soul of honour and loyalty. No one so far as I know has ever accused him of a personal breach of trust; not quite the claim which could be made on behalf of some other leading 'loners', such as Joseph Chamberlain, for example, a man with whom Enoch Powell has sometimes been compared. We shall have special occasion in a moment to return to the comparison, but let us for a moment mark the contrast. When Chamberlain was called Judas, not even fellow disciples could repudiate the charge. No one ever dreamt of levelling any such accusation against Enoch Powell.

The examination of his political conduct has been persistent, especially in the form of political biographies. Few worthwhile books are written about living politicians, yet already there are several in which Powell appears as hero or villain, and each has helped to expose a corner of his mind and nature. No complete portrait emerges from any of them, and yet his magnetism loses none of its potency; so there will be more to come. He himself is (leaving aside for the moment any controversial attributes) the greatest master of clear exposition in British post-1945 politics; yet he has not explained himself. He seems to scorn excuses, apologia, memoirs, essays in autobiography. In the country at large he is a household word, a figure of fame or infamy; in the House of Commons, he can compel attention, even from those who detest what he appears to say or stand for, as no one else has done since Aneurin Bevan, almost alone, faced the all-powerful Winston Churchill with the wartime Parliament at his back. To elevate Enoch Powell into such company may at first seem a sacrilege, but most of those who have sat in the Parliaments of the past two decades would not dissent. And yet again, has there not been in his career, is there not in his character or perhaps his political philosophy, some indelible, inexorable flaw? The search for the truth about him remains absorbing and elusive.

Roy Lewis, a kindly, sympathetic and, one might guess, fully-converted Powellite disciple (even in the sense, as someone put it, that there's 'a Powell policy for everything') chooses to start his book auspiciously with the tremendous moment when Powell refused to fight in the 'fraudulent' election of February 1974, called by Edward Heath. ('One might say his whole life had been a preparation for February 1974'.) For the country at large, and for Powell's own constituency of Wolverhampton, the declaration was startling enough; for Powell himself, it must have been an indescribable agony. Maybe the action could be said to follow logically from some of his earlier quarrels with Heath, as Roy Lewis gropingly indicates; but how could this weigh in the balance against so much else? Powell cherished his individual association with his constituency as an essential part of his life and his parliamentary creed. He understood too, so much better than all the exponents of consensus and coalition politics, that allegiance to party is an essential ingredient of the British political system. He must have known that he would expose himself to charges of near-betrayal from his closest friends, apart even from the avalanche of Conservative fury which he invited upon his head.

Moreover, what hope could he have that he would ever survive the gamble? One of the oldest maxims of British politics is that politicians, and especially those who wish to take proper risks elsewhere, should guard their base: here was Powell, surrendering his without a fight, inexcusably, quixotically, wantonly. Many others before him have challenged their own party leaderships, left their own parties, crossed the floor of the House of Commons; but they have customarily done it with a reasonable and legitimate circumspection. Enoch Powell in February 1974 broke every such precedent and precaution. He did the deed in a manner likely (as most of us thought at the time) to inflict the minimum immediate injury on his opponents and the maximum lasting injury on himself.

Would he indeed ever return to the House of Commons; would he not be left to roam the political wilderness, a Hamlet without an Elsinore? He did not leave the path open for a return to his old party nor did he prepare to remodel his own party to suit his own design nor did he seek out the way to join a new one; the matchless trapeze artist of the age had fallen between three stools. He acted alone and indeed he selected a course where none of his followers could conceivably follow. Ambition should be made of a more willowy stuff; indeed, of a different fabric altogether.

Truly, one deduction to be drawn from this occasion, rightly raised to the place of honour in any record of his life, is that Enoch Powell cannot be intelligently defined as the high Tory turned populist, the opportunist without scruple, the arch-demagogue. Events have too often destroyed the accusation. Surely he likes applause and the proof of public support: is not this the meat on which all democratic politicians must feed? But often Powell seems ready to toss aside a popularity too easily gained, and to pursue some circuitous diversion in order to find his own solitary path. He has an unshakable, almost pedantic, sense of rectitude in personal dealings, and this strain does not accord readily with the notion of a ruthless, scheming careerist.

Turn aside for a moment from this aspect of his personality to one of his own esoteric writings, a learned essay contributed a few years ago to the *Historical Journal* on the subject of the so-called Kilmainham Treaty of 1882, agreed between Parnell and Gladstone, the essay being a by-product of Powell's own book on Joseph Chamberlain. Ever since reading that volume, I have nursed the suspicion that Powell grew disenchanted with Chamberlain, maybe even after he had signed the contract and started the work. At first thought, the attraction for him of Chamberlain, as hero or exemplar, must have looked obvious and overpowering: the shared interest in Birmingham, Ireland, the unity of the United Kingdom, not to forget, of course, the common hazards courted by a politician challenging the leadership of his own party. But Powell's book falls very far short of hero-worship, and sometimes comes nearer to distaste or condemnation. His concluding sentences are surely not intended as an encomium. 'The pathos of Chamberlain's political life was not the less for his having never clearly perceived that he had turned his own weapons against himself. It was the pathos of Ajax, not an Achilles.'

And the later gratuitous contribution to the *Historical Journal* strikes a harsher note. It offers fresh evidence on how the wretched Captain O'Shea used and misused the relationship between his wife and Parnell for purposes of blackmail and deceit, and how Chamberlain himself was at least partly privy to these subterfuges. That Enoch Powell, the Unionist MP for South Down, should insist so fastidiously on setting the record straight, to the honour of the arch-Home Ruler Parnell and the dishonour of the arch-Unionist Chamberlain, shows a quality rare in a politician, or an historian for that matter. Nothing but a passion for truth could have persuaded him to write that learned treatise. Chamberlain was of a coarser breed altogether, and certainly no similar passion and no sense of scruple governed his conduct. Rather he left a stain of dissemblement wherever he went. No wonder the sympathy between subject and author proved so imperfect, despite their common cause.

But to return to Roy Lewis's biography and *his* hero; he paints no warts or weaknesses on that bold countenance; usually and wisely he lets Powell's natural eloquence speak for itself. It is an impressive spectacle on a series of stages: the Powell of the 1960s anticipating by more than a decade the intellectual triumph of the monetarists among the Conservatives; another Powell of the same epoch forecasting the collapse of the Americans in Vietnam and indeed the evaporation of another Empire nearer home; the Powell of the 1970s defining more dazzlingly than any rival or associate the threat of the Common Market to the British Constitution and then the same Powell living to see his prophecies fulfilled in the spirit, if not the letter; the Powell of the late 1970s, with one hand seeking to purge the Ulster cause of its Paisleyite fanaticism, and then, with the other, hurling the hardest stones against Scottish and Welsh devolution – and this too from the Ulster glasshouse; or the Powell of the 1980s stating the case against the nuclear deterrent with a crystal logic no one else could equal: these and more. Considering the range of leading topics on which he has not shirked the test of offering settled and far-reaching judgements, it is an accomplishment of the first order. No one of his generation has done so much to check the subordination of the art of politics to the dictates of the technocrats, the managers, the crushing bureaucracies – the modern equivalent of what Edmund Burke berated as the rule of sophisters, economists and calculators.

Yet some qualifications of major consequence are required; we must dig deeper into the mystery than any of his biographers have yet attempted. Other aspects of the man and his politics must be explored by future biographers – or present-day politicians. 'We are all monetarists now,' is the slogan sometimes paraded as the new conventional wisdom, and if the claim were ever proved valid and the doctrine were applied *and found successful*, Enoch Powell would be entitled to the credit in a degree so far not even hinted at even in his own perorations. It is true that he had seen the blinding light before Keith Joseph or Nigel Lawson had ever heard there was any such place as Damascus. It is true that he has put the case in better English than Mrs Thatcher's best speech-writers will ever contrive. It is true that it is pleasanter to let Powell expound the pure milk of the word than to be condemned to endure Hayek, Friedman, Schumpeter and the rest all conglomerated into one or even that assortment of American or Middle European prophets of the 1920s who preached the same monetarist gospel with much the same assurance – and calamitous results. And as the old doctrine is applied, and the results are hardly less calamitous, Enoch Powell must bear the guilt no less than his late-developing pupils, the Jacks and Jills now in office.

It is not by these dead doctrines that the economic life of our nation, and indeed of the Western world, can be revived, and if they continue to be applied, with the full rigour of Powellite logic, great stretches of our beloved country will be wiped off the industrial map altogether — most of Ebbw Vale and much of Ulster, for a start. I long for the moment when he might stop and look at what is happening. It would be part of my thesis, if I ever contributed to a volume on the lives of Enoch Powell, that he became a wiser man when he crossed the Irish sea. And what would he do if he saw with his own eyes how the needs of the living nation, and more particularly that precious part of it which he represents so skilfully and loyally at Westminster, clashed with his suffocating economic theory? It would be a Powellite speech to outdo all that had gone before: that one assuredly will be worth reading many, many times as he invites us to do with the others.

The last burning topic is left till the end; it is almost too hot and too tender to touch: the item omitted from the list of great prophecies cited earlier and yet the most devastating of them all. Would Enoch Powell ever have made his reputation on the spacious scale now acknowledged if it had not been for the 'race' speech delivered in Birmingham in 1968, if he alone of all British politicians had not dared to treat the question in the terms and style he did? Roy Lewis, his biographer, had little difficulty in proving that that speech was not, on Powell's part, the calculated sensation designed to challenge Heath and the Tory leadership which some, like Lord Hailsham for example, have alleged. He can prove that in playing 'the numbers game', Powell has sometimes been right about the figures. He can show that Powell is no racist, a man obsessed with hatred for others with different coloured skins. Nor was that speech the act of an opportunist reaching for the popular cry — that would be the most shameful explanation of all, and is surely one belied by the whole of the rest of Powell's political life. So why did he do it? Why did the man who made another of his reputations with the Hola speech allow his imagination to desert him? Why did he fail to comprehend what fears and hatreds and antagonisms his words would help to spread, what furies and divisions and ferocities in the nation he wished to serve? Why did he harden his heart, like some Ancient Pharoah?

I do not know the answers; one day a great biography or autobiography may give us the true ones. Meantime, I believe it is the tragic irony of Enoch Powell's political life — or the pathos, to use his own word about Chamberlain — that the issue which made him famous is also the one which has barred his path to the highest office in the state. Without the Birmingham speech, the Tory kingdom would sooner or later have been his to command, for he had all the shining qualities which the others lacked. Heath would never have outmanoeuvred him; Thatcher would never have stepped into the vacant shoes. It was a tragedy for Enoch, and a tragedy for the rest of us too.

Once – but only once, so far as I can see – he did apply his mind, for publication, to these high autobiographical themes. He was being interviewed by Terry Coleman of the *Guardian* who put to him the suggestion that twice, in 1968 and in 1974, he had gone over a precipice. Back at once came the retort that there was a great contrast between the two occasions: 'In 1968 I didn't know there was a precipice. It was an elephant pit – but in 1974 I drove over the precipice knowing that the road I was on was bound to take me over a precipice, and telling everyone, and myself, "Look, there is the end of my public life."'

'Telling everyone' must be dismissed as an exaggeration; that is never the Enoch Powell way. Telling and arguing with himself, in the true 'loner' style, would be more accurate. But the conclusion still stands. He did believe that in deserting his own party and inviting the electorate to vote 'Labour' he was committing political suicide, and, according to most of the precedents, he was correct in that judgement. Joseph Chamberlain was never forgiven by his old associates for a far less abrupt and barefaced breach of allegiance.

In this sense the whole Ulster period was a kind of life after death, an uncovenanted bonus, a man playing with all his consummate talents a quite unexpected role. All else was made subordinate to the service of the people who sent him to represent them in the British Parliament, and for this task his grand rejection of Heathite Conservatism was no handicap at all. He had ceased to be a loner, and was quite entitled to parry the charge, as he did, that he, like Joseph Chamberlain, had become a political failure.

# George Orwell

*Swift:* It has been my especial misfortune to be edited usually by clergymen who thought me a disgrace to their cloth. They were tinkering at my writings long before Dr Bowdler was even born or thought of.

*Orwell:* You see, Dr Swift, you have put them in a difficulty. They know you are our greatest prose writer, and yet you used words and raised subjects that they couldn't approve of. In a way I don't approve of you myself.

*Swift:* I am desolated, Sir.

*Orwell:* I believe *Gulliver's Travels* has meant more to me than any other book ever written . . .

> Jonathan Swift, an imaginary interview by George Orwell, 2 November 1942
>
> from Orwell's *The War Broadcasts* Edited by W. J. West

I am deeply indebted, as must be evident, to Bernard Crick's biography *George Orwell: A Life* published by Secker & Warburg in 1980 and scarcely less to the Oxford University Press edition of *Nineteen Eighty-Four*, published with a critical Introduction and Annotations by Bernard Crick in 1984. These references are not intended in any sense to dismiss the writing of others who knew

Orwell so well, such as T. R. Fyvel, George Woodcock and Ian Angus, who with Sonia Orwell edited the Collected Works in 1968. It is sometimes alleged that the belated discovery of *The War Broadcasts*, from which the above quotation is taken, alters considerably our knowledge of Orwell and especially our knowledge of his association with Swift. I doubt it. After all, the famous Orwell essay on the subject was published four years later and contains a more ambitious criticism than anything attempted in the imaginary conversation.

George Orwell owed a great debt to Jonathan Swift, and, honest man that he was, he readily acknowledged it. Swift was the foremost exemplar of Orwell's much-vaunted plain, downright style. He read *Gulliver's Travels* for the first time on the night before his eighth birthday, and returned for inspiration or respiration to his model and master again and again, most notably in a well-known essay written in 1946, just after he had at last found a publisher for *Animal Farm* and before he embarked on *Nineteen Eighty-Four*. No *Gulliver's Travels*, no *Animal Farm* and no *Nineteen Eighty-Four*. The more the matter is examined, the more the likenesses and the linkages appear.

Indeed, in that same essay, Orwell singled out as 'Swift's greatest contribution to political thought' his attack upon what we now call totalitarianism. Swift, he said, had 'an extraordinary clear prevision of the spy-haunted "police state", with its endless heresy hunts and treason trials, all really designed to neutralise popular discontent by changing it into war hysteria'. True enough, but even so, was not the compliment slightly, if unconsciously, backhanded? Swift was not previewing some distant future; he was satirising the state system, especially the English state system, which he saw around him and, in particular, the methods employed when that English state went to war, in Europe or in Ireland.

A few pages later, however, Orwell, with Swift as his guide, took a much larger stride towards modern times, when he gave his account of Swift's supposed utopia: 'The Houyhnhnms, we are told, were unanimous on all subjects. The only question they ever *discussed* was how to deal with the Yahoos. Otherwise there was no room for disagreement among them, because the truth is always either self-evident, or else it is undiscoverable and unimportant. They had apparently no word for "opinion" in their language, and in their conversations there was no difference of sentiments. They had reached, in fact, the highest stage of totalitarian organisation, the stage when conformity has become so general that there is no need for a police force.' The stench of *Nineteen Eighty-Four* is there, overpowering.

And yet immediately after this quoted sentence comes another of shattering disillusion. 'Swift,' says Orwell, 'approves of this kind of thing' – that is, totalitarianism carried to the highest degree – 'because among his many gifts neither curiosity nor good nature was included.' Swift believed in the static society in which 'we know everything already. So why should dissident opinion be tolerated? The totalitarian society of the Houyhnhnms, where there can be no freedom, and no development, follows naturally from this.'

Every Swift admirer (leave aside, for the moment, the Swift-lovers who may be eager to answer for his good nature even more than his curiosity) will be itching to protest with all the vehemence at his or her command. If Swift did cherish such an idea of a future society, if he did offer in advance some plausible excuse for the Stalinite horror, must there not have been some demoniac aspect of his mind or soul, something diseased in his own mental outlook? And was this not the very charge made by some of Swift's contemporaries or some of his most eager and early defamers, such as Dr Johnson? And is this not the charge now delivered and sustained, almost sanctified by Orwell? He does not refrain from using the actual, awful word: diseased.

He plunges deeper still, even more unpardonably: 'The political expression of such an outlook must be either reactionary or nihilistic, because the person who holds it will want to prevent society from developing in some direction in which his pessimism may be cheated. One can do this either by blowing everything to pieces, or by averting social change. Swift ultimately blew everything to pieces in the only way that was feasible before the atomic bomb – that is, he went mad.' In short, the Swiftian utopia doesn't work. It is too violently offensive to human instinct, human nature, call it what you will. The idea itself was enough to drive even its author out of his senses.

We are now confronted with a Swiftian irony of Brobdingnagian proportions. The great and justly acclaimed twentieth-century satirist, whose phrases have challenged the totalitarian philosophy of our time more potently than anyone else's, pays wonderful tribute to his English (or Irish) forebear, and yet accuses him in the same breath of being one of the unwitting authors of, or apologists for, our monstrous present-day ordeal. What excuse can there be?

The short answer is: Orwell ought to have known better. If, instead of accepting current academic verdicts about Swift, he had applied his iconoclastic mind to the personal question, he would have formed a different diagnosis. He himself had asked the question: 'Why is it that we don't mind being called Yahoos, although firmly convinced that we are not Yahoos?' Had he struggled a little longer for the answer, might he not have discovered that Swift too did not call us Yahoos; that Swift appreciated, quite as well as Orwell himself, the potential menace of the so-called totalitarian utopia; that he detested these conceivable developments just as surely as he condemned police-state tendencies in his own day; that it was our true human nature, with its inborn instinct for rebellion against war and poverty and oppression, which he sought to protect and proclaim; that his own natural goodness was such that at least he never went mad?

Indeed, one of the exciting discoveries about Swift is that he got saner as he grew older. Maybe in his brilliant youth he did believe unshakably in the conservative values, the static society, the uselessness and therefore the peril of dissent, the dark pessimism of orthodox Christianity. But the spectacles of war and poverty and oppression which he saw around him broke, not his reason, but his heart and, maybe, his faith. Ireland, especially, changed his temper and his style. No *Drapier's Letters*, no *Gulliver's Travels*. It was the passion stirred in the first which shaped the masterpiece.

George Orwell should have understood better maybe than any other writer since Swift's own time. He cherished all his adult life some rigid articles of literary faith, as Swift had done, but the way his mind and creed developed was even more significant. We must turn to Orwell's own story, as he told it or as others told it for him, and we may recall at once how he himself asked that no one should attempt the task of writing his biography, and we may pause for a moment to consider why the request was made. It was, since he never posed, a part of his diffidence, but it was also due to the streak of self-confidence, almost arrogance, which mixed with the shy manner. He knew he had fulfilled the strange ambition of his youth to make himself into a great political writer. He knew better than anyone else what agonies and obstacles he had encountered on the way. Most aspects of that life story he had reconstructed himself –

in *Homage to Catalonia, Down and Out in Paris and London*, and elsewhere – and he trusted no one to tamper with the effects he had laboured so hard to achieve. Direct autobiography he scorned – 'only to be trusted when it reveals something disgraceful'. And he would argue too that the very greatest writers, like Swift, always struggled to efface their own personalities. 'Good prose is like a window pane,' he said, but the greatest autobiographers have always been great egotists.

The case could easily be piled higher still; so why was his will defied? The answer is that his fame had extended worldwide in a manner which neither he nor even his most enthusiastic contemporary admirers could ever have conceived possible. He had become a household name, a household word, a set of household ideas, across the whole planet, and he died only thirty-five years ago! How could such a literary-cum-political phenomenon fail to arouse endless curiosity and re-examination?

So a legion of writers stepped forward to answer the demand – friends or half-friends who knew him, literary would-be biographers at first denied access to necessary material, and then an official biographer – to use a horrible term for any writer about Orwell – at least one who had received the essential encouragement from Sonia Orwell, whose previous qualms seemed so well-based. And yet how could she ever have fixed for the purpose on Bernard Crick, a Right-wing Socialist academic, surely one who would start with a whole range of imperfect sympathies with the down-and-out, anarchistic George Orwell? And was not the reader forced to quail all the more when he discovered that the book opened with a twenty-page disquisition on the art of biography written in a circuitous style which would certainly never have escaped Orwellian censure? ('Truth,' we were told, 'often has to deal in dull negations, unlike the glittering results of intuition and characterology.' Is there truly such a word? Not in my Oxford dictionary.)

Despite all these alarms and absurdities, Bernard Crick's book was a triumph of the first order. It was an absorbing, scrupulous, original record of how a reserved, impecunious English eccentric who had had the utmost difficulty in getting some of his chief writings published at all set his own imprint on the age of Hitler and Stalin. Indeed his words became part of the folklore, just as Orwell had intended. He had once marvelled at Rudyard Kipling's huge and enduring popularity; how he added unforgettable phrases to the language: 'East of Suez', 'the White Man's burden', 'palm and pine', 'the road to Mandalay'. Orwell's phrases, which he had designed even more deliberately, became more extensively part of our modern experience: 'double-think', 'some more equal than others', '1984', 'big brother is watching you' – it is hard to recall how, in this totalitarian era, we framed our thoughts before he had fashioned these instruments for us.

Bernard Crick's book traced all the facets in the connection between this eventual worldwide usage and the tentative beginnings. But best of all, in my prejudiced judgement, was the way he placed at the centre of his story of this passionate, self-created political writer, the *Tribune* Socialist. That is what he was and that is what he stood for. That was the truth which, without Bernard Crick's valiant exertions, might have become suppressed and distorted beyond recall.

It was in the *Tribune* years, between 1943 and 1945, when no other paper in the land for which George was prepared to write would have printed what he wanted (and even at the *Tribune* office there were several alarms, magnificently allayed by Aneurin Bevan's wisdom) that he also wrote *Animal Farm* and struggled painfully and at first vainly to find a publisher. *Tribune* sustained his pride when all Establishment doors, Right, Left and especially Centre, were slammed in his face, and when T. S. Eliot could write from Faber & Faber's office: 'Now I think my own dissatisfaction with this apologue is that the effect is simply one of negation.' Another suggestion from another worthy publishing house was that perhaps the pigs could be changed to another less offensive breed of animal. Thus the sensitivities of the Kremlin might be smoothed.

Such was one important strand (largely suppressed, since so many have an interest in the suppression) in the mood of the England of 1944 when the best traditions of English liberty were upheld in the near-bankrupt *Tribune* office, by Aneurin Bevan whom we now learn was blacklisted by the BBC, and by the young Frederic Warburg in a publisher's office scarcely more prosperous. The year 1944 deserves special note. His powers were rising to their peak, and his care of his beloved England rose to its highest pitch too. How he would flay her and how he would caress her. His blood boiled at the human degradation inflicted upon great masses of

Englishmen and women beneath the averted noses of their masters, at the suffocating class system which so nearly brought his country to destruction in 1940. But he would also remember: 'The outstanding – and by contemporary standards – highly original quality of the English is their habit *of not killing one another.*' How gentle and true his fellow countrymen could be. His patriotism was somehow interwoven with his ideas of how to write; they had the same purity and firmness. Language, he said, should be the joint creation of poets and manual workers, but in England they hardly ever met. So he wrestled to create a new style, to lift political pamphleteering to an art, to make words the weapons for smashing class barriers and saving his country. 'I hate to see England either humiliated or humiliating anybody else,' he wrote, and how could the patriotism of an English Socialist be better expressed – in the 1940s or in any other age, for that matter. 'It was Orwell's way,' as his truly close friend Tosco Fyvel perceived, 'to catch and reflect a moment of history. In *Homage to Catalonia* he had caught a revolutionary socialist movement. In *The Lion and the Unicorn*, in a larger war, he caught a patriotic English socialist moment – a moment in that dramatic year when England gathered herself from what seemed imminent defeat by Hitler.' *The Lion and the Unicorn*, by the way, was published in February 1941, at the height of the bombing of London before any prospect of respite appeared, East or West.

That for many of us was George Orwell at his greatest, the Orwell of the war years who understood so well the mood of the English people, and yet risked so much of his own ease to tell us, even at such a moment, the supreme truths we didn't want to hear. 'A power of facing unpleasant facts': that was the real quality, a singular quality, which he most often claimed for himself, with every justice. A similar inspired combination of his understanding of the English and the need to summons them to action appears in the last paragraphs of *Homage to Catalonia*, first published in 1938. 'And then England – southern England, probably the sleekest landscape in the world. It is difficult when you pass that way, especially when you are peacefully recovering from sea-sickness with the plush cushions of a boat-train carriage under your bum, to believe that anything is really happening anywhere. Earthquakes in Japan, famines in China, revolutions in Mexico? Don't worry, the milk will be on the doorstep tomorrow morning, the *New Statesman* will come out on Friday. The industrial towns were far away, a smudge of smoke and misery hidden by the curve of the earth's surface. Down here it was still the England I had known in my childhood: the railway-cuttings smothered in wild flowers, the deep meadows where the great shining horses browse and meditate, the slow-moving streams bordered by willows, the green bosoms of the elms, the larkspurs in the cottage gardens; and then the huge peaceful wilderness of outer London, the barges on the miry river, the familiar streets, the posters telling of cricket matches and Royal weddings, the men in bowler hats, the pigeons in Trafalgar Square, the red buses, the blue policemen – all sleeping the deep, deep sleep of England, from which I sometimes fear that we shall never wake till we are jerked out of it by the roar of bombs.'

During the next five years after the *Tribune* period, from 1945 to 1950, the last before his death, he was starting to become famous and almost affluent. He found himself detached from, if not hostile to, his old *Tribune* associations. He believed that we, like the rest of the human race, were guilty of many misdeeds and backslidings. Above all, no doubt he felt we were relapsing into the shameful pro-Stalinist sympathies from which he had done so much to rescue us, or at least that we had ceased to keep this argument on the high plateau it deserved. The charge would not have been so easy to clinch, since the *Tribune* of those years did engage in a reasonably rough debate with the unreconstructed Stalinites or Stalin-lovers in the Labour Party's ranks. But Orwell's attitude, his distance from practical politics, may be gauged by some of his comments on Aneurin Bevan's activities in the new post-1945 Labour Government. He criticised the Cabinet as a whole for its Fabian tastes, for its refusal to embark on the immediate abolition of the public schools and the House of Lords, and of Aneurin Bevan in particular for having allowed himself to become immersed in 'all this administration about housing and hospitals'. Such was the Orwell of 1947 on the establishment of the National Health Service. The best excuse for him is that all the while he was embarking on his own last great exertion of writing *Nineteen Eighty-Four*. I remember now only vaguely the impression when I first read it. My recollection was that, along with the horror, it left a taste of sourness, even defeatism, and that even the world-acclaimed Orwellian clarity had in those last pages lost a little of its lustre.

But now, move ahead to 1984 itself. Start afresh, first of all, without any sour recollections or preconceptions, as Orwell himself would have wished, with his own most carefully designed text. The stench, the wretchedness, the suffocation, the horrific climax are truly overpowering. Winston Smith and his lover, with their flickering glimpses of common sense and truth and courage, are not allowed to prevail. Less still even is any sure hope permitted to stir amid the listless murmurings among the proles. The whole picture is bleak and black and terrifying, and no one in his senses can doubt that this was part of the effect Orwell intended to produce. The torture scenes are surely among the most terrible in all literature; all the powers he had learned as a realistic reporter he used to make these scenes real too. A few critics once tried to dismiss them as melodrama; reading them in 1984, it is hard to see why.

Here, I believe, is the first and last imprint which *Nineteen Eighty-Four* must leave upon us. So does it not truly mean a descent into morbidity? Is not pessimism on such a scale ineradicable and insufferable? May it not even be, as one of Orwell's earliest and fiercest critics, Isaac Deutscher, alleged, that Orwell himself dabbled in 'the mystique of cruelty', that *Nineteen Eighty-Four* did mark the moment when, gripped maybe by the disease which brought his own early death, his power of prophecy overcame his humanity, and he surrendered to despair? And, if this most serious charge is true, how much would it undermine not merely the claims of *Nineteen Eighty-Four* but of Orwell himself; how much would it diminish his formal stature as both a writer and as a man? If *Nineteen Eighty-Four* is the product of a diseased mind and a cowardly soul, would it not cast a strange retrospective backward judgement across the rest of his work?

Of course, a quite opposite conclusion is the right one. Orwell was a model of courage as well as a master of the English language. His character is part of his writing; the one can never be torn from the other. *Nineteen Eighty-Four* is not, in my view, his masterpiece or anything like it; but it was brave to the point of heroism. Maybe it was even that touch of foolhardiness which interfered with his artistry.

And anyhow, whatever verdict is now passed on *Nineteen Eighty-Four* as a work of art, no one whose view is worth hearing would question Orwell's greatness. Bernard Crick added an introduction to the 1984 edition which presented the book in its proper critical and biographical context. He showed, or rather *proved*, from Orwell's other writings of the time, some of them absurdly neglected, how he remained to his dying day a committed, democratic Socialist; how he would upbraid others, Arthur Koestler for example, for their seeming readiness to abandon hope in practical politics. 'To take a rational political decision one must have a picture of the future,' he himself wrote in one of his essays on Koestler. He never ceased to search out his own political path, 'a kind of secular moral realism', as Crick called it: 'It is foolish to be too optimistic. It is cowardly and unhuman to despair – that is Orwell's line both as an author and as a man.' Bernard Crick held that balance well throughout 1984 when strange storms blew from many quarters and which, had he not adopted so strong a foothold, would have blown him and Orwell into shapes beyond all recognition.

1984 began, in the very first week of January, with the *Daily Mail* printing doctored extracts from *Nineteen Eighty-Four* designed to suit the 1984 opinions of the *Daily Mail*, whatever defamation might thereby be inflicted on the reputation of George Orwell. The whole book was presented as an anti-Soviet, anti-Socialist tract and nothing else, with the very same Professor John Vincent, who had made his journalistic reputation on Mr Murdoch's *Sun* during the worst 'Gotcha' days of the Falklands War distortions, let loose each day to underline these implications in case any *Daily Mail* reader had been too dull-witted to appreciate them. Not merely was Orwell's text shortened; his diction was improved too. Professor Vincent, alas, did not find it necessary to draw attention to Orwell's original delinquencies. Some of the specific exclusions had an especial interest. Nothing was allowed to be left of the references to the useless manufacture of atom bombs or the pursuit of 'the cold war' (another of Orwell's inventions, on Bernard Crick's claim). Nor were the 1984 *Mail* readers allowed a taste of what happened in one section of Minitrue: 'Lower down there was a whole chain of separate departments dealing with proletarian literature, music, drama and entertainment generally. Here were produced rubbishy newspapers containing almost nothing except sport, crime and astrology, sensational five-cent novelettes, films oozing with sex, and sentimental songs which were composed entirely by mechanical means on a special kind of kaleidoscope called a versificator. There was even a whole section . . . engaged in producing the lowest kind of pornography.'

Bernard Crick's own comment on this event must be recorded.* 'I share Orwell's view that the masses are controlled – or that people are massified – by prole feed. We're not clear whether that is what they "really want", for that is all they are given. A large part of his book is a great cry of rage that the Education Acts, the Reform Bills and cheap printing should have resulted in – the popular press. The disparity between formal literacy and the content of print does chill the bones: and that it should be done to Orwell himself!' Indeed. To forge Orwell in 1984: only the *Daily Mail*, the Forger's Gazette, could have dared.

Truly, it is hard to dissent from Bernard Crick's verdict that the *Daily Mail* had perpetrated 'the worst atrocity'. Nothing can ever touch it. Yet there was another charge against the Bernard Crick odyssey – the biography of 1980 and the 1984 defence of *Nineteen Eighty-Four* – which can match in irony what it lacks in deliberate perversion. He was accused of transmuting the grand anti-Stalin, anti-Socialist prophecy into a Swiftian satire. Strange impeachment, the tables turned indeed! Such accomplishments do not happen so readily, so inconsequentially, so accidentally, in our history or our literature or any other combined operations of the human race. Swiftian satires are not quite the tame affairs which the 1984 assailants of Bernard Crick might be eager to suggest. I cannot refrain from recording here what actually happened, in the year 1985, in Dr Swift's own Dublin, at a meeting called to raise funds for the famine victims in Africa. One speaker dared to read Swift's *Modest Proposal for Preventing the Children of Poor People in Ireland, from Being a Burden to Their Parents or Country: and for Making them Beneficial to the Public.* This Modest Proposal is indeed the most terrible curse pronounced on the money changers since, according to the reports, Jesus of Nazareth drove them from the temple. In Dublin, in 1985, the whole audience rose to their feet and left in protest. But that's just by the way.

Orwell himself had every intention of writing a Swiftian satire on the world around him and all its most evil propensities. Swift was

---

* They appeared in *Granta 14*.

his model, the one who had formed the rare idyllic partnership between poet and worker. Swift, the poet, Swift, the patriot, mastered the common speech of the people in a way few had done before. He became part of the folklore of his countrymen. His phrases, his words, the ideas he expressed so simply, formed part of their tradition, their political instinct. Orwell had the same aspiration in his age. And taking *Animal Farm* and *Nineteen Eighty-Four* and his other writings together, and taking as his subject a mankind and a womankind (not that Orwell often allowed women their proper place; Swift was slightly ahead of him) and facing an even more desperate world than Swift's searing imagination could envisage, he achieved a satire worthy to be set beside the master's. (He himself once wrote to a friend that he 'ballsed it up rather' in *Nineteen Eighty-Four*, but no such indictment will ever be justified.) Swift shaped Orwell's life, his style, his achievement, and in 1984 it was hardly possible to mention one without the other.

So the two men can share some of the same glory. And Swift, we may be reminded, took wise precautions to help guide us here too. He wrote a famous epitaph for himself, which stares down at us from the black marble on the wall of St Patrick's Cathedral in Dublin. He was well aware of the advantage and the dangers of such a form of composition. He knew that, once inscribed, no amended second edition would be possible, and he knew he was provoking an argument, although it is inconceivable that he could have imagined how endless and mighty the argument would be. Some considerable authorities pronounced his carefully chosen words 'terrible'; Yeats called them 'the greatest epitaph in history', an estimate which most fortunately did not inhibit him from translating them into his own version.

> Swift has sailed into his rest;
> Savage indignation there
> Cannot lacerate his heart.
> Imitate him, if you dare,
> World-besotted traveller; he
> Served human liberty.

Who will deny the claim? George Orwell did dare; his savage indignation was of the same order; and he too served human liberty. He was not also, as Swift was, a comic genius but there are precious few of them anyhow, and Orwell made no claim to be included in that exclusive category. And Swift, we must note, did not seek to cite that item in the famous epitaph. It is as servants of human liberty that they stand shoulder to shoulder, and woe to any who would put them asunder.

# James Cameron

Which does she want to kill first – me or the
NHS?

> James Cameron's last words, or almost the last.
> They appeared in the article in the *Guardian*
> printed after his death in January 1985,
> recording his last experience in hospital.

For the reasons stated in what follows, I would
prefer not to cite all James Cameron's books. His
greatness as a journalist was not comprised in any
one of them. However, his *An Indian Summer*,
published by MacMillan in 1974, holds a special
place.

Full-time working journalists seldom produce great books, even good ones, and the reasons are not hard to find. They write for the day and the week, grow disrespectful of words and too quickly exhaust such little patience as they may have. The routine of earning a living saps the precious lifeblood and offers few opportunities for replenishment. But every now and again an exception to the rule appears; men like H. W. Nevinson or H. N. Brailsford, who could hardly describe an individual incident or scene without setting it in a wider context of comprehension and leaving their own imprint.

The leading candidate for entry into this exclusive company in the post-1945 world was James Cameron. Yet it was with a mixture of excitement and trepidation that I started upon his 'experiment in biography', *Point of Departure*, published by Arthur Barker in 1967. The book was not truly an autobiography at all, as Cameron himself acknowledged in his first sentence. He lacked the engrossing egotism required for the task. 'In many ways I am more of a fool now than I ever was,' he said in his Foreword. What oceans of self-pity and fascination a Rousseau or a Boswell would have wrung from that single admission! But Cameron, the master of brilliant, cascading eloquence, could be tight-lipped about himself. There are hints and gleams of self-revelation, but the reader aches for more.

No dispute is conceivable about his journalistic credentials. At an early age he was ghost-writing for his father, who gained an increasingly meagre livelihood from serial fiction. He himself started on the *Red Star Weekly* in Dundee, of which each page had to be soaked in human gore. One of his gifts, incidentally, is to recall places; he describes the impact of Bonnie Dundee, 'the brutal melancholy, the façade of unparalleled charmlessness, an absence of grace so total that it was almost a thing of wonder'.

Thereafter, he did every job a newspaper offers, menial and romantic. Somehow, by a magic process which he did not disclose, he fashioned the most individual style of any reporter of our time. And yet he did not scorn to learn also how to write a story when he didn't have one, the essential requirement for the peace of mind of reporters, not to mention editors. He became a supreme professional, able to jump on a plane at a moment's notice and unravel some imbroglio at the other end of the planet. He could pick up the fresh mood of a place within hours. Heat and cold, hellfire and prodigious bouts of drinking, could not break his wiry frame or stop him from catching his deadlines. Yet he was the reverse of the hardbitten, cynical newspaperman. The more words he manufactured, the more tender and discriminating they became; the more bestial the horrors he was compelled to witness, the sharper his sensitivity.

He saw the bomb, with the portrait of Rita Hayworth on its casing, dropped at Bikini, 'a kind of slapstick nightmare', and labelled himself 'the first of the atom bomb bores'. He went to Korea to report how the United Nations prospered, only to be transfixed by the infamies of Syngman Rhee. To persuade the world that the North Vietnamese were made of flesh and blood, he staked the fortune he hadn't got, all his precious time and energy, to get in and out of Hanoi. Back in London occasionally, amid such exploits, he would declare reckless war on one after another of his bosses, starting with Beaverbrook. The rest of Fleet Street admired but never emulated his daring. No practising journalist was ever so devastating on the abstruse theme of newspaper ethics. But along with the reports, the campaigns and the invective, he could also present unforgettable glimpses of the road to Tibet or the last days of the *News-Chronicle*, of Albania, the U2 Conference, or Bardot or Miss Bardot 'as I came to think of her'.

I trust I may be excused for quoting the first two paragraphs of his piece on 'Brigitte'. The whole appears in his so-called autobiography and runs to just about 1500 deathless words. Not one of them truly should ever be altered. But the three introductory paragraphs may be exactly quoted, since they indicate his tone of voice, and the way his wit obtruded and captivated at the least likely moments. This is the way he talked, and in a sense always talked, more especially when he had just returned from some central scene in the world comedy – Khruschev's Moscow, in this instance. He went on talking like this to the day he died. But herewith Brigitte in 1954:

The news some years ago that Madame Jacques Charrier was soon to become a mother had an especial piquancy for all students of foreign affairs, and I for one heard the announcement with a warm appreciation. I had been a student of the career of Madame Charrier, as she was then, for some time, ever since she had been a fresh, eager, public-spirited young woman called Brigitte Bardot, and walked into my life across the Okhotny Road in Moscow, many long trips ago.

It is not generally known, except to those of my acquaintances who have now heard the event described so often that they flinch at my approach, that Brigitte (or Miss Bardot, as I came to think of her) was once a Fraternal Delegate to a Moscow Conference. The word Fraternal is not one I would have used myself. She was, in a sense, an envoy. Nowadays, to be sure, there can be few people who have not found themselves a delegate of some sort to the Soviet Union; even so there tends to be a lack of glamour in the occupation. Certainly in those days Union business was rarely in the hands of small blondes with square mouths; indeed very much to the contrary.

I had been despatched during the winter of 1954 on some undertaking or other which involved much plodding around places like Kharkov and Stalingrad and Rostov-on-Don, not on the whole centres of much bohemian delight. Nor did I await any more rich diversion back in Moscow, a city where I have usually found it only too easy to be well-behaved.

But *Point of Departure*, even with such polished gems as this embossed in it, was not Jimmy at his very best. His love of individuals and the human race in general, his insight into individual hearts, needed to be stirred to raise his writing to the highest pitch. Another title, *An Indian Summer*, which appeared in October 1974, offered even more enticing prospects, partly because India had always seemed to occupy so central a place in his journalistic life, and partly because the middle-aged fool of his own confession had been freshly-incarnated in the eyes of his Fleet Street friends.

He had married Moni, the wisest act of his life. She had taken him on a honeymoon to her native land, and one which had ended publicly in the vast horror of Bangladesh (that is, two or three horrors before the most recent one) and privately in a most excruciating motor-smash. A bundle of skin, bones, wood and wire was somehow transhipped back to London and there magically stuck together by English medicine and Moni; and yet, for all his courage and her care, how much of the Cameron genius could survive such buffetings?

And how would India survive too? Perhaps that was the worst source of doubt, and the apparent disproportion in the questions is not false. No British writer of recent times had written more lovingly of India; no journalist had reported more sympathetically the dilemma of India's leading statesmen – he was the close friend of Jawaharlal Nehru back in the critical, liberating days of 1947. And yet he would never refrain from lashing those he loved. He would write his own independent truth though the heavens fell, as he had done in Korea, in Algeria, in Vietnam, in Israel, and none of the legions of victims in those lands could touch his heart like India, now more than ever.

All these pressures, susceptibilities, memories and broken hopes and dreams, were woven together into a single thread in *An Indian Summer*. It is not an autobiography, although the personal tenderness is allowed to shine through in a few gleaming references. It is a book about ancient and modern India, brave, beautiful, astringent, withering and, just occasionally, savage. 'Thus I formed,' he recalls, 'an acquaintance with a man whom as the years went on I was increasingly to admire, and even revere, until the tragic days. From Pandit Nehru I learned more about India than from anyone, and a great deal about the essential sadness of power. He was profoundly responsible for the achievement of Indian independence, and alas even more responsible in time for its vitiation and decay. Jawaharlal Nehru made India, and lost it.'

Terrible words those, for sure, and not in my judgement to be accepted as the final verdict on one of the truly greatest men of the century, but they were written with a candour and clarity which compelled attention and forced the argument. *An Indian Summer* started as a personal Odyssey and encompassed eventually the whole modern, tragic history of the sub-continent.

However, by some extraordinary art, indictments so daring that they make one catch one's breath, reminders of the grinding wretchedness and the fatalism of India, perceptive probings into Hindu history and into Hindu practice today, were mingled with scenes of Chaplinesque slapstick. Perhaps those of us who knew the author recall especially on these occasions his accent and tone, and the manner in which conversation could turn without a tinge of offence from the most horrific themes to gaiety and back again. How Jimmy dined, for instance, with the young Maharaja in a new kind of Barmecide feast, is as unforgettable as other more desperate moments: 'During the meal an odd thing became apparent: while one group of bearers was serving us, another bearer was serving His Highness. What was more, His Highness was clearly getting a better class of dinner. One did not have to be envious to see that we were getting cold and listless chapatis and dhal. HH was getting aromatic partridge; what was more, one perceived outside in the corridor a servant fanning a charcoal brazier on which he was making piping hot *phulkas* with which the young man was being plied, though none came our way. When the meal was over, we were offered Indian whisky, HH was given Scotch.'

*An Indian Summer* is an Anglo–Indian classic fit to take its place beside Forster's *A Passage to India*, and will be returned to again and again by those it had captivated or enraged and finally overwhelmed with such a flood of human compassion and tragic sense and comic inspiration. Page after page of his writing provoked laughter when they might have drawn tears. He had the perfect disinterestedness of a Don Quixote, and most of the other endearing qualities of that knight besides. But he was also, if it can be imagined, a Don Quixote with an uncontrollable self-critical humour, and an endless capacity to report and satirise all the crimes and follies of the age, a lonely crusader against all the hideous realities of the post-Auschwitz, post-Hiroshima world.

Almost everything or anything he wrote may stir some fresh, previously unsuspected revelation – not the kind of claim which can be made about most other journalists, living or dead. Only a very precious few, such as Jonathan Swift or William Hazlitt, can be held to have raised journalistic writing to such a level. But the comparison is not inapposite. Much that he wrote on the greatest themes of the age *is* imperishable, and one reason perhaps is that his truest kinship was not with Nehru but with Gandhi.

Not so long before Mahatma Gandhi's assassination Jimmy had a conversation with him which shaped his whole life. The two words, Mahatma Gandhi, go together, and reporting that conversation, he explained why. 'In those days to the political world outside the word India equated almost automatically with the word Gandhi, which had gone almost into folklore. "Mahatma" was an honorific existing nowhere else; it roughly means "great soul", but it has no formal standing, cannot be conferred or really defined. Gandhi never asked for it but he could never reject it. It is true that he occasionally deprecated it, with befitting modesty, while greatly enjoying the deprecation. Somebody once used the phrase: "The man of towering modesty." Only after all these years I dare admit that it was mine.'

One remark made by Gandhi in that interview seemed, for Jimmy, to have a special relevance. He said: 'Surely you must appreciate by now that my belief in *satyagraha*, non-violence, is an active thing, a militant thing in its way. It is possible for a violent man, but never for a coward. The political question is nearing its end: let us see a little further. All life implies some sort of violence; we must select the path involving the least. But there again you must go a little deeper . . .'

James Cameron's journalism always seemed to be going a little deeper. I felt he must often have stopped, amid some international crisis beating about his head, to recall Gandhi's advice, which meant more to him than anyone else's.

# Arthur Koestler

———◦◉◦———

Malraux said of Koestler that he was a person
perpetually in search of a country.

Stephen Spender,
*The Thirties and After* (Fontana, 1983)

Iain Hamilton's *Koestler* published in his lifetime,
by Secker & Warburg in 1982, did not win Koestler's complete approval. That was too much to
hope for; but it is a fair book and should encourage
everyone to turn back to Koestler's own writings.
As with George Orwell, it is hard to imagine how
we could have conversed in the Hitler–Stalin epoch
without their guidance.

Who will ever forget the first moment he read *Darkness at Noon*? For Socialists especially, the experience was indelible. I can recall reading it right through one night, horror-struck, over-powered, enthralled. If this was the true revelation of what had happened at the great Stalin show trials, and it was hard to see how a single theoretical dent could be made in it, a terrifying shaft of darkness was cast over the future no less than the past.

But *Darkness at Noon* did not make its worldwide intellectual conquest until roughly a decade later. It was published six months before Hitler's armies invaded the Soviet Union, and its full explosive force was necessarily for a while submerged. It renewed its assault when peace came (selling 400,000 copies in liberated France, for instance) and reached its peak of influence at the Berlin 'Freedom' Congress of 1950 (a meeting of 'American police spies and literary apes,' as one old Communist called it) where Koestler's ideas more than anybody else's set their stamp on the way all Europe, East and West, conducted the great debate.

Quite a feat for a shy, fragile, rootless, self-conscious, guilt-ridden Hungarian Jew who arrived near-penniless on our shores sometime during our finest hour in 1940 to join the Pioneer Corps, once he'd escaped from Pentonville, his favourite prison – and he was a connoisseur. He came to us to take on Hitler before he tackled Stalin.

What went before and what came after in the world Koestler helped to transform, the incisiveness of almost all his political writing, all this and much else is excellently chronicled in Iain Hamilton's book. But a biography must be something more. What about the innermost soul, which he himself has taken pains to expose? How much is left; how much concealed? And what of the suspicion that his conduct, his character even, may be deeply flawed? My answer is that every word of the book is absorbing on this personal level too, but here I suppose, I am required, as we say in the House of Commons, to declare my interest.

I first met Arthur Koestler in that same 1940, and fell an immediate, swooning victim to his wit, charm and inordinate capacity for alcohol. He was in Pioneer Corps uniform and in his best fighting spirit, but since the encounter occurred in the Savoy Grill, I suppose we met momentarily as equals. With him, though, such scenes of composure never lasted long. A year or so later I signed him up to write a column for the *Evening Standard* under the title: 'This is the voice of Sidney Sound, your neighbour on the Underground'. Within weeks he had ruptured my relationship with proprietor, management and, as they alleged, a considerable chunk of the reading public. The column came to an abrupt end, but not, as yet, my friendship with him.

He was the most pulverising arguer I have ever met, bar none. Others might seek to entice and persuade, thus offering loopholes of illusion or dignity for their victims. Others might be said to wield a rapier, bludgeon or some such old-fashioned instrument. But Koestler got you in a corner, with all escapes blocked, and machine-gunned with fact, analogy and superabundant debating skill. Sometimes his passion and his logic would consume themselves and everyone in sight, in mounting, insensate, satanic virulence.

Iain Hamilton faithfully chronicles these episodes – the vast, drunken, rhetorical orgies in which some hidden Koestlerite drive sought escape and some new intellectual flight was pursued to imbecility. A cloud of witnesses are here to testify, and one of them clinches the charge beyond dispute. For the biographer has the use, with Koestler's concurrence, of the intimate diary of Mamaine, who loved him as he was never loved and left him as he was never left. On their long-postponed wedding day, in his beloved Paris and in one of his milder moods, he managed to drive off in the early evening and leave his bride to have breakfast in the cafe on the *quais* with Stephen Spender ('I've always wanted to spend the night with you, it's too bad it was your wedding night').

It was this same Koestler who in Berlin in 1950 denounced his fellow intellectuals with such magisterial authority: 'It is amazing to observe how in a crisis the most sophisticated often act like imbeciles. . . . Faced with destiny's challenge, they act like clever imbeciles and preach neutrality towards the bubonic plague. Mostly they are victims of a professional disease; the intellectual's estrangement from reality. And having lost touch with reality they have acquired that devilish art; they can prove everything that they believe, and believe everything that they can prove.'

A dazzling Koestlerite indictment indeed, but how much of it could be validly turned against himself? One of his greatest admirers, almost a disciple, Emanuel Litvinoff, asked about Koestler's second volume of autobiography: 'Are the Koestlers, the Malraux, the Weissbergs and the Silones the right people to lead Western Europe into sanity?' An ironic, implicit answer is supplied in the account here of that Berlin Congress in 1950. Koestler himself noted in his diary at the time: 'If Berlin survives, of which there is little chance, a new European spirit might be born there.' Yet another witness of the scene, a practising, pragmatic politician, did more to save Berlin and much more to help Europe back on the road to sanity. He was Willy Brandt, and his name symbolises a form of democratic Socialism which Koestler sometimes implies has perished from the earth.

The moral is, I suppose, that Koestlerism, like all other delightful intoxicants, should be taken in temperate doses or even in association with other similar potions. Koestler remains the most deadly of all the great anti-Communist writers. Often he lacks George Orwell's commonsense or Ignazio Silone's compassion but *Darkness at Noon* is an artistic-cum-political achievement which neither of them could rival and, in the presence of it, who can care a straw about alleged defects of character?

One day – Iain Hamilton would not claim to offer more than an interim portrait – the whole man, the artist and the political fighter and the philosopher and the reckless pursuer of the temptations of the moment, may be presented to us. And whatever happens, we in this country have our special cause for pride. Koestler chose to write in English, and designed for his own purpose a sharp and vibrant individual style. He chose England, 'the land of virtue and gloom', in preference to 'the delectable nightmare' of the United States. And, having in *Darkness at Noon* given us the most ferocious instruction in the politics of freedom, he closed that splendid volume and opened up others more intellectually adventurous still. He even prescribed a peace pill to help us subdue our deepest and darkest instincts of aggression.

This new intellectual life started with *The Sleep Walkers* in which he knocked about so unmercifully the rationalist anti-clerical hero, Galileo. When I first reviewed that thunderbolt of a book in *Tribune*, I promised to produce a second review once I had worked out the proper reply. Alas they are still waiting for it. What Koestler professed to do in this field – and what he largely achieved – was to bring together the most modern knowledge on the working of the human mind as discovered and tabulated by a whole variety of experts. Man refuses to be reduced to a machine, a commissar's plaything, a predictable reactor to chemical doses and potions, a brainwashed mass. Koestler, who had spent half his adult life describing the totalitarian juggernaut, devoted the other half to a search for the elusive individual. Ancient learning and the latest news from the science laboratories were scoured to confirm the same conclusion: 'One could fill a whole dictionary with quotations, from Pythagoras to Einstein, all of them testifying to hunches of unknown, extra-conscious origin.' How could anyone rebut a sentence like that? And who but Koestler would dare invoke with such assurance the history of the hunch?

However, let me descend for a moment from these lofty planes to some personal incidents. One of the pleasures in life still to be relished was to see his lacerating genius at work when someone else was the target. I recall a glorious occasion, just after the war, when, leaving the House of Commons at the early hour of 10.30 one night and bumping into Joseph Alsop, as all the world must know, one of the most respected of America's top columnists. As he tapped his umbrella impatiently in Palace Yard, I said: 'Would you like to come to a night club and meet Arthur Koestler?' 'Koestler,' he replied, 'is my hero of heroes. He has told the world the truth about the cold war. He is the prophet of our times, the man I'd most like to meet of any on the face of the planet.' So we set off together to the Gargoyle, where Arthur Koestler and Dylan Thomas had laid a good foundation for the night's work. Dylan Thomas in such combats could not quite match Arthur, who, without provocation or pause, turned upon Jo Alsop, no mean controversialist, as he liked to consider himself, and lambasted American ineptitude in dealing with the Communist menace. Three hours later the eminent columnist was declaring, as he tapped his umbrella on the pavement of Piccadilly Circus, that he had never been so insulted in his life. He made off into the night and never met Koestler again, while the three of us reeled round the corner to my top flat at No 62 Park Street, there to glory in our several ways at the Alsop discomfiture. Koestler and I played chess, while Dylan Thomas took my copy of *Darkness at Noon* from the shelf and wrote a few insulting paragraphs to which Arthur replied in kind. Someone later stole that volume. If it should ever find its way into the auctions, it should make a fortune.

The final soreness left by that episode may be imagined. I offer another to compensate for it. Once, within fifteen minutes on the same No 11 bus journey, Arthur persuaded me, without leaving the faintest tincture of doubt in either instance, (a) that the only cure for asthma must be to go to a psycho-analyst; and (b) that the effective cure should not be adopted, since it would certainly produce something worse. Wait for it and, great Marxist dialectician that he was and remained, Koestler could yet supply his own incontestable antithesis, or even a synthesis, something not at all easy to come by in these hard times.

# Harold Nicolson

. . . he was for ever hampered by those doubts which assail the intellectual who mixes with the world of action . . . doubts above all regarding his own prescience and judgement.

On Benjamin Constant,
by Harold Nicolson

Harold Nicolson was not, like some others in this section, an obvious comrade-in-arms. But I was entranced by some of his books, for instance, *Benjamin Constant or The Congress of Vienna*, long before I fell for a while beneath his personal spell – I went to speak for him at a by-election in North Croydon in 1949 – and that of his diaries, celebrated here.

All who have derived so much delight from the wit and grace of Harold Nicolson in his other writings will reach eagerly for his *Diaries and Letters 1930–39* (Collins), and they will not be disappointed. The flow continues, and will only be finally contained in two more substantial volumes. It is an astonishing feat, for ever since 1930, according to the editor, Nigel Nicolson, his father sat down after breakfast to bash out a few hundred words on his typewriter. Even assuming that the best of the three million words available are being selected, such scandalous fluency should, in all fairness, become insipid at last. Instead, the diary triumphs at three or four different levels.

First, the direct comments and observations of the diarist on the varied assortment of personages he bumps into on his social round. For example, T. S. Eliot: 'He looks like a sacerdotal lawyer – dyspeptic, ascetic, eclectic . . . without pose and full of poise.' Or A. E. Housman: 'dry, soft, shy, prickly, smooth, conventional, silent, feminine, fussy, pernickety, polite, sensitive, tidy, greedy, and a touch of a toper'. Or Bernard Shaw ('His cheeks as pink as a girl's. His eyes as simple and unmalicious as those of an animal') hailing a young twenty-three-year-old Laurence Olivier as the great actor of the future. Two other youngsters make notable entries. John Strachey: 'His great hirsute hands twitched neurotically as he explained to us, with trembling voice, how unpathological he really was'; and Anthony Eden, after his resignation in 1938: 'He does not wish to defy the Tory Party and is in fact missing every boat with exquisite elegance.' And what a dinner party that must have been just after Hitler's entry into the Rhineland with Maynard Keynes and Guy Burgess – 'Keynes is very defeatist.'

Which glimpse leads to another entrancing series of revelations. What fatuous prophecies our major prophets can make! What heads of clay our idols sometimes uncover! Keynes (in 1931) foretold general breakdown in the United States, with the whole country 'reverting to a Texas type of civilisation'. Sir Horace

Rumbold, British Ambassador in Berlin, explained (in January 1932) how 'the Hitlerites had missed the boat'. Beaverbrook (in 1930) prophesied the early demise of the *Daily Herald*. Harold Macmillan (in 1931) suggested that Oswald Mosley's New Party would be coming into its own just about five years later. Churchill (in 1938) told how, if war came, London would be a shambles in half an hour. And William Mabane, a rising star in the Chamberlain firmament, described (in 1938) how the wind had gone out of Winston's sails, how he was 'becoming an old man'. The diarist added: 'He certainly is a tiger who, if he misses his spring, is lost.'

Honest man and honest editor, they do not suppress a good number of the diarist's own imbecilities, and these add fresh charm and credibility to the tale. He made an ass of himself over Mosley's New Party, but offers much detail to confirm how wide across all parties was the fascination which Mosley exercised, how great was opportunity missed, partly through neglect of Nicolson's advice. Then he joined MacDonald's National Labour Party, of all absurd contraptions, and had to listen to Ramsay explaining (in 1936) how 'the ball will soon be at their feet'.

In the late 1930s Nicolson also became a London luncheon party gladiator, carrying the good fight for a decent foreign policy from one West End party to another, properly clouting the assorted Hitler-lovers he would find round those tables and recording with contempt how many of his own class put their supposed class interests before England's honour. In politics, he was almost a statesman, almost a democrat, something of a snob, something of a joke. When he fought his first election in 1935 he explained to his amiable, affronted Tory chairman: 'I am very bad at *prolonged* deception.' When elected to the House of Commons, he made a brilliant maiden speech, but soon found himself flapping ineffectually in 'our dear old aquarium'. Despite a reputation for vitriolic invective, he had no combative qualities. Even his snobbery had a compensating aspect: he would get into trouble with Americans for regarding bankers as 'rather low-class fellows'.

Altogether, his charm, his honesty, his eloquence and his wit did not fade: so while he followed the politicians, helped out the hostesses, made a fine husband, reared a loving family and watched an old world die, he still found time, almost against his will, to fulfil his destiny – to show the angels how to write upwards of 1000 words a day, 5000 at a pinch.

We left our hero, at the end of his first volume of memoirs, smiting Philistines, Municheers and every denomination of Hitler-lovers and appeasers all the way from Lady Cunard's luncheon table to Lady Colefax's, and the final impression was that the lights would soon be going out all over SW1, especially in these innermost haunts of gossip and chicane. Not a bit of it. So stiff was the upper lip of the British upper-crust that something of the same sort went on right through Armageddon. In *Diaries and Letters 1939–45* (Collins) the odyssey of Harold Nicolson is continued from Brooks's to the Beefsteak, from Pratt's to the Carlton, from Boulestin to the Savoy Grill, even to the Travellers', which, beneath the storms of war, became 'a battered caravanserai, where the scum of the lower London clubs are served inadequately by scared Lithuanian wait-resses'.

Nothing daunted him. And nothing need daunt the vast company of his delighted readers. Through those years, London was the centre of the universe, and Harold Nicolson had an advantageous place close to the very heart where he could measure almost every palpitation. He was, after all, a member – an *embattled* member, he says with not so much as a wink – of the best club of all which put on a show to make even White's look seedy. For it was the House of Commons that won the war. Historians with their fine talk of Alamein or Stalingrad and unfolding destinies may cavil at the claim, but they must read and rebut Nicolson first. He records how Captain Margesson, Chamberlain's Chief Whip, retained his sway right up till May 1940. When dazed MPs were still asking the strange question '. . . but whom could you put in Chamberlain's place?' Nicolson writes – on 4 May, a bare six days before Hitler's tanks went through the Ardennes – 'Churchill is undermined by the Conservative caucus.'

Even at the height of the Norway debate, which finally overthrew him, Chamberlain's messenger raced upstairs to the meeting of the Tory rebels with an offer: vote for the Government tonight and the PM will see you tomorrow and, maybe, sacrifice Hoare and Simon to save his own skin. So it was still touch-and-go then whether destiny would ever have a look-in, and the identity of the messenger on this fateful errand adds spice to the tale. He was Lord Dunglass, Chamberlain's Parliamentary Private Secretary; in a later incarnation, Sir Alec Douglas-Home.

And how was it that the handful of Tory rebels ever became a force sizeable enough to divert the gulf stream of history? Nicolson offers clues which might easily have been lost forever: Anthony Eden hovering and havering in the wings; Margesson snarling at any would-be new conspirator; the rebels suddenly discovering their strength in a secret session; Churchill himself, deferring, flattering, respectful, almost fearful of the assembly which had scorned and ostracised him. Here are the essential scenes which Hansard and the official histories usually miss.

Churchill, of course, is God, and Nicolson devotedly describes how the point was at last conveyed to and accepted by the most incorrigible Chamberlainites. One secret of his slowly-established mastery was 'the combination of great flights of oratory with sudden swoops into the intimate and conversational'; another was his constant attendance in the Smoking Room where he would knock back adulation and sycophancy with the double brandies, and yet somehow not quite become intoxicated. Nicolson, for all his idolatry, was not afraid to criticise. He has his own evidence of how Churchill so nearly made a complete ass of himself about de Gaulle and why his own sympathies were normally on the side of the impossible Frenchman. A host of other figures flit across these pages and Nicolson can often pin them down with a phrase: a vain Lord Beveridge and a snorting Lady Astor; Lloyd George explains his sedate son Gwilym ('You see, he is not a Welshman. He is a Scandinavian . . . His mother is directly descended from the Vikings.'); Guy Burgess, always good for a gay evening ('I tell him there is no chance now of his being sent to Moscow.'); these and many more of war-time London's fashionable waifs and strays.

Finally, suffusing the whole and not at all to be overlooked as one of the most beguiling features of the book is the character, the pathos, of the author himself. He was, as he suggests, a Bohemian among politicians, a respectable Establishment figure among the Bohemians. Clearly he aspired to high office, only to be pushed out of the lowly one he had as if he were a dud. Constantly he laments the lack of iron in his makeup. He itched to be 'formidable', and was more often comic; there is indeed a Bertie Wooster streak in our drawing-room D'Artagnan. It would be easy to mock; he provides all the ammunition. But instead one stops to marvel at the achievement. Honesty, decency, modesty, magnanimity, are stamped on every page, as evident as the wit. These are not the normal virtues of successful diarists or would-be politicians, but Harold Nicolson possessed them all and, what's more, can make them as entrancing to read about as the seven deadly sins.

Speaking on behalf of the Amalgamated Society of Book Reviewers, Literary Hacks, Reputation-mongers and Licensed Logrollers, I hereby insist that a further reason why our hitherto-unheeded wage claim should be considered forthwith – without any reference to a philistine Prices and Incomes Board, what's more – is that we are now faced with the last, the very last of the Harold Nicolson *Diaries and Letters, 1945–62* (Collins).

For the past few years the mere mention of one of these volumes as a forthcoming item in a publisher's list has been enough to lighten the soul. *That* week, we have noted, we shall be granted sybaritic relief from the galleys. The book itself will slip down so easily; not real labour at all, but more like the softest vin rosé served with sunshine on the banks of the Seine. And as for the review, how many reviewers have been able to pass themselves off as debonair habitues of what they presume to be London society by a judicious mixture of quotation and plagiarism?

There was, for example, the ineffable moment when Harold Nicolson screwed up his never-too-readily accessible courage to join the Labour Party; later to be dismissed as the cardinal error of his life. He had to break the news to his would-be-Conservative MP son, his incorrigibly Conservative wife and his even more crusted eighty-five-year-old mother, Lady Carnock, who believed in 'privileged classes with nice clean Sunday-school discipline for the poor'.

The first two interviews went remarkably well, considering, but Lady Carnock re-established a proper appreciation of the gravity of the deed. 'I never thought,' she seems actually to have said, 'that I should see the day when one of my own sons betrayed his country', whereupon his brother Frederick Archibald, the second Lord Carnock, added for make-weight: 'I suppose you will now resign from all your clubs.' But the thought perished, the reader will be re-assured to hear, even before it crossed Harold's mind.

His odyssey continued unchecked from the Beefsteak to Brooks's, from Pratt's to the Carlton. He had in fact joined the Labour Party for what in those days seemed the oddest of reasons: in order to qualify for promotion to the House of Lords. When that came unstuck, he even resorted to the desperate extremity of fighting a by-election at North Croydon and felt 'like a cow being led gar-landed to the altar'. It was there that he gave his immortal reply to a heckler: 'No, I do not think that it is quite fair to say that the British businessman has trampled on the faces of the poor. But he has sometimes not been very careful where he put his feet.' It was there he discovered 'how difficult the proletariat are' and how 'I do not like the masses in the flesh'. So was he a hopeless snob? Harold's son Nigel, who edits the book with skill and loving care, passionately denies the accusation, but the ever-honest Harold is not so ada-mant. He suffered from the indelible effects of a public school education, could always be carried away by the mention of Oxford 'even on a pot of marmalade'.

A better defence, to restore relations with the enraged sansculot-tes of North Croydon, is that he could turn the same astringent gaze on the upper classes, too. How gratified he was to see that the Duke of Windsor had 'lost that fried-egg look around the eyes' and that the Duchess too had softened, that 'the taut, predatory look had gone'; to note that Winston saw the young Tories as 'no more than a set of pink pansies'; to characterise Attlee, off to Potsdam, as a 'lonely little snipe'. And when, finally, he was given a tuppenny-ha'penny knighthood instead of the precious renewed pass to the best club at Westminster, which he coveted, does he not convince us how truly he would have preferred 'a dozen bottles of champagne or a travelling clock'?

Royalty was a theme he was born to: he was loyal to the fingertips. And yet the biographer of George V is not afraid to confess his alarm at the discovery that for seventeen years his hero 'did nothing at all but kill animals and stick in stamps'. How to translate such source material into words offensive to neither piety nor truth? The passage in the book began thus: 'These years succeeded each other with placid similitude . . .' What a master! And then there are the new Winstonisms, for which he always had a specially well-attuned ear. Churchill, it seems, in the 1950s, gave fortnightly luncheons at the Savoy to his Shadow Cabinet. (Did Ted Heath, too, I wonder, ever stage such bacchanals in Bexley?) On one occasion he said: 'The Old Man is very good to me. I could not have managed this [Korean] situation had I been in Attlee's place. I should have been called a warmonger.' At that, Sir David Maxwell Fyfe asked innocently: 'What Old Man?' To which Winston replied: 'God, Sir Donald.' It seems, adds Harold, he always called David 'Sir Donald'.

Writing about the odious Pepys, Nicolson remarks that 'to be a good diarist one must have a little snouty, sneaky mind'. So it has always been supposed; such has been the tradition from the Creeveys to the Channons; yet it is his own achievement, rather, to have written one of the best diaries in the language, without betraying a single friend, even such a one as Guy Burgess. When once he was being scolded for being malicious in his descriptions of people, Aneurin Bevan protested: 'Harold is not malicious at all. He is the angel of pity.' And let that be the final word. Except, maybe, to add that since he always professed to have a 'naturally pagan soul', the other angels may count themselves lucky that they will not have to endure a rival who could write them off the face of Heaven.

# Lady Astor

Her eyes are very pale blue and sharp even when they are distorted by laughter. Her gaze has the power of going through walls and souls. She often wears blue to match her eyes. This is her favourite colour. She always has a gentle scarf loosely round her neck, and it ranges from a pale to a rich azure.

> Chiquita, the Roman Catholic daughter-in-law she first ostracised and then came to love best.

*Nancy Astor; Portrait of a Pioneer* by John Grigg, published by Sidgwick and Jackson in 1980, does truly present a portrait. The text and the pictures are necessary together to give even a hint of the loveliness of Lady Astor.

So many people (and places) had love–hate relationships with Nancy, Lady Astor, that we might suspect she had invented the idea herself to suit her special social-cum-political requirements.

From a distance her utterances or attitudes could appear absurd or offensive or insufferable, but when one met her face to face all criticism was apt to be swept aside by a single flick of her mingled charm and wit. Sometimes the same endowments seemed to operate inversely; bosom friends or adoring members of the family could be sent reeling by an insensitive blow. 'When I read my Christian Science lesson in the morning,' she said, 'I feel I can go out to raise the dead. But what happens? I go out and raise the devil.' Of course it was a joke and she could make marvellous jokes against herself. But the wit could also turn to sadistic glee, to something like savagery.

Few more pitiful tales have ever been told of the peculiar afflictions which the ultra-rich may suffer than the account given here of the final years between Nancy and Waldorf, Viscount Astor, who had bestowed upon her all the offerings which a vast fortune and overflowing devotion could supply. But one prize was not within his gift. He could not decree that the Sutton constituency of Plymouth, which she had represented in Parliament since 1919, would continue to be held by her in what used to be called the Conservative interest. He had his own quarrels at the time with the local Conservatives. He understood the spirit of the age better than she did. He feared for her, passionately; believed defeat in the election could break even her flaming spirit. For once in his married life, he put his lordly foot down. So, on 1 December 1944, the twenty-fifth anniversary of her entry into the House of Commons as the first woman to take her place there, she said at a celebratory dinner: 'I have said that I will not fight the next election because my husband does not want me to . . . Isn't that a triumph for the men?' Momentarily the rebuke was mild, but not for long. She screamed like a child robbed of its toy and went on screaming almost to her dying day, rarely ceasing to hold Waldorf responsible.

Her excuse, if conceivable excuse there can be for such conduct, is that she did love Plymouth. When she was first elected, she said: 'I ought to feel sorry for Mr Foot and Mr Gay [her two opponents] but I don't. The only man I feel sorry for is the poor old Viscount here.' But that was her last tear for him on that account. She herself was thrilled. She was brilliantly good at the game; as a parliamentary candidate just about the best there ever was, superabundantly energetic, effervescent, good-humoured, captivating. The poor old Viscount – he had vainly sought to do a Tony Benn and resign his peerage – was not in the same league.

And for nearly twenty years the people of Plymouth, or at least a good number of them, loved her in return. But they did not want to be owned by her and the Astor millions. It was a distinction she did not always have the wisdom or taste to draw, in personal and political matters. She could be impossibly possessive, about her children, her favourites, her constituency, everything else.

The Foot mentioned above, by the way, was my father, and if he hadn't lost his heart already to my mother he would have lost another one in that election, along with his deposit. He loved Lady Astor ever afterwards, and there was never so much as a streak of hatred in the mixture. He was stunned to see some of his own favourite Puritan causes – temperance, anti-Popery, Plymouth's greatness as a Protestant city – defended in such style. A Daniel come to judgement: better still, it was Portia herself with a touch of the Queen of Sheba.

He was even prepared to forgive her – a dispensation allowed in no other case whatever – for being a Tory. Or was she ever a real one? The monstrous series of misdemeanours or worse in the age of appeasement may be overlooked. Was she not one of the forty Conservatives who, in that momentous vote of May 1940, went into the lobby with the Labour Party to destroy Chamberlain and make Churchill the nation's leader? A deed all the more creditable in her case, since she had a permanent hate–hate relationship with Winston Churchill. When she first knew him in pre-1914 days she ventured the characteristic, comprehensive verdict that he united 'the worst blood of two continents'. John Grigg supposes that this comment reached Winston's ears, and she had other well-known counts against him too. She always held that Lloyd George was a greater war leader, and who will say she was wrong? Not the biographer of Lloyd George, John Grigg, for a start.

Winston also came to Plymouth in the Second World War and shed tears ('gin tears', she called them) at the spectacle of the city bombed like no other; she said audibly: 'It's all very well to cry, Winston, but you got to do something.' When years later he had the chance to address the Virginia Legislature on the historic links between Virginia and England he managed to achieve the feat without mentioning her name. Such was Churchillian magnanimity.

Perhaps it was her feminism more even than her views about war lords which he could never stomach, and yet that was her greatest glory. She faced, alone at first, both the ridicule and the freezing hatred of the male House of Commons. She bombarded the ramparts of prejudice with just the right combination of insolence, scorn, repartee and courage. She never wavered in her championship of the rights of women, never missed a golden moment to advance the cause. When General Montgomery once tackled her: 'Lady Astor, I must tell you I don't approve of women politicians,' she gave him an El Alamein of a reply: 'That's all right, the only General I approve of is Evangeline Booth.'

John Grigg tells the whole story afresh with judgement, intelligence, candour and sympathy. He dodges no awkward issue, tolerates no tactful suppression, seeks no escape from Nancy's own colourful diversions – her red scares, her white hopes, her black sheep – the last being fittingly headed by her first-born, Bobbie, who would make the endearing claim (or was it just a touch of his mother's wit, of which he had plenty?) that he could never quite remember whether he had been seduced by Lord Kitchener, and could therefore never look upon the famous Kitchener poster with a suitably patriotic eye.

The photographs help and so do a few brilliant descriptive passages, to which the author pays generous tribute, from a much too-little-known classic on the whole Astor tribe by Michael Astor and an outsider's dazzling insight supplied by Chiquita, one of the wives whose religion was such that neither Nancy nor Waldorf would attend the wedding. And yet all the family in unison and multitudes besides, would agree on one proposition, if no other: that nothing and nobody can quite recapture the excitement and loveliness which was Lady Astor.

# *Ivan Maisky*

——⊃°◐°⊂——

. . . the trouble about Maisky is that he knows
nothing about Russia. He knows a lot about
England, a very great deal . . .

> Sir Robert Vansittart
> 13 October 1939, quoted
> in W. P. Crozier's Political
> interviews, *Off the
> Record* (Hutchinson, 1973)

For us to push Russia out of Europe would be
'fatal'. I said that though I had no desire to mention
names, I thought that was the Prime Minister's
policy.

> W. P. Crozier
> 22 June 1939
> Conversation with
> Sir Robert Vansittart

Ivan Maisky, Soviet Ambassador to Britain for eleven years, was the most intelligent and agreeable diplomat I ever met. The point is mentioned to parry criticism that my review of his *Memoirs of a Soviet Ambassador: The War 1939–43* (Hutchinson), may seem too biased or fulsome.

He was experienced, astute, strong-nerved, and he occupied a post of exceptional importance throughout the most perilous years in the history of his own country and ours. He saw the epics of Dunkirk, the Blitz, Stalingrad and the rest from a unique vantage point. He can present his own individual profiles of Churchill, Beaverbrook and many more. Better than most foreigners, he had the chance to catch the changing flavour of wartime London.

All this is certainly in the book but it is not so easy for those who knew him to judge how much of himself he allows to appear or whether he is merely jogging our memories. For he was an enchanting, inscrutable little gnome of a man who could speak volumes with a shrug of the shoulders. 'Don't quote me,' he would say to the journalists, when he used that precise gesture.

His ruling passion was a burning love of his own country and somehow he combined this with a sure hint – doubtless part of his secret – that England was his second love. He had also an excellent sense of humour with which he played upon English idioms and prejudices. Once, when the waveringly neutral Turkish Government had veered afresh towards the Axis powers, he greeted me with the observation: 'I see the Turks have become unspeakable again.'

Quite a fellow, I trust you may believe already. But how much of his truth is allowed to pierce the jargon and the reticence imposed on Soviet officials? The answer is: enough to shake several of the orthodoxies accepted at the time or approved since by British officialdom.

Take the question of the great Second Front controversy. This was, after all, the major behind-the-scenes strategical argument of the whole war, despite the efforts of Churchill and the British War Office to dismiss it as a dangerous absurdity. It lost its all-pervasive force only because the Soviet armies survived, contrary to the forecasts of Churchill and the British experts. It cut a deadly wound in the Anglo–Soviet alliance which festered for years afterwards. Maisky recites the facts with more insight than rancour.

He also recalls the row in the winter of 1942 when Churchill and Roosevelt were upbraided by liberal Britain and America for daring to hire Admiral Darlan's dubious services in North Africa. Just when the outcry was reaching boiling point, a friendly message came from Moscow explaining how military diplomacy must use for its own purposes 'not only the Darlans, but even the Devil and his grandmother'. Tears of joy poured down Churchill's cheeks: 'Oh, Stalin! You understand me so well.'

Maisky disclaims any similar affinity. From the days of the Nazi–Soviet Pact, through the terrible years of the Red Armies' retreat, to the harsh, inexplicable moment when he was recalled from London without even being allowed to report direct to the Kremlin, he increasingly suspected and girded against 'the great man cult'. No word of Stalin-worship appears in these pages. Rather, the suffocations of that era still leave their mark. 'High authorities,' says the discreet ambassador in an aside 'do not like receiving unpleasant information from their men on the spot.' Yet Maisky, so far as one can judge, risked much to report faithfully what he knew, and take his own initiatives. On a dozen or more critical occasions his intrepid diplomacy tipped the balance favourably for the Allied cause.

Here also are occasional distortions, suppressions and propaganda-judgements which will stick in British and American gullets. But before anyone makes much of them, let us note the contrast between the reports sent back from the London of 1940 by the United States and Soviet Ambassadors in our midst. In the darkest and finest hour of British history, when so much turned upon what the outside world would believe about us, the American said Britain would give in and the Russian said the opposite with eager assurance. That was Maisky's compliment to the people he had learned to understand. No one ever paid us a better one.

# Vanessa

For who would such a nymph forsake
Except a blockhead or a rake?

> Jonathan Swift,
> writing about his Vanessa, after
> whom mine was named.

*The Animals Came in One by One*, by Buster Lloyd-Jones was published by Secker & Warburg in 1966.

Why so many poodles round about the place? London seems alive with them.

Not, let me hasten to add, before the office where this is written sinks beneath the deluge of protests, that I have any objection to their self-conscious, sophisticated charm. Poodle popularity is well-assured and understandable. Unlike politicians, they need no public opinion polls to sustain their egos. It should be recognised, however, that the phenomenon may have a more recondite, not to say sinister, explanation. Common Market propaganda may be responsible. All unawares, we may be the victims of a Gaullist conspiracy. And before anyone interrupts to dismiss such suppositions as nonsense, let him study *The Animals Came in One by One* by Buster Lloyd-Jones, a man whose opinions must be treated with the utmost respect.

He is at his best on the subject of fashions in dogs, a theme which previously I have never seen adequately treated. He reveals, for example, how dachshunds suffered in the early days of the Second World War. Cartoonists tended to treat them as treacherous, evil German sausage dogs, and so, just when suspect aliens were being crowded into the Isle of Man, vast numbers of wretched dachshunds were scheduled for destruction at the Battersea Dogs' Home. Only when chauvinistic emotions subsided did they return to favour. On the other hand, in the cramped conditions after 1945, labradors, dalmations and alsatians never quite regained their pre-war esteem. How could asthmatic bulldogs be expected to climb the steps of modern blocks, or was their decline just another example of Britain's retreat from a world role?

And still the nagging problem of the poodles remains; unanswered, I fear, even by Mr Lloyd-Jones. Given that the British people are in one of their introvert moods, given that they wish for no reminders of wide spaces and the outer Empire, why should they not be content – as they were in the 1920s – with scotties, spaniels and wire-haired terriers? Why poodles?

But before the question grows too obsessively, let me also hasten to add that these inquiries form only a part of Mr Lloyd-Jones's interest. He is an expert on the whole range of domestic animals – cats, tortoises, monkeys, parrots and the rest. At the age of four, he made up his mind to become a veterinary surgeon. How he put that ambition into effect, against immense obstacles, is an amiable, heroic tale, packed with acute observation and instruction. 'You will never meet a fat tiger,' says Mr Lloyd-Jones, carrying conviction right away. He explains then how he has cured animals of all descriptions of all the diseases of civilisation, how he learned to feed and to rescue the sick by watching the healthy, how he would send limping dogs into the sea, how he discovered that wild garlic killed worms, and that pekes ached to escape from cream buns to chase rabbits.

His experience is vast and bizarre, and his conclusions, however odd, are obviously hard to contest. He has seen spaniels changing sex, and other breeds engaged in 'abnormal' sexual practices, quite shocking to orthodox poodle-faking poodles. He says chows are one-man dogs. He tells of a lamb which cavorted with boxers, of an aged sixty-year-old parrot which learned good manners in her dotage, of tortoises which would ecstatically wake up the whole house in the mating season. And most outlandish of all, of course, are the owners – the husband of the mistress of Fifi, the black poodle, who had been compelled to give up his meat ration throughout the entire war; the vegetarian purist who would never allow leather in the house and insisted that her five pomeranians should be vegetarian too; the pug owner who pressed, unavailingly, for the discovery of some means to stop pugs snoring.

Dogs, insists Mr Lloyd-Jones, often intervene in human relationships, but here he is back on more familiar ground. 'Who do you love best?' asked my animal-addicted sister: 'Vanessa (a Belgian water-hound-cum-Welsh sheepdog) or your wife?' Then she added, tactfully offering an escape from the sharp dilemma: 'Ah well! Maybe the choice will never arise.'

# Some True Prophets

# THE CHARTIST
# *William Lovett*

If war is the only path to civilization, what mockery is it to preach up the religion of Christ. If brute force is to be the instrument of human happiness, why talk of cultivating, the mental and moral nature of man?

> William Lovett, in a pamphlet
> he published in 1844

This lecture was delivered on 8 August 1977, in Penzance, a few miles from Newlyn, where Lovett died a hundred years before. An essential Welsh footnote was added in 1985.

When I was invited to join in this centenary meeting to commemorate the death (and the life) of William Lovett, I could not refuse, for both personal and political reasons which I would like briefly to indicate.

On Newlyn cliff there stands a tablet: 'To the Honoured Memory of William Lovett. As a National Leader in social reform he suffered imprisonment for advocating liberties which we now enjoy. 1800–1877.' It so happens that in the year 1848 William Lovett was honoured 'as an expression of gratitude for public services, and of respect for private work'. He was presented with a handsome silver tea service, a purse of 100 sovereigns and an illuminated address. So it was arranged that, in 1948, he should be further honoured in his native town of Newlyn by the fixing of the slate tablet I have described. And it was also arranged that the unveiling of that tablet should be done by my father.

My father was invited to perform the ceremony no doubt primarily because of his West country connections. (The two greatest loves of his life, apart from my mother, were Devon and Cornwall, and he would never choose finally between the two.) But my father was also a Methodist, and so was William Lovett. That was doubtless another reason for the invitation. William Lovett was brought up in Newlyn by the strictest of Methodist mothers but it is worth remembering that, contrary to the misconceptions fostered in some quarters, Methodism often had the most radical and even near-revolutionary associations. Or perhaps this derives from the special quality which Methodism had in Cornwall or Wales or among the Celts generally.

Where would the English be without the Celtic influence and where, even more, would British Socialism be without the revolutionary strain which has come from Ireland or from Wales or from Cornwall? I hope I will not be accused of racialism in any sense whatever in making these preliminary comparisons. But it is an unchallengeable, historical fact that when William Lovett from

Cornwall went to London he joined forces with others who bore famous Celtic names, such as Feargus O'Connor or Bronterre O'Brien or George Julian Harney or, most eloquent of all, Henry Vincent and Zephaniah Williams from Gwent and a host of others who certainly could not boast of any pure Anglo-Saxon ancestry. The history of British Socialism cannot be written without constant reference to the Celts, and perhaps I may say in passing that this was one reason why I was so eager to see a Devolution Act passed through the House of Commons, to help keep the Celts within the United Kingdom. The blood of our Labour Movement cannot tingle properly without them, devolution or no devolution.

A second reason why I could not refuse the invitation derives from what William Lovett said himself about the history of our Labour movement. When, at the moment of his departure from a most active public life, he settled down to write the story of his *Life and Struggles*, he remarked that one mainspring of his determination to tell his story derived from the knowledge that 'hitherto, little is found in history or in our public papers, that presents a fair and accurate account of the public proceedings of the working classes; for if the Whig and Tory papers of the day ever condescend to notice them, it is rather to garble and to distort facts, to magnify follies and faults and to ridicule their objectives and intentions'. (All that sounds excruciatingly familiar, doesn't it, and it was written 100 years or more before such horror comics as the *Daily Mail* or Murdoch's *Sun* sought to pass themselves off as national newspapers.)

It is only in comparatively recent times – thanks to the work of the Webbs, the Coles and the Hammonds and in more recent times still to such a wonderful book as E. P. Thompson's *The Making of the English Working Class* – that a real start has been made in the prodigious task of compiling a true working-class history on the scale which the other classes take for granted. And William Lovett was one of those who helped us to set out along this road when it still looked hopelessly stony. His book was described by E. P. Thompson as 'essential reading for any Englishman' – by which, of course, he also means essential reading for the Welsh, the Scots, the Irish and the Cornish too; Mr Thompson's single fault is that he sometimes writes of the freeborn English as though they could somehow have made good on their own.

However, there is a third, more directly political reason why I was eager to accept the invitation. Few words in our language have been more sadly debased than the name 'Radical'. Once it could strike terror into the ranks of wealth and privilege. Now it has been purloined even by the palest and pinkest critics of current orthodoxy. A Radical nowadays may merely be one who can be distinguished by his respectability from a Socialist. William Lovett's autobiography is the classic reply on these matters of definition. It can restore to the term 'Radical' all its colour and power. It can show how the word can be turned to deeds; how political thought can be transformed into revolutionary action. Not that William Lovett was ever a red-hot revolutionary or anything like it. Indeed, he was sometimes accused, quite falsely, of apostasy to his cause. But I hope to touch upon that great argument later. Let me first recite a few of the facts.

William Lovett never forgot his Cornish roots, but his Cornish childhood, I fear, was a grim affair. He spent long Sundays in the 'reading of texts, prayers and portions of scripture', and was assured by his mother that his soul was in danger when he ran off and played truant with the other boys and broke his ankle on the Newlyn sands. He was instructed in the power of Cornish ghosts and goblins, and lamented that while being stupefied with such supernatural horrors there were no proper book shops in Newlyn, or even in metropolitan Penzance for that matter. He tried his hand at rope-making, and as a fisherman and as a carpenter. But all these various efforts failed and at the age of twenty-one he collected passage money for the journey to London and arrived there with thirty shillings in his pocket and no prospects whatever; even the sailor's dress, as worn by the young men of Penzance, told against him. However, his character already had a streak of Cornish granite in it. He was a strong, upstanding youth with a touch of gentleness and melancholy in his countenance. Young Gregory Peck could have played the part to perfection.

During the next fifteen years the near-penniless Cornish exile became the leader of working-class politics in London. It was a superhuman achievement of combined application and imagination, of patience and idealism. He had, first of all, to teach himself a trade, and he became an expert craftsman, a cabinet-maker, at first excluded from an apprenticeship in the Cabinet Makers' Society by some primitive pre-entry closed shop system, but later winning his way into the confidence of his fellow-craftsmen to become their President. He secured a wonderful wife by the same patient methods, rejecting her first requirement that he should accept the sacraments of the Established Church, but continuing his wooing so successfully that eventually her allegiance to these idolatories was worn down. And apart from earning his living, gradually he became absorbed into one form of working-class political activity after another, and by herculean striving found time for them all – fighting for a free press, against the militia draft, against the ravages of drunkenness, and for the opening of museums on Sunday.

To each of these splendid causes he made his own special contribution. He was, for example, one of the first openly to resist the militia draft on the grounds that he had no representation in Parliament – 'no vote – no musket' was his slogan – and he was the very first to petition Parliament for the museums to be opened. And, more extensively and formidably, when, as he believed, the whole swelling reform movement was being sidetracked by the miserably inadequate Whig Reform Bill of 1831, he joined the newly-founded National Union of the Working Classes and Others which had as its modest objective 'the repeal of all bad laws' and an 'effectual reform of the Commons House of Parliament'. Already, before the 1832 Act became law, William Lovett had raised the banner of much more far-reaching reforms to last throughout the century. He was completing the political education which would place him at the centre of the historical stage.

But frequently he was compelled to turn aside from the main struggle, or such was the accusation levelled against him. Lovett, more than almost any of his contemporaries, retained his belief in universal suffrage as the major objective, to which all else must be made subordinate. He never wavered in accepting that sense of priorities. But he was shaken time and again by the assaults unleashed by the Whig Establishment against the trades unions, revealed first of all in their action against the men charged at Tolpuddle and, a year or so later even more dangerously, if less notoriously, in the fresh attempt made by the government of the time to reverse the repeal of the Combination Acts – in other words, to make all forms of trades unionism illegal. It was the variant of the 1830s of the Industrial Relations Act of 1971 – a fresh, full-blooded

offensive against the central principles of trades unionism. William
Lovett understood in his bones how an attack on this industrial
flank had to be beaten off before any other advances could be
attempted. He knew that the trade unions were the first essential
bulwark of the nascent working class movement. All too often
reformers of those times, with their eyes on the ends of the earth,
would be ready to be diverted from some immediate defensive battle
on behalf of a group of workers locked-out or on strike. But William
Lovett knew reality too well to be deceived by such Utopianism,
soaring through his political imagination could be in other spheres,
and he could sometimes show himself a sterner fighter than Feargus
O'Connor himself and at least one more to be feared by their
common enemies.

By dint of these exertions along with all the others, he made
himself the indispensable committee man, the ever-assiduous organiser; in particular the secretary of the London Working Men's
Association, an institution which deserves to occupy many more
pages in our history books than several other better-known and
better-documented bodies. Incredibly, between its foundation in
June 1836 and 1839, only 297 members were registered on its
official list, in addition to some thirty-five honorary members. But
this small London band, led by the great Cornishman, changed the
face of England, and not merely London. The London Working
Men's Association sent out missionaries all over the country and
helped to give birth to 150 kindred associations elsewhere. It issued
manifestos concerned with the affairs of workers in other lands; for
example, to the workers in Belgium under the leadership of Jacob
Katz; to the Polish workers, then engaged in one of their great
revolts; to the Canadians, then at the mercy of Whig coercion; and
to many others besides. It issued a proclamation on adult education,
a subject most dear to Lovett's heart, and appealed to all Christians
to rise above their sectarian jealousies. It issued a splendid denun-
ciatory address under the title of 'The Rotten House of Commons',
which I am sure from my knowledge must have been a plain breach
of Parliamentary privilege. And when Queen Victoria came to the
throne it proposed to present a special address to her in person, but
Lovett and his friends were deterred by the requirement to appear in
court dress, which some officious official had the nerve to insist
upon. 'With every respect for those forms which make personal

cleanliness and respectful behaviour necessary qualifications to approach Her Majesty we have no means, nor the inclination, to indulge in such absurdities as dress sword, coats and wigs,' wrote William Lovett to the Home Secretary. And that was that.

But, above all, what William Lovett did as secretary of the London Working Men's Association was to draw up and present at a public meeting at the Crown & Anchor in the Strand on 28 February 1837 the petition to Parliament which became known later and immortally as 'The People's Charter'. The People's Charter, written by William Lovett (although doubtless a few other hands contributed) is the most important democratic manifesto in British history. The only other British document which could be held to be compared with it is Thomas Paine's 'Rights of Man', but that was a one-man thesis, literally penned by Paine in a garret, whereas William Lovett's document was the genuine product of a full-scale working-class debate.

My father used to tell me that the test of a man's radicalism was which way he would have voted on the issue of the execution of Charles I. I used to reply to him, stealing the idea from H. N. Brailsford's book on the Levellers, that a better test would be which side a man would have chosen at Burford, when the Levellers in turn resisted Cromwell. An even better test still, or at least a less bloodthirsty one, is whether the student can recite the six items of the People's Charter. They were, to relieve your embarrassment:

1 Manhood suffrage
2 The ballot
3 Payment of Members
4 Annual Parliaments
5 Equal Electoral Districts
6 The abolition of property
   qualifications for MPs

All of these items, with the exception of the perhaps superfluous or excessive requirement of annual parliaments, have now been translated into effect. Together or separate, they can be made to sound as mild as the milk of human kindness itself. But at the time when William Lovett wrote them and the London Working Men's Association proclaimed them, they were derided or condemned as an outrage against all the proprieties. In the desperate, hunger-stricken

1830s, before nineteenth-century capitalism had acquired its self-confidence, they were regarded as a direct threat to the innermost citadels of the established order. So the threat brought a devastating counter-assault. William Lovett himself was spied upon and imprisoned by a panic-stricken government. Chartism was crushed, its leaders scattered, traduced and driven near to desperation or despair and, worse still in one sense, a true record of those events was wellnigh effaced from the history books. Victorian England bitterly resented the blood-red charge sheet which the Chartists had delivered against her. Even Sidney Webb, writing what he called 'The Historical View of Socialism' in the first Fabian essays published in 1889, managed to achieve the feat with only a footnote reference to the Chartists.

However, before leaping to these later events, let me return to one special aspect of William Lovett's role in the writing of the Charter. If he had had his way, it would have incorporated an insistence on genuine universal suffrage, in other words, *one woman – one vote* as well as *one man – one vote*. That was provided for in his original draft, and it was only the fear that manhood suffrage might thereby be jeopardised which persuaded him reluctantly and momentarily to relinquish his demand. William Lovett never lost his capacity to reflect the pressure of the women's movement which was surely so much stronger than the history books, written by men, have ever properly recorded. William Lovett sometimes translated this aspect of his politics into verse. In 1842 he wrote a poem, 'Women's Mission', in which he asserted that man 'must at once his gothic laws annul', and he wrote that 153 years before a Labour Government finally sought to make a legislative end of gothic conditions of sex discrimination and unequal pay.

William Lovett's role in the Chartist struggle is the central feature of his life, but two other strands were interwoven with it, and it would be a travesty to transfix everything on the Chartist theme without mentioning them. He was a great believer in working-class education and especially self-education, and the necessity had been borne in on him ever since he had failed to discover a decent book shop in Penzance. His disillusion with some of his fellow-Chartist leaders made him work all the harder in this cause and he spent another lifetime teaching himself and teaching others. He lived to see the first national Education Act of 1870, introduced by the timorous Liberals, and felt it to be as pitifully pallid a reflection of the achievement he wanted in that field as the Reform Act of 1832 had been of the kind of real democratic advance he yearned to see.

He lived too to establish – in 1844, before Marxism gave to Socialism its international stamp – a new society called the Democratic Friends of All Nations. Italians, Poles, Germans, Frenchmen, Russians, were all to be gathered under the international banner of the Cornish cabinet maker. 'To the Working Men's Association,' he wrote, 'belongs the honour, I believe, of first introducing the mode of international address between the working men of different countries that has since been practised by other bodies so beneficially.' He would have been ashamed of any Socialism which was not international in its embrace, and so should we be. He looked to Ireland, to Italy, to Canada, to Spain, to the people of Africa and America, for fellow-victims who needed the succour of the London Working Men's Association, and for allies in the same world-wide cause to outlaw 'the race-destroying curse of war'.

However, it was in his own land that he knew the most urgent battle must be fought. He never sought escape or distraction from the peremptory realities, as he saw them. He was ready to stand and argue, not only with the obstreperous police forces of Melbourne and Peel, Whig and Tory administrations alike, but in the ferocious contests with his own fellow-Chartists. These, as so often happens, were the most bitter battles of all. William Lovett, incredible as it may seem now, was branded as a traitor by some of his fellow-Chartists and the wound must have touched his heart. But he would not abate his faith: 'Whatever is gained in England by force, by force must be sustained; but whatever springs from knowledge and justice will sustain itself.' The argument swayed back and forth, at the great meetings of the Chartist Conventions, on 100 platforms, and in 10,000 conspiratorial back rooms, north and south, among William Lovett's devoted associates in London and those who cried out in their agony for much stronger action from the great festering cesspits of industrial Britain. One of Feargus O'Connor's accusations against him, incredibly again, was concerned with his turning aside to help defend the trades unions. It was then that William Lovett, the mild Methodist, could not offer the other cheek. He gave his answer to O'Connor's egotism. 'You tell the country,' he wrote, 'that you alone have organised the Radicals of London – and told the Londoners the wonders your genius has performed in the country. You carry your fame about with you on all occasions to sink all other topics in the shade – you are the great "I am" of politics, the great personification of Radicalism – Feargus O'Connor.' That outburst expressed one of his deepest political instincts: 'The masses in other political organisations,' he wrote on another occasion, 'were taught to look up to great men (or to men professing greatness) rather than to great principles. We wish, therefore, to establish a political school of self-instruction among them, in which they should accustom themselves to examine great social and political principles, and by their publication and free discussion help to form a sound and helpful public opinion throughout the country.'

As the years passed, the charges against him sank into proper proportion, and at the time of his death, one of his old Chartist opponents, and the greatest of them, Julian Harney, described William Lovett as 'first in honour' among all the Chartist leaders. No other tribute can ever equal that.

That is what Harney said almost on his deathbed. Several years before, on 8 August 1877, William Lovett was buried in Highgate cemetery, not so far from where, a few years later, Karl Marx was laid to rest, if that is a proper expression. Karl Marx derived his culture and his immortal anger from the literature of the world, from the Greeks, from Shakespeare, from 100 other sources, and above all, from the Bible. William Lovett derived his from the primitive religion of a secluded Cornish fishing village, and from that same Bible too. But both had eyes to see and hearts to feel, in the face of the horror of England's industrial revolution. It was not so incongruous that they should find nearby resting places in the same cemetery.

Julian Harney, the friend of Marx who paid such tribute to William Lovett, also gave his conclusion on the whole Chartist struggle – 'It may be said that the Chartist agitation – which had for its aim the reform of Parliaments – was so much energy wasted. I think not. The Chartist influence extended beyond the Six Points, and to it we largely owe the extirpation of innumerable, some of them abominable abuses, and a great widening of the bonds of freedom.'

This is the great tradition of our Labour movement. All the

freedoms we cherish were fought for by the Chartists, less than 180 years ago – the right to vote, the right of women to vote, the right to vote secretly, the right to be ruled by a representative Parliament, the right to associate freely in trades unions, the right to a free press – and all these rights and freedoms, in the eyes of the Chartists, had to be fought for *together*, and woe to those who would put them asunder.

Of course, they had to fight for their freedoms against *somebody*. The point cannot be overlooked. And those somebodys were the Tories and the Whigs, and usually the two banded together. In each of the fights for all the rights listed above, Tories and Whigs (which was the impolite name for Liberals) were, in the age of the Chartists, on the wrong side of the battle lines. The very word *democracy*, in the mind of the opponents of the Chartists, was hated and feared.

And now for one final conclusion which may not be so widely approved. Perhaps the reason why these rights and freedoms are, on the whole, better established here than in most other countries in the world is that William Lovett and his allies eventually won the argument about the way our freedoms should be fought for. He pleaded that it should be done without resort to violence, by the politics of persuasion, by an unfailing confidence in the power of free debate. More than ever he seems to be right in the age of hand-made explosives, nuclear horrors and such final obscenities as the neutron bomb.

The more the facts are unearthed, the more the greatness of William Lovett emerges. Indeed the more the violence of those times beneath the surface is revealed and the nearness with which it broke above the surface, the more impressive becomes the strength of character which men like Lovett – not that there are many like him – had to show in order to help guide the tumult into effective channels. How strong was that ferment is shown afresh in more recent studies, some of them initiated or conducted by local historians in Wales. In 1985, one study *The Last Rising*: The Newport Insurrection of 1839, by David J. V. Jones gave a new perspective to Chartist history. It helped to show, as Lovett's whole life helped to show, how much earlier and stronger was the demand for democracy than most observers had supposed, and how ruthlessly it was suppressed.

Local histories, written by local historians, have been having a

splendid renaissance. At least, that has been our experience in South
Wales, and the fashion was set, I'm proud to say, by Oliver Jones, a
native of Tredegar, born in the same year as Aneurin Bevan, a
self-taught agitator and Marxist like Aneurin, who in the last few
decades of his life taught himself how to write history. Once, as a
small boy, Oliver sat in the cabinet-maker's shop in Church Street,
Tredegar, and heard an old man tell how, as a youth, he had
marched with the Chartists down to Newport. Many of the mountains and caves round Tredegar, Ebbw Vale, Brynmawr and Blaina
shake with the memories and traditions of the Chartists. Oliver had
lived with this heritage all his life. He could never accept the lies and
libels about the Newport rising – when, in November 1839, panic-
stricken soldiers outside the Westgate Hotel had opened fire on a
force of miners and iron workers, killing at least twenty-two and
wounding many more.

A most strange orthodoxy indeed came to be accepted about that
event. By any reckoning of the masses of people involved or the
number killed in cold blood, it was the biggest class-war clash of the
century. It was much bloodier than Peterloo, more savage than
Tolpuddle, more dangerous, as some terrified Minister in the
Commons testified, than the battle of Sedgemoor, the last battle
fought during the Monmouth rebellion on British soil.

It was, maybe, a full-scale planned insurrection, designed not
only to release the Chartist leader, Henry Vincent, in jail in Newport, but to unloose a much more far-reaching vengeance for the
infamies which the Monmouthshire 'men of the hills' saw perpetrated all around them: a collective deed done in a mood of burning
anger. Such revolutionary acts, even if not finally conceived as such,
have changed the course of history. Yet, strangely, the rough truth
became obscured, and for a variety of curious reasons. Some of the
other Chartist leaders themselves did not know what had happened
or had an interest in hiding it. Feargus O'Connor called it 'a Whig
trick', and Julian Harney talked of 'the Newport business' as 'all
part of a government conspiracy'. William Lovett, the most trust-
worthy witness among the leaders, could add nothing of note.

So the historians had some excuse for their own distortions.
Julius West, in the 1920s, reduced the whole affair to a fairly
innocuous gathering of some 200 people. G. D. H. Cole, for most of
us one of the greatest of modern Socialist historians, spoke of it as 'a

small affair, led by a small man'. Even a later and better-informed scholar, Professor Williams, writing his biography of the Newport Chartist leader, John Frost, still imagined the rising to be a monster demonstration, a kind of modern miners' gala, and nothing more. But the facts, assembled with sufficient imagination, do not fit that conclusion. Oliver Jones felt as much in his bones as he walked the troubled hills of Gwent; the mood of revolt was much more widespread and insistent than the experts allowed. And now comes another Jones – no relation except in spirit and Celtic comradeship – who brings to bear on the subject all the art and diligence of modern scholarship. He uses for his purpose (and with proper acknowledgement) the individual work of local historians like Oliver Jones, but he binds it all together into a single, persuasive, original work.

'What is definite,' asserts David Jones, after his survey of all the doubts and qualifications, 'is that on this morning of November 1839, the British authorities inflicted greater casualties on the civilian population than at any other time in the nineteenth and twentieth centuries.' And some people were perceptive enough to see some of these ramifications at the time. What had been contemplated, said Macaulay in 1846 – and he must have had 1839 and especially Newport in mind – was 'a great war of classes in this country. All the power of imagination fails to point the horrors of such a contest.' The preparations embraced all the iron and mining townships and villages of Monmouthshire and Brecon (and a few in Glamorgan), and touched most of them in every aspect of their lives, in their pits and foundries, their homes and chapels.

The churches and some of the chapels, I'm sorry to say, were turned into citadels to defy the infidel Chartists. Many of the would-be revolutionaries, even in the most Eastern valleys, addressed meetings and conspired in Welsh, but it was never an anti-English campaign. The truly democratic appeal of Chartism was much too potent for that. Such antagonisms only arose when, as David Jones deftly suggests, the victors wished 'to replace the vernacular with the tongue of the civilised imperialists'.

Indeed, what happened after that bloody morning in Newport is almost as riveting as what went before, although this is not the writer's principal theme. He shows how the Whig government panicked, how they called in as judge the hero who had conducted the infamous trial of the Dorchester labourers, how the jury was picked and packed, how John Frost, Zephaniah Williams and William Jones and all the other Chartist leaders held their heads high, facing death and persecution and exile; how most of them returned to be acclaimed in their own townships – although it is only now, in David Jones's discoveries, that full honour may be accorded to them for the large, long-ranged *democratic* vision which they served. That, after all was their cause, the Charter for which William Jones called for three cheers when he left the court, the flag which they wished to see raised above Newport Church. I must confess I did not quite notice it there in its proper allocated place when I was last in Newport. But Newport's main square now, to its eternal honour, is named after John Frost, while 'the men in the hills' have Chartist emblems at every turn, thanks to Oliver and David and our new race of historians.

# THE DREAMER
## *Alexander Herzen*

It is not reason, it is not logic that leads nations, but faith, love and hatred.

Ideas that have outlived their day may hobble about the world for years.

Art, and the summer lightning of individual happiness: these are the only real goods we have.

You can work on men only by dreaming their dreams more clearly than they can dream them themselves, not by demonstrating their ideas to them as geometrical theorems are demonstrated.

Our enemies must know that there exist independent human beings who will never give up free speech; not until an axe has passed between their head and their body, not before a rope has wrung their necks.

These are individual sentences selected from Herzen's own Memoirs, introduced later.

The best books of all are those you can *wallow* in, huge, rambling conglomerations in which a man exposes his whole mind and which can take the reader to another world in another age but which still cast gleams of light on the present and the future. 'I love best, juicy, helpful books, companions for life,' wrote Idris Davies, the Rhymney poet. He was right.

Tolstoy's *War and Peace*, Montaigne's *Essays*, Gibbon's *Decline and Fall*: every addict can supply his own list of honour, and when the miracle happens and an addition is made, the proper reaction is not just to write a review but to shout Hallelujah and compel everyone to join the chorus. Such is the effect of *My Past and Thoughts: The Memoirs of Alexander Herzen* (Chatto & Windus, 4 vols.), which started at ten guineas, and maybe is much more by now. And don't wince too long at the price. These four beautiful volumes are put on the market not by mere publishers but by inspired benefactors of the human race.

Alexander Herzen was born in 1812, the illegitimate son of a ferocious Russian aristocrat whose jeers can still scald. 'Mockery, irony, cold, caustic, utter contempt, were the tools which he wielded like an artist.' One can feel that tongue, and the real lash that fell across the backs of his serfs, and the society which the old man had morosely abandoned. 'They were all quite cultured, well-educated people; having no work in life they flung themselves upon pleasure, pampered themselves, loved themselves, good-naturedly forgave themselves all transgressions, exalted their gastronomy to the level of a Platonic passion and reduced love for women to a sort of voracious gourmandise.'

The first 600 of these pages might indeed have been written by Tolstoy himself. They fix the Russian framework, the abiding love of his native land, from which the most fervent internationalist of the century never escaped. They fix too Herzen's own special tone, a peculiar brand of protective irony, his armour against an unjust world – 'it is the retort to humiliations undergone, a reply to insult, it is the reply of pride, not of the Christian'. But this was just the beginning.

He came to Paris with true revolutionary reverence, in search of 'the mighty titanic poetry of 1793'. Yet for a moment the holy city seemed eternally gripped 'in the unclean worship of material gain and tranquillity'. Paris looked as contentedly bourgeois and affluent as in, say, early 1968. But the date was 1847. Within a few months 'all Europe took up its bed and walked'. The Paris of 1848 and of 'the cross-eyed cretin Louis Napoleon', the Rome of 1849 and Mazzini, the Geneva where the exiles congregated amid that stupendous eruption which shook the whole continent – all these people and places he describes not only with an astringent eye but with a passionate and compassionate heart. It is enough for an epic, but again the story has only just begun.

He was forced to settle in stolid London and came to terms with the fog. 'Life here is as boring as that of worms in a cheese.' How could he tolerate these English with their potato-dough parliamentarianism, not to mention his fellow-emigrés. 'Expect nothing of *them*; they are dead men burying their dead.' Yet one by one they came alive and stride like giants across the scene and he himself reveals why Tolstoy saw him standing 'head and shoulders above all the politicians of his own and of our time'. In a back street off the Caledonian Road he printed the first independent Russian newspaper ever published, produced a pebble and sling to challenge Tsardom, and prepared the way for 1917, in defiance of all sceptics.

One of these, a famous one, refused to join him at 'the international soiree in commemoration of the great revolutionary movement of 1848', held in St Martin's Hall, Long Acre, on 27 February 1855, and addressed by the revolutionary élite of Europe, headed by Victor Hugo, Mazzini, Kossuth and many more, all assembled without passports or immigration vouchers in confident, liberal London. Only Karl Marx refused to come: 'I will nowhere and at no time appear on the same platform as Herzen since I am not of the opinion that old Europe can be rejuvenated by Russian blood.'

But Herzen could look after himself in controversy with Marx or anyone else. In his old age, some nihilist rivals from his homeland told him to stop flapping his enfeebled wings in the cause of his beloved, stick-in-the mud democracy. Herzen rebuked this 'syphilis of revolutionary lusts', lamenting the ease with which his young opponents despaired of everything, 'the ferocious joy of their denial and their terrible ruthlessness. Despite their excellent spirits and noble intentions ambitious ones can, by their tone, drive an angel to blows and a saint to curses.'

Page after page here offers a dazzling contribution to present-day debates, and yet interwoven with the history and the politics runs another story altogether, the private life of Alexander Herzen which became so scandalously public; how he loved and was loved, how he was cuckolded and then seduced, how he made himself a laughing-stock and still rivets our respect. His wife wrote to her lover: 'Everything in Alexander that was lighthearted, carefree, childlike – I have torn it from him like a skin, and left him raw and bleeding.' She did indeed. But somehow the lightheartedness of the childlike Herzen, along with his strange wisdom and courage, are restored and enshrined in this book which will surely be read as long as anyone wants to know how human beings may withstand individual crucifixion and the cruel march of history.

# THE ROMANTIC REALIST (1)
## *Heinrich Heine*

I am accused of having no religion. No, I have them all.

Heine

In our condition we must choose to flourish in this world or the next one; there is no middle course.

Stendhal

The last major biography of *Heinrich Heine* was written by Professor Jeffrey L. Sammons of Yale University in 1980, but for the reasons indicated here Heine lovers, old and new, should turn to the writings of Dr S. S. Prawer.

When Karl Marx left Paris, in January 1845, en route for Brussels and London, he wanted to take little Heinrich Heine (he was five foot two inches tall) with him in his luggage, and if he had had his wish, much glory and excitement would have ensued. Doubtless they would have quarrelled, and the invectives from two masters of the craft would still scorch. But, in their short nine months of acquaintance, each had seen the genius in the other, and their association still plays its part in moulding Heine's fame.

Today the two Germanies strive to fix their protective, possessive clutches upon him; rival collected editions of his works pour forth from the presses in Berlin and Düsseldorf: East Germany must have some trouble with his assaults on censorship, the most searing ever written ('Where books/Are burned, in the end people will be burned as well'); Düsseldorf, thanks one must suppose to some still simmering anti-semitism, would not use the name of its greatest son to grace the university. Hitler sought to reduce him to the status of 'author unknown': no easy dethronement for a poet who had been set to music more often than any other since the Psalmist. Finally, the Jewish establishment has struggled, more excusably, to restore the balance: did not the most irreverent critic of religion who ever lived, not excepting Marx himself (Heine prompted that phrase about 'the opium of the people') take precautions on his deathbed to seek a return to Jehovah's bosom?

Yet a still stranger fate has now befallen him. No one ever lashed academic backs more fiercely than Heine; at Düsseldorf they still bind up the wounds. Yet what scorpions would he have reached for to chastise the American manner and method in these matters? A decade ago Jeffrey L. Sammons, Professor of German at Yale University, produced his massive *Heinrich Heine, the Elusive Poet*, a most aptly entitled literary study. Later he offered a no less massive, meticulously researched modern biography, in which the poet and the politician and the journalist and the iconoclast – in short, Heine in all his various incarnations – once more eluded him.

Considering his vast labours, I hesitate to write this churlish conclusion. Yet old Heine-worshippers like myself must be warned. The man allowed to peep out from these learned pages, despite the light cast by occasional gleaming diamonds of direct quotation, is a pitiable caricature: devious, secretive, self-pitying, incapable of true intimacy, cantankerous in personal controversies and usually on the wrong side, a deeply flawed personality, lacking judgement or ethical standards. Once in a famous declaration the real Heine said that poetry was for him only a sacred plaything: 'You shall lay a sword on my coffin, for I was a soldier in mankind's war of liberation.' Professor Sammons does not refrain from interpolating into these sentences a charge of disingenuousness. Again, even more famously, Heine asserted: 'God will forgive me; *c'est son métier.*' Professor Sammons has the nerve to cast a shade of doubt on the authenticity of the immortal epigram.

All too frequently, I fear, Heine's joyous irony is lost on the plodding professor, or there is no appreciation of how, with the flick of a little finger, he could send his enemies reeling. And not to be accepted at all is the final verdict that the wandering Heine *did* return to the God of his fathers. 'There is, of course,' the professor acknowledges in a rare note of qualification, 'a tension with blasphemy.' There was indeed. Heine had sometimes said that there ought to be two Gods, one for the healthy and another for the sick. Just about the same time he could still write to one of his closest friends: 'I lie twisted up day and night in pain, and if I believe in God, sometimes I don't believe in a good God. The hand of the great tormentor of animals lies heavily on me.'

Once he is safely prostrated on that mattress-grave, his biographer begins, it must be said, to show a few traces of imaginative sympathy, or perhaps he captured them from the loving pages left by Camille Selden or the others who came, like Theophile Gautier, and saw him lift the paralysed lid of his eye with his hand, which was the only way he could see. He was there for eight years, tortured by time, which he called 'the worst syphilis', and, more than likely, by a real syphilis too. The miracle is that even thus he made wondrous additions to his already incomparable achievements.

He was truly the wittiest German who ever lived, and, if that compliment appears insufficiently glowing, let us say he was the wittiest Jew, which is certainly saying something. He wrote about love and food and drink and sometimes mixed them all up together in the most lascivious of soufflés, and, for further measure, he had wisdom; breathtaking, prophetic wisdom. He prophesied Socialist revolution in an international language which still tingles with excitement, and yet never relaxed his ferocious judgements on the horrors men and women could inflict on one another.

Such a pity Karl Marx never succeeded in bringing him to London; for one thing, he might have exorcised the hellish ideas about us which Heine had picked up on his own by paying calls on English bankers and the House of Commons. Heine in turn might have continued the education which the German censors so foolishly interrupted of Marx and all 'these other godless self-gods'. England, moreover, has been marvellously magnanimous and perceptive in understanding Heine, more so than his own countrymen. Not so long ago, Dr S. S. Prawer of Queens College, Oxford described how Marx, the lover of literature, had soaked himself in Heine, and not so long before that he wrote another book on Heine himself, *The Tragic Satirist*, in which his greatness is properly estimated and extolled, right up to those same last moments on the mattress-grave. One caller found him reading a medical work on his own complaint: 'but,' said Heine, 'what good this reading is to me I don't know, except that it will qualify me to give lectures in Heaven on the ignorance of terrestrial doctors about diseases of the spine'. Heine indeed had a special touch about deathbed scenes. He had one for the incomprehensible Hegel whom he pictured saying: 'Only one person has understood me,' and then adding at once peevishly, 'and he didn't understand me either.'

But one person does understand Heine himself. Dr Prawer has added to his picture of the tragic satirist a more elaborate counterpart in *Heine's Jewish Comedy*. How to give a proper enticing whiff of the feast which this book offers! The author's title was naturally chosen for that purpose. It is intended to combine the tastes of Dante's *Divine Comedy* and Balzac's human one, with Heine's own special spice added to the dish, and for those who are already Heine-lovers (and Prawer-admirers, and in this country the two should already be indistinguishable) all this should be enough to attract customers in pursuit of sheer enjoyment.

But the book could be read also, with equal delight by Jews or non-Jews, as an introduction to the wondrous world, the earthly paradise of Heinrich Heine. Dr Prawer modestly adds the sub-title: A Study of his [Heine's] Portraits of Jews and Judaism. It is all that and much more, and a further extensive hint is given in the first quotation from Heine himself, offered as an epigraph on the whole volume. '[A people] demands its history from the hand of the poet rather than that of the historian. It does not ask for faithful reporting of naked facts; what it wants is to see these dissolved again into the original poetry from which they sprang. The poets know this, and they secretly take a malicious pleasure in remodelling, in whatever ways they see fit, what the people's memory has preserved; as a means, perhaps, of pouring scorn on historians proud of their dryness and on state-archivists as desiccated and dull as the parchment of their documents.'

Here then, for a start, is an essay on Jewish history, gleaming with wit on almost every page, and still deeply moving. So often in his lifetime that wit cut near the bone, and may not subsequent horrors make the whole too excruciating to be borne? But not so: the wit was, always or almost always, interwoven with a never-failing human compassion, and how the Jewish establishment struggled to the end to restore Heine, despite all his offences and furies, to their bosom! They had some justification. Moses was always one of his real heroes, and became as time passed the greatest prophet of all. 'How small Sinai appears when Moses stands on it.' And then again: 'O Moses our teacher! *Moshe rabbenu* exalted fighter against servitude! Hand me hammer and nails so that I may nail our complacent slaves in red-white-and-gold livery to the Brandenburg Gate by their long ears.'

Nobody ever used those hammer and nails to better effect than Heine against stupidity, hypocrisy, barbarism, money-making for money-making's sake, and a whole decalogue of similar sins. 'The Jews, who snatched their Bible from the great conflagration of the second Temple and dragged it about with them in exile as a portable fatherland throughout the whole of the Middle Ages – they kept this treasure well hidden in their ghetto, whither German scholars, those who preceded and those who began the Reformation, crept secretly in order to learn Hebrew and thus find the key which would unlock the shrine that held the treasure.' Yet these quotations, I fear, may leave a slightly too impersonal a flavour. *Heine's Jewish Comedy* is also a marvellous substitute for what the world lost when Heine abandoned or deliberately destroyed his memoirs, confessions, call them what you will.

Heine had much particular to say on this topic. He was bitterly opposed to the publication of writings which the author himself had not authorised. He scorned the art of self-characterisation, and said once at least that it was downright impossible: 'I would be a vain fop if I crassly emphasised all the good I know of myself; and I would be a complete fool if I laid bare to the whole world the many failings of which I am no less conscious. And then: however willing one may be to be candid and frank, no man can speak the truth of himself. No one has yet succeeded in doing this – neither St Augustine, the Prince Bishop of Hippo, nor Jean-Jacques Rousseau from Geneva . . .' And yet again, despite this honest disavowal, despite the incidents or offences which Heine needed to suppress, he tells us as much of himself as anybody. The poets are usually in a class of their own in this field – Wordsworth and Byron, for example, and Heine himself. They can hardly open their lips without telling us more or maybe they often tell it, as Dr Prawer convincingly proves, in their portraits of other people.

Did any man ever leave behind a richer, more comic, more varied gallery of portraits and self-portraits? Who but Heine – as Dr Prawer asks – would have thought of an 'intoxicated' Sermon on the Mount? Who but Heine would have given us the vision, not of the prophet Jonah, but the whale that swallowed him? Who but Heine – with the assistance of Moses, the lawgiver – gave the right of Jewish citizenship to the whole of humanity? Such claims and questions are piled high one upon another through these pages, and only as we reach the end may we recall again that Heine wrote as much for the Gentiles as the Jews, as much for the rest of Europe as his fellow Germans, as much on political as religious issues; for all humanity indeed in those last great arguments with the Aristophanes of Heaven.

It is hard to recall any great figure in history, or literary history especially, who suffered a physical fate more cruel than Heine's. For eight years on his mattress-grave, he was tortured, but he still continued to hurl his thunderbolts of wit back towards that same heaven. It is neither a tragedy nor a comedy, but a human triumph almost without parallel.

My first introduction to Heine was when a copy of his *Works of Prose*, edited by Hermann Kesten, with a preface by Louis Untermeyer and published by L. B. Fischer, New York, arrived in the *Evening Standard* office in 1943. No one had ever told me before what wonders were in store. No one had ever told me that his prose could be as exciting as his poetry, and how both could be understood by those who could not read German; after all, Heine himself had taken pains to cross European frontiers, to hit blind, boring nationalism and racialism where it hurt, to win an international audience. I suppose the first time I read his name so that it stuck in my consciousness was on almost the very last page of P. P. Howe's *Life of Hazlitt* when he remarked how William Hazlitt, for so many decades after his death in 1830, in his own country, had been 'neglected and forgotten'. However, 'in France both he and his work were known; in Germany Heine championed his memory'. The kinship between Heine and Hazlitt (as between Hazlitt and Stendhal – they were all three 'unfrocked Romantics', as Heine described himself) is a theme all its own but one not so easily followed since the references are not at once evident. But the tone and temper show immediate, exciting affinities.

Not so long after that first Heine introduction, I also started a friendship with Vicky which lasted for the next twenty-odd years till his death. I always pictured little Vicky as a kind of Heinrich Heine or vice versa, and Vicky indeed loved Heine and could recite his poetry with real passion and understanding. The Jewishness, the wit, the Socialism, and the agnosticism of the two of them intertwined in seemingly endless permutations. I could never read Heine or Don Quixote without recalling Vicky's picture of the knight who kept his humour whatever provocation there might be for his melancholy. And when Vicky died, it was proper to apply to him those immortal words which Heine applied to himself as 'a son of the Revolution' and which Professor Sammons sought to qualify: 'I doubt that I deserve the laurel wreath, for poetry has always been an instrument with me, a sort of divine plaything. If you would honour me, lay a sword rather than a wreath upon my coffin; for I was, first of all, a soldier in the war for the liberation of humanity.'

But let me return to the *Works of Prose*, read in 1943. Page after page opened new delights and vistas. No one could describe so well 'the great seven-league-boots ideas', which the French revolutionary armies had carried across Europe and which seemed reborn with a new vitality in the Europe to be liberated in the 1940s. And Heine, like Hazlitt, for all his admiration of Napoleon's achievements in the overthrow of the old regimes, would never bow down before such authority: 'Remember this, you proud men of action. You are nothing but unwitting assistants to the men of thought, who often in the most humble silence have prescribed all your work for you in the most definite manner. Maximilian Robespierre was nothing but the hand of Jean-Jacques Rousseau, the bloody hand which from the womb of time drew forth the body whose soul Rousseau had created. The restless fear that marred Master Jean-Jacques' life – was it perhaps caused by a presentiment of the sort of midwife which his ideas needed to come bodily into this world?' Or better still, the irreverence of the Jew who still loved his people. 'I think perhaps this God-pure spirit, this parvenu of Heaven who is now so ethical, so cosmopolitan and universally cultured, harbours a secret resentment against the poor Jews who in their synagogues keep reminding him of his one-time obscure national connections. Perhaps the old gentleman wants to forget that he is of Palestinian extraction, and that he was once the God of Abraham, Isaac and Jacob, and that his name was then Jehovah.'

However, perhaps these were tastes subsequently developed. One passage, one picture, one portrait captivated me at once, as it must have done multitudes of other first readers of Heine. It appeared in *Works of Prose* under the single title *Jessica*: 'When I saw this play presented in Drury Lane, standing back of me in the box was a pale British beauty who violently wept at the end of the fourth act and frequently cried: "The poor man is wronged!" Hers was a face of the noblest Grecian cut, and the eyes were large and black. I never could forget them, those great black eyes that wept for Shylock!'

Heine saw Edmund Kean perform his famous role as Shylock in 1826. Maybe he had already been influenced by Hazlitt's account of Kean's first appearance in that role a dozen years before, the combination which transformed *The Merchant of Venice* into something beyond even Shakespeare's imagination. But Heine carried the transformation further still: 'When I think of those tears, I must include *The Merchant of Venice* among the tragedies – although its frame is decorated with the gayest masks, satyr pictures and cupids, and even the poet really wanted to write a comedy.

Perhaps Shakespeare intended to present a drilled werewolf for the amusement of the mob, a despised mythical creature that thirsts for blood, loses his daughter and his ducats over it, and is made ridiculous in the bargain. But the poet's genius, the world spirit reigning in him, always stands above his private will, and so it happened that, despite the glaring burlesque, he voiced in Shylock the justification of a hapless sect, which for mysterious reasons was burdened by Providence with the hate of the lower and the higher rabble, and did not always want to requite his hatred with love. But what am I saying? Shakespeare's genius also rises above the petty quarrel of two religious parties, and actually his drama shows us neither Jews nor Christians but oppressors and oppressed, and the madly agonized exultation of the latter when they can repay their arrogant tormentors with interest for insults inflicted. . . . Truly, except for Portia, Shylock is the most respectable character in the whole play. He loves money; he does not hide this love but screams it out in the market-place; but there is something he values more highly than money: the satisfaction for his offended heart, the just retribution for unspeakable insults.'

Yet these extracts can give little true impression of the mighty climax, the mighty Marxist climax (before he'd even met Marx) to which Heine carried his inspiration and all let loose by the black eyes which wept for Shylock.

They hate the rich, and are glad if religion lets them yield to this hate with full feeling. In the Jews the common people have always hated only the possessors of money; it was always piled-up metal which drew the lightning of their wrath down on the Jews. The spirit of each time merely lent its slogan to his hatred. In the Middle Ages, that slogan wore the dark colour of the Catholic Church, and the Jews were killed and their homes looted 'because they crucified Christ' – with exactly the logic of some black Christians in San Domingo, who at the time of the massacre ran round with a picture of the Saviour on the cross and screamed fanatically: *'Les blancs l'ont tué, tuons nous les blancs!'* My friend, you laugh at the poor negroes; but I assure you that the West Indian planters did not laugh then, and they were butchered in expiation to Christ exactly like the Jews of Europe a few centuries earlier. But the black Christians in San Domingo also were right as to the matter! The whites lived idly amidst the fullest pleasures, while the negro had to work for them in the sweat of his black brow, and as a reward got only a little rice-meal and very many lashes. The blacks were the common people.

We are no longer living in the Middle Ages; the common people, too, are growing more enlightened, no longer kill Jews on sight, no longer extenuate their hatred with religion; our time no longer is so naively and hotly devout; the traditional grudge is clothed in more modern phrases, and in beer halls as in chambers of deputies the mob inveighs against the Jews with economic, industrial, scientific, even philosophic arguments. Only hard-boiled hypocrites still give their hatred a religious colouring and persecute the Jews for the sake of Christ; the great mass admit candidly that material interests are the basic issue, and seek by all possible means to hamper the Jews in the exercise of their industrial faculties. Here in Frankfurt, for instance, only twenty-four members of the Mosaic faith may marry each year, lest their population increase and too much competition be created for the Christian tradespeople. Here the real reason for anti-Semitism emerges, with its real face, and this face wears no gloomy, fanatical monk's mien but the flabby, enlightened features of a shopkeeper afraid of being surpassed in his doings and dealings by the Israelite business acumen.

But is it the Jews' fault that this business spirit of theirs has developed so menacingly? It is wholly the fault of that madness with which in the Middle Ages the importance of industry was ignored, trade regarded as ignoble and the money business in particular as ignominious, and accordingly the most profitable part of these industries, the money business, was surrendered to the Jews – so that they, barred from all other trades, necessarily had to become the shrewdest merchants and bankers. They were forced to become rich and then were loathed for their riches; and though by now Christendom has dropped its anti-industrial prejudices – and in trade and industry the Christians have become as wealthy as the Jews, and equally great crooks – the traditional people's hate has clung to the Jews; the people still see in them the representatives of money and despise them. You see, in world history everyone is right – the hammer as well as the anvil.

Mostly in anticipation of Marx, sometimes in tune with him, sometimes in passionate protest against revolutionary inhumanity or the crimes committed in its name, Heine lashed his own age and dared to prophesy a great Socialist future for the common people. And all the while, whatever agonies he might be suffering, he defied the gods of intolerance, bigotry and persecution who would rob men and women of their joys and exhilaration, as for example, when he set out for Italy with Rossini having already captured his mind and soul: 'For in truth, in order to love, and through love to understand modern music, one must have seen the Italian people with one's own eyes, their heaven, their character, their customs, their sorrows, their joys . . . Speech is forbidden to the poor Italian slave, and it is through music alone that he can give expression to the emotions of the heart. All his hatred of foreign domination, his longing for freedom, his rage at his powerlessness, his sorrow at the memory of former lordly magnificence, all this, is embodied in those melodies.' The revolution in which Heine believed had Rossini as its composer.

Heine's *Italian Travel Sketches* are the lightest and loveliest he ever wrote: the music of Italy, the poetry of Italy, the food, the politics, above all the women of Italy fill his pages more joyfully than any others. 'It was the richest period of my life, a period when, heady with confidence and drunk with good fortune, I sang on the peaks of the Apennines and dreamed wild dreams of great actions which would echo through the world to the remotest islands.'

Yet there were strange gaps in the record of his travels, or so it appeared to me. Most especially, what happened to Heine in Venice? A few glancing references said he had been there, but could Heine of all people have seen La Serenissima which inspired his beloved Rossini, and written nothing on the subject? Yet most of his biographers, including the best, were silent on the subject. One reason seemed to be the same which prevented him proceeding to Rome. For whilst he was in Florence, he had an irrational longing, combined with an irrational fear, to see once again the father he adored. He turned back and made for Venice where the news that Samson Heine was dangerously ill awaited him. He hastened on homewards to Hamburg, arriving too late to find him alive.

What he did write about Venice appeared in none of the *Travel Sketches*. It was tucked away at the end of one of his essays brought together under the title, *Shakespeare's Maidens and Women*, the same essay indeed which had included the passage on Jessica. At last I found it, and once found, it is never to be forgotten. Heine understood the persecution of his people as well as any of the prophets, and how well he understood too how Shakespeare had understood.

When thou goest to Venice and wanderest through the Doge's palace, thou knowest well that neither in the hall of the senators, nor on the Giant's Stair, wilt thou meet Marino Faliero. Of the old Dandolo thou wilt indeed be reminded in the Arsenal, but on none of the golden galleys wilt thou seek the blind hero. Seest thou on one corner of the Via Santa a snake carved in stone, and on the other a winged lion, which holds the head of the serpent in his claws, you may remember the proud Carmagnolo, but only for an instant. But far more than all such historical persons wilt thou think in Venice of Shakespeare's Shylock, who is ever living while they are long mouldered in the grave. And when thou crossest the Rialto thine eye will seek him everywhere, and thou deemest he must be there behind some pillar with his Jewish gaberdine, his mistrusting, reckoning face, and thou believest many a time that thou canst hear his harsh voice – 'Three thousand ducats – well!'

I, at least, a wandering hunter of dreams, looked around me on the Rialto to see if I could find Shylock. I had something to tell him which would have pleased him; which was, that his cousin Monsieur de Shylock in Paris had become the greatest baron of all Christendom, and received from their Catholic Majesties the Order of Isabella, which was originally instituted to celebrate the expulsion of Jews and Moors from Spain. But I found him not on the Rialto, so I determined to look for my old acquaintance in the Synagogue. The Jews happened to be just then celebrating their holy Feast of Expiation, and stood wrapped up in their white *Schaufäden-Talaren*, with strange, mysterious noddings of their heads, looking like a company of spectres. The poor Jews who stood there fasting and praying since early in the morning had not tasted food nor drink since the yester-evening, and had also first of all begged pardon of all their acquaintances for any evil things which they might have said of them during the past year, that God might in like manner forgive them their sins – a beautiful custom, which very strangely exists among his race, which has, however, remained afar from the teachings of Christ . . .

Though I looked all around in the synagogue of Venice, on every side I could nowhere see the face of Shylock. And yet it seemed to me he must be there, hidden under one of those white *talars*, praying more fervently than any of his fellow-believers, with stormy, wild passion, yes, with madness, to the throne of Jehovah, the severe, divine monarch. I saw him not. But towards evening when, according to the belief of the Jews, the gates of heaven are closed and no further prayer can enter, I heard a voice in which tears flowed as they were never wept from eyes. There was a sobbing which might have moved a stone to pity – there were utterances of agony such as could only come from a breast which held shut within itself all the martyrdom which an utterly tormented race had endured for eighteen centuries. It was the death-rattle of a soul which, weary to death, sinks to the ground before the gates of heaven. And this voice seemed to be well known to me – as if I had heard it long long ago, when it wailed just as despairingly, 'Jessica, my child!'

No visitor to Venice should ever omit his visit to the ghetto. He can find there Moses, Shakespeare, Shylock and Heine himself.

# THE ROMANTIC REALIST (II)
## *Count Stendhal*

I once showed a person of this overweening turn
(with no small triumph I confess) a letter of a very
flattering description I had received from the
celebrated Count Stendhal, dated Rome. He
returned it with a smile of indifference, and said,
he had a letter from Rome himself the day before,
from his friend S—!

> Hazlitt's essay on Intellectual
> Superiority, from his *Table Talk*

Gita May's *Stendhal and the Age of Napoleon* was
published by Columbia University in 1977. It may
be a good introduction, but Stendhal is a master at
introducing himself. Start with *Red and Black* in
any of the excellent English translations (the very
best, in my opinion, the most recent by Robert M.
Adams), and never stop.

*Stendhal and the Age of Napoleon* does not fulfil the expectations roused by such a trumpet of a title. But how could it? For all its horrors and infamies and garishness, the age of Napoleon still retains its power to enthral; for multitudes of Frenchmen, Italians, Germans, Englishmen and many more, and for some of the most daring and farseeing spirits in their midst, it was an age, not only of war and cruelty but also of liberation. Stendhal watched the whole performance with just the right mixture of enthusiasm and astringency, and with a wit at his command not excelled by that of any other observer whatever, even in a Europe where he faced such competitors as Heinrich Heine or William Hazlitt.

The combination of scene and author should produce a book in a million, but, alas, Gita May has not achieved that. She has an excuse: Stendhal himself shied away from the fullscale development of the theme; he dallied with it, and yet he, the great exponent of persistence in some other fields, set it aside quite inadequately attempted. One reason for his reticence, maybe, is that, had he drawn his portrait of the Emperor warts and all, he would have given aid and comfort to the great man's dwarflike successors, with whom the war was still on. Stendhal had many moods of waywardness; but he would never betray.

It was one of his own confessions or boasts that he conducted his love affairs as if they were military operations, and it was certainly true that he went off to his wars as if they were love affairs; in short, an incurable romantic, if ever there was one, nurtured almost from the moment when he was torn from his loving mother's breast, on Rousseau's *La Nouvelle Heloise*, the real Bible of the Romantic movement. And yet, in Stendhal's case, the words must be qualified the moment they are uttered. He could suddenly turn realist, in love or war.

No one after the age of thirty he asserted (speaking obviously for himself) could tolerate any longer the flowery rhetoric of Rousseau's *Heloise*. And that, let it be noted, was *not* an older man's cynicism.

Stendhal never grew old; despite all provocations and disappointments, he grew serene instead. With him the exhilarations of youth never faded, but his tastes and understanding changed. In particular, his appreciation of the way to write formed itself into his own style, so different from Rousseau's. He would never abandon the Romantic faith of the Revolution: who amongst those who had ever truly felt what it was like to be alive in that blissful dawn would ever forget it? But he could not help seeing also the weaknesses and limitations of the cause, and more especially the deficiencies of those who espoused it with an egotistical obsession.

Besides, he had other distractions which surely involved no element of schizophrenia in his romantic ardour. Reading and writing and searching for his rightful place in literature, were agreeable pursuits, but real love affairs were better. Politics was always his passion, but unlike some politicians, he had room for other passions too. 'Whatever some hypocritical ministers of government may say about it,' he wrote, in one of those footnotes into which he could compress a whole novel, 'power is the greatest of all pleasures. It seems to me that only love can beat it, and love is a happy illness that can't be picked up as easily as a Ministry.' So even when he was dissecting the politicians so astutely, he retained a peculiar and, many would claim, a proper sense of priorities.

When Moscow was burning, he could still be on his bed devouring one of the famous, gushing, successors to Rousseau's novel, *Paul et Virginie*, and when Napoleon was returning from Elba, the devoted disciple, Stendhal, spent most of the 100 days in a Venetian paradise, in the arms of the once inaccessible Angela Pietragrua, to an accompaniment, for good voluptuous measure, provided by the young Rossini prophesying the Italian risorgimento. Politics, despite Stendhal's evident addiction, was seen in proportion. Given the choice, would he not have preferred to have seduced Mathilde Viscontini Dembowski than to have conquered Italy, and, given his hints and intimations of her ineffable, unattainable charms, who wouldn't? More than almost any other great writer, Stendhal had a premonition of how a much later generation would re-value his neglected work, but his extraordinary self-knowledge and confidence never deterred him from immediate pursuits, and the perils he might court and the follies he would commit in the process. Fame was not the spur; it was the sedative.

But again it is necessary to qualify the conclusion before it becomes settled. (Never neglect Stendhal's own maxim: 'I'll nearly always be mistaken if I think that a man has only a single character.') Politics for him was never a side-show; it not merely filled the stage, but diffused its influence throughout the whole theatre and throughout society itself. Wherever he turned, and all through his life, and in defiance of all the accusations of dilettantism, his political judgement was perpetually in action, sharp and original. His political aphorisms retain a sensational potency. He was a kind of Machiavelli of the Left, whose exposure of the way the political mind works has a permanent validity. But, of course, like any good politician, he was concerned, not with the music of a distant drum, but with the immediate enemy, the one which had to be fought and crushed here and now. His enemy was, first and foremost, the priest-ridden society of the restored Bourbons, and, thereafter, the seedy financial manipulators of the Orleans monarchy. He was much more concerned to give them their devastating due than merely to glorify the dead Napoleon. 'A Ministry cannot overthrow the Bourse, but the Bourse can overthrow the Ministry.' So he wrote with Marxist contempt and finality, decades before Marx.

However, considering how he despatched Napoleon's successors to eternal ignominy, it remains regrettable that he did not deal comprehensively with Napoleon himself. Clearly he pondered the possibility; consider, for example, an entry in his notebook, way back in 1805, soon after the Emperor-crowning ceremony which Stendhal might have been expected to deplore as fiercely as any of his fellow atheist-republicans: 'When Milan [Napoleon] was thinking of re-establishing religion in France, he employed some caution in dealing with the enlightened people with whom he had attempted to fortify his government; he consequently summoned Volney to his study and told him that the French people had asked for a religion and that he felt he owed it to their happiness to give them one. "But, Citizen Consul, if you listen to the people, they will also ask you for a Bourbon." Thereupon Napoleon flew into a rage, called his servants, had him thrown out, even – so they say – kicked him and forbade him to return. There is a good example of the ridiculousness of the advice-seeker. Poor Volney was ill as a result, but that didn't stop him, as soon as he had recovered, from drawing up a report on the matter, thinking that the affair would be brought up in the

Senate. It became known, and he was told to desist if he didn't want to be assassinated; since then, he has scarcely left his home – *If true for a future Tacitus.*'

But the new Tacitus held his hand. Napoleon was spared anything distantly tinctured with the full Stendhalian treatment. For that, the world had to wait for Tolstoy, who however had learnt much from Stendhal about war and military men, and all the various accompanying horrors and vanities. One of the reasons why Stendhal shrank from the full-hearted defence of his hero was that he had seen for himself, and understood better than anyone had given him credit for, what war was really like. It was that unromantic truth which he preferred to tell in the early chapters of *The Charterhouse of Parma.*

Of course there could and should have been a full-scale Stendhalian judgement on the Age of Napoleon; no one was so well qualified to do it. 'It was in France,' he himself wrote, 'that the despotism of Napoleon was most poisonous; he feared the works and the memory of the republic over which the people stood guard; he hated the enthusiasm of the Jacobins.' That was the discernment of Stendhal; he was a true son of the Revolution and of Rousseau, of whom his fellow-observer and kindred soul, William Hazlitt had written: 'He was the founder of Jacobinism which disclaims the division of the species into two classes, the one the property of the other.' Stendhal so well understood the driving force of that doctrine that he devoted to it his greatest work, *Red and Black.* Napoleon made his successors look like absurd and insignificant figures, but he could not blot out the stupendous events which had preceded his entry onto the stage. Stendhal treasured those memories as the inspiration of his youth, and perhaps that is a further reason why he would not trust himself to embark on such a full-scale Napoleonic study. Neither opponents of the Jacobin cause nor deserters from it would get any comfort from him.

Gita May's book is a straightforward biography of the subject rather than a special new estimate of Stendhal's Napoleonic associations. Yet it offers several excellent fresh glimpses of the world he gazed out upon, from the windows of Dr Gagnon's house in Grenoble, to the last days in Civitavecchia when he was still at work on 'an unfinished masterpiece', *Lamiel.* And if *Lamiel* eventually receives a belated elevation in the acclaim accorded to Stendhal's writings, as has happened previously to several of the others, Gita May will deserve some of the credit. Others before her have recognised Stendhal's championship of the rights of women. No one has enlisted *Lamiel* in the service of that good cause in quite the same way, and it is fitting that the latest contribution to Stendhalian studies should seek to recruit him not as one parading the musty emblems of Napoleonic grandeur but as a true prophet of twentieth-century liberation.

# THE CARTOONIST
## *Will Dyson*

———◇•◉•◇———

Will Dyson was one of the closest friends Aneurin Bevan made when he came to London in the early 1930s. When Will died, Nye was grief-stricken; standing at his own fireside, he took a glass in his hand, toasted his friend and then threw it into the dying embers.

The world had to wait a long time for a proper presentation of Will Dyson, in word and drawings, but when it came, the work was done perfectly – in Ross McMullin's volume, published by Angus & Robertson in 1985.

Nothing to touch the glory of the great cartoonists! They catch the spirit of the age and then leave their own imprint upon it; they create political heroes and villains in their own image; they teach the historians their trade and warn the best of them against the fatuities of hindsight; thanks to their potency, they provoke the bitterest feuds between their victims and the medium they serve; thanks to the variety of their art, they have proprietors and editors at their mercy and may enforce contracts the like of which other journalists never saw. All others on the same stage, fellow politicians and fellow journalists alike, are, in their heart of hearts, if they have such, deeply jealous. For the cartoonists, the truly great ones, achieve their effects by methods with which their fellow craftsmen cannot hope to compete.

I am prompted to these comments by a book on one of the three greatest cartoonists of the century – at least among those who have practised their craft in Fleet Street – and yet one who is the least well-known. I did know (and naturally boast of it) and study with some care the two who were most widely acclaimed for their pre-eminence in their lifetimes, David Low and Vicky. David Low, I believe, would win the suffrages of all his fellow practitioners as the master craftsman. He combined brilliant draughtsmanship with a political insight which rarely failed, and his wit never lapsed, even if his political passions sometimes did. He studied the political scene with unfailing sensitivity, as I can testify from the time when I was his editor on the *Evening Standard*. He would not rush to conclusions but could rarely be budged once he had reached them. He treasured his reputation for radical consistency, and with every good reason. He did as much as anyone to overthrow the Lloyd George Coalition in the early 1920s and as much as anyone to hoot Hitler and Mussolini and their British backers off the stage in the 1930s.

Vicky was much more volatile; not in his political allegiance which was indeed even more sturdy and incorruptible than Low's,

but in his moods. He could move from deep depression to hilarity, from tragedy to farce; but it was never, in my opinion, some superficial manic-depressive condition. These transformations had something to do with his art as a cartoonist. He did truly believe – although we would all mock him when he said it – that he would suddenly lose his touch, and that this moment of terror might be allied to some wretched political disillusion, for he studied that scene even more diligently than Low. It was as if he knew – although he was the most modest of artists – how magical was his gift, and how suddenly and irremediably it might pass from him.

All of which bring me to the one whom I have always regarded as the third in the trinity, and one whom the other two, I am sure, would be eager to claim as their fellow craftsman and comrade-in-arms. Ross McMullin's biography of Will Dyson, a beautifully produced, illustrated and constructed volume, gives us a better chance than might ever have been hoped for to make the judgement.

His career fell into three sharply defined sections, each in a sense blotting out the other, which is why his general fame has been impaired. Yet there were no desertions from his original faith, no apostasy, no abandonment of his own vision. Once the full story is unravelled with Ross McMullin's skill and sympathy, his real greatness is enhanced.

His most splendid period, giving expression to all his faculties, was when he arrived from his native Australia in pre-1914 London, and worked for the Socialist *Daily Herald* in its fiery youth and most blissful dawn. The *Herald*, of course, at that time was not one of the leading newspapers; it was an impecunious upstart. All the more remarkable was Will Dyson's achievement, as may still be tested today, in producing the cartoons which embody best the spirit of the age, in Labour politics first and foremost but in much else besides. Here enshrined indelibly is what the Suffragette fight felt like, what freshly confident trades unionism felt like. Here were the unforgettable scenes in *The Strange Death of Liberal England* several years before a mordant and often misleading observer wrote a famous book of that name. Will Dyson brought with him from Australia a strong streak of working-class ardour already quite in order there, and he helped both to reflect and instil it here, for the most compassionate and civilised causes. Many of the cartoons from this period can still make us catch our breath, by their poignancy, by their ferocity.

But then, when the 1914 war came, Will Dyson soon found himself cut off, not from the bulk of his working-class followers either here or in Australia, since most of them came to back the war as he did, but from his closest associates in the Labour Party and on the *Daily Herald*. He found himself drawn into the work of an Australian war artist – not by money (he wasn't paid), not by any process remotely corrupt, not by emotional blackmail, but by sheer conviction induced by what he saw with his own most sensitive eyes.

'I'll never draw a line that does not show war as the filthy business it is,' he himself said, and no one who looks at the pictures in this book will dare to question the claim. The record is here, and doubtless the original pictures (in the Australian War Museum) are even more deeply moving. Nothing tawdry, nothing flag-wagging; indeed the mystery is how they should ever have been published at the time. They look now much more like anti-war pictures fit to illustrate the reports which came later from, say, Siegfried Sassoon or Edmund Blunden. They were an artist's response to the war faithfully discharged, whatever the risk to himself.

If anyone, then or thereafter, questioned his allegiance to his former Socialist principles, they need only mark what he did immediately after the Armistice. He returned at once to the service of the same Socialist cause, at the offices of the *Daily Herald*. He did so even though some editors, even the great George Lansbury, did not always appreciate his services, and even though, in those same momentous months, he suffered the agony of his young and beautiful wife being struck down by the influenza plague which killed more people than the war itself. From that blow, he never quite recovered; but some of his cartoons still seemed to be inspired. It was just at this time he did his most famous one of all: the picture, under the heading 'Peace and Future Cannon Fodder', of Clemenceau, Lloyd George and Woodrow Wilson entering the Palace of Versailles, with a peace treaty in the gutter, and the child standing by, and Clemenceau saying: 'Curious! I seem to hear a child weeping.' The child was labelled '1940 class'.

However, despite these flashes of brilliance, the Will Dyson of this third phase never equalled the consistent achievements of the pre-1914 or the war period. His heart was wounded, and he sometimes turned aside from using the talent he knew best. He rejoiced, as he said himself 'in the freedom from the Oriental tyranny of editors'. His wit and effervescence were still there; 'he looked like Voltaire, and talked like Voltaire,' said one observant admirer. He admitted to David Low that he had failed to concentrate his gifts: 'You win, Dave. You're the pure merino. I'm a bit of a cross-breed.' Too many people took him at his own estimation, and thought that the fire had gone or, perhaps even, that it had never burnt so brightly as his pre-1914 admirers had supposed.

The alternative evidence, the proof, is here in this beautiful volume. As in the old cartoon books of David Low and Vicky, it is not only that ancient controversies catch fire again and light up our modern times. We can also see how the true artist must pour his whole heart and soul and spirit into the task, and may run the risk, as poor Vicky did, of draining it altogether.

# THE ANTI-VICTORIAN
## *Lytton Strachey*

The true Pope threw his wig into the corner of the room, and used all the plainest words in the dictionary. He used them carefully, no doubt, very carefully, but he used them – one-syllabled, Saxon words, by no means pretty – they cover his pages; and some of his pages are among the coarsest in English literature. There are passages in the *Dunciad* which might agitate Mr James Joyce.

Lytton Strachey
The Leslie Stephen Lecture
for 1925 on Alexander
Pope.

One hundred years after Lytton Strachey's birth, the Oxford University Press published *The Shorter Strachey*, which should be enough to encourage readers to turn to Strachey ad lib, and Michael Holroyd's splendid, massive two-volume biography can help them on the journey.

When Lytton Strachey was born, in the year 1880, the Victorian age was at the peak of its power and glory. The British upper classes still kept their grip on society with little sign that it would ever loosen, and sexual customs and manners were, overtly at least, of a most prim and respectable kind. Somehow, class, sex and the age itself intertwined, and since those times all three have taken a terrible pummelling. Oddly, incredibly, the truth seems to be that no one did more to knock the stuffing out of the three jumbled together than one who made no claims to be a popular or political figure in any sense whatever, but who knew, subconsciously perhaps, that the artist may be the most powerfully revolutionary figure of all. 'The essence of all art,' wrote Lytton Strachey, in another connection, somewhat over-stating the case, 'is the accomplishment of the impossible. This cannot be done, we say: and it *is* done. What has happened? A magician has waved his wand.' (He wrote these sentences about someone who would not at first seem to qualify for the revolutionary title at all: Alexander Pope. But read his marvellous essay on the subject and all doubts are dissipated.)

The magician who waved his wand to sweep aside the influence of the Victorian age over the minds of his countrymen was Lytton Strachey himself, and he did it in a most peculiar manner at a most peculiar time. His *Eminent Victorians* was published in May 1918, just at a moment when the British people, emerging from the experience of the most terrible war in history, might not have been expected to accept kindly an attack upon some of their national heroes and heroines, and especially since the criticism came from a despised 'conchie'. When Bertrand Russell first received his copy of *Eminent Victorians*, he was a prisoner in Brixton jail, and as he turned over the pages, he laughed so loudly that the prison wardens complained. But Bertrand Russell, like Lytton Strachey, was part of the sub-species which had not been able to share the national sentiment of wartime. How could it be – or rather, may it not be an absurd misapprehension to suppose – that *Eminent Victorians did* have anything distantly approaching the degree of national influence hinted at above? It took some time for the national reaction to follow, and perhaps *Eminent Victorians* never became a best-seller in the exact sense of the term; but it soaked deeply into the national consciousness. Outside Brixton jail, after a while, the general glee was scarcely more controllable; almost single-handed that volume mocked Victorian hypocrisy off the stage.

But, of course, *Eminent Victorians* was not some isolated academic study nor could it be unaffected by Strachey's own experience in the war period. He could laugh but he could also fight, and one of his true heroes showed the way. 'Consider that life and take courage,' he once wrote of Voltaire to a friend in Paris, and it was in an essay on Voltaire, written during the war, that he expressed his contempt for tyranny in every form. Voltaire was the inspiration to which he constantly returned and, contrary to the general supposition, he could emulate the crusader as well as the satirist. Voltaire was always at his side in that London of the First World War when he started to reveal unsuspected qualities of ambition and fortitude. Pitifully frail as he was, he prepared to deliver his blow against the enemy, the impact of which smarts to this day.

Somehow he had learnt a prodigious contempt for the British upper classes. Crossing the Channel just before 1914 he noted the manner of two young Etonians: 'There was a look in their faces which showed both were born to command and that none of their commands would ever be any good to anybody.' How he despised the elegant vapidity of our rulers, their hypocritical moral systems, the craving for power and the negation of intellect which helped bring the war and the slaughter. The reason why *Eminent Victorians* was, and remains, a classic, is that it expressed this spirit of a new age in a tone desperately difficult for his contemporaries to challenge. The upper classes were flayed in the best upper class accent. (Although what he wrote in his own diary was: 'God blast, confound and fuck the upper classes.') He had derided our Victorian rulers, trusting that the echo of his laughter would shame their successors too. It took years for orthodoxy to get its breath back.

But turn aside for a moment from these major targets to the subject of Strachey and sex. No one who reads Michael Holroyd's

biography of Strachey – one of the great biographies of the century
– can doubt that his homosexuality and his resentment at society's
attitude to the phenomenon played some part in shaping his iconoclastic temper, and why not? Indeed one good excuse for re-reading
all his writings – and any excuse is a good one – is to look back with
the latest autobiographical knowledge to see how these feelings
must have influenced his writings in an age much less tolerant than
our own. And furthermore, there is the fact that Strachey was
always eager to write about sex in a way few English writers have
done – apart from anything else he realised that it was a topic of
perpetual, potential high comedy. But let us beat about the bush no
more, if that is a proper term in the context; let us use *The Shorter
Strachey* to vindicate the theme. At the ripe and randy age of
eighteen he read a paper to the Apostles at Cambridge in which he
posed the question thus:

> Can we, after our 2000 years of experience, formulate a rule? Can we
> say to the artist 'Within these limits you may select as much of life, and
> reject as much of it, as you will: beyond them you cannot go'? Can we
> say to Antony, 'You may enjoy the limbs and the head and the breasts
> of Cleopatra as much as you like, but there are some parts of her
> which you will never enjoy; for with these you have nothing whatever
> to do'?
>
> Since the institution of Christianity and fig-leaves, there has been a
> remarkable unanimity as to which these parts precisely are. With an
> outer limit at the extreme top of the stomach on the one hand and at
> about the middle of the thighs on the other, the forbidden zone
> gradually deepens in intensity, enclosing within its boundaries the
> whole region of the bowels and most of the essential parts of the
> human economy, until it reaches the culminating and central point of
> the sexual organs. Here indeed is the undiscovered country, the North
> Pole itself. The eyes of our Antony, baffled by a thousand veils, turn
> away in despair. The instrument which would penetrate here must be
> infinitely more delicate, more gentle, more insinuating, than any with
> which nature has endowed him; he must be content with remi-
> niscences, with allusions, with dreams: what is he that he should cry
> for the real thing?
>
> But why the dickens shouldn't he, and get it too?
>
> I wish to give an illustration.
>
> Suppose tomorrow morning nursery-maids in Kensington Gar-
> dens, clerks on buses, ladies and gentlemen driving in their carriages

and cabs to the shops and to the City, were to notice that an extraordinary change had, during the night, come over the central figure on the Albert Memorial. Suppose their astonished eyes were to perceive that that imposing golden form was no longer in the sitting posture, had risen to its feet. But that is not all. Imagine they saw too that it had discarded that princely robe, those knee-breeches, those stockings which we have all admired so, that it stood there in the garb of nature, in the garb in which Augustus and Hadrian and Marcus Aurelius thought fit to appear before the millions of their subjects, thought fit to be remembered when they had long since ceased to walk the earth, had long since passed to the abode of the immortal gods. Imagine this, and imagine the accumulated force of horror and disgust and fury in the breasts of passers-by. Imagine the indignant rush up those sacred steps, the blind fingers tearing, overturning, destroying . . . but to contemplate our late beloved Prince in such a situation is too painful; I draw a shuddering veil.

There; but that's just a taste. A few pages later he suggests that an entertaining essay could be written on the theme of 'the sexlessness of historians', and immediately he cites the case of Macaulay, about whom on other counts he is brilliantly laudatory as well as perceptive: 'His sentences have no warmth and no curves; the embracing fluidity of love is lacking.' True enough: but there is a kinship between Macaulay and Strachey himself which he illustrates in a later piece (first published in this volume) on one of Macaulay's villains, Warren Hastings. Macaulay's portrait is, says Strachey, 'a picture which, once seen, is seen for ever'. And now read, for example, Strachey's own portrait of Asquith, written in May 1918, but not published until fifty years after his death. Squeals of protest deluged *The Times* correspondence columns even then: what would have happened if the portrait had circulated in the victim's lifetime? Published now, it will hang for ever in the English portrait gallery, along with those from the other masters, Clarendon, Gibbon, Carlyle, Froude and Macaulay himself, whom Strachey has subjected to a douche of their own imperishable art – not forgetting that all of them at one time or another were inclined to take themselves too seriously too long. Strachey, great historian though he truly was, would never make the same mistake. He was always on the alert to keep matters in proportion, thus: 'Clio is one of the most glorious of the Muses; but, as every one knows, she (like her sister Melpomene) suffers from a sad defect; she is apt to be pompous. With her buskins, her robes, and her airs of importance she is at times, indeed, almost intolerable. But fortunately the Fates have provided a corrective. They have decreed that in her stately advances she should be accompanied by certain apish, impish creatures, who run round her tittering, pulling long noses, threatening to trip the good lady up, and even sometimes whisking to one side the corner of her drapery, and revealing her undergarments in a most indecorous manner. They are the diarists and letter-writers, the gossips and journalists of the past, the Pepyses and Horace Walpoles and Saint-Simons, whose function it is to reveal to us the littleness underlying great events and to remind us that history itself was once real life. Among them is Mr Creevey. The Fates decided that Mr Creevey should accompany Clio, with appropriate gestures, during that part of her progress which is measured by the thirty years preceding the accession of Victoria; and the little wretch did his job very well.'

However, I have been led astray from the study of Strachey and sex. He will, I assure you, constantly lead you back there and by the most surprising detours. He detected the homosexual trait in Prince Albert, learnt Freudian psychology – from Dostoievsky rather than Freud himself – and applied it to the Virgin Queen, insisted upon a preference for Robert Burns to T. S. Eliot, proved himself a disciple of Stendhal no less than Voltaire, and yet could also be, as Cyril Connolly called him, 'a passionate Elizabethan'. A matchless mixture indeed: and the citation of Robert Burns reminds us that his bursts of humour could be even better than the wit. Some lines from Robert Burns kept intruding while he was reading a *Life* of Lord Salisbury – 'One of those extraordinary men of action, so certain, so unreflective, so untemperamental,' one of the very type he most abhorred. But 'a line of Burns has kept floating in my head as I've been reading, I don't know why – except its incongruity. "Laddie, lie near me!" Were Burns and Lord Salisbury both human beings? . . . Laddie, lie near me! The words act as a kind of incantation, dispelling the folly of the virtuous and the harshness of the wise.' Yes, sometimes the comedy is so rich that it seems like well-constructed slapstick, if there is such a thing, and then, a moment later, with himself as the hero, the absurdities of homosexual love can change to pitiful agonies. For, believe it or not, this clown could at a pinch play Hamlet too, at least for one or two unfinished scenes. One hitherto *unpublished* scene of this character is included in *The Shorter Strachey*; and it would be enough on its own to send addicts to buy this volume.

I trust it may also create a whole new generation of Stracheyites. 'It is,' he wrote, 'too late to be prudish: Catullus, Rabelais and a hundred others stare us in the face.' Lytton Strachey will keep his place in the company of great comic writers, the clowns who prefer that role to Hamlet, when all his unreadable detractors are reduced to footnotes.

FOUNDING MOTHER
# Dorothy Wadham
## and Kindred Glories

———◦◖◦◗◦———

The English language is going to conquer the world, I believe . . .

> Idris Davies, the poet from
> Rhymney; a diary entry made
> in 1939

I reviewed together three memorable books about Oxford,* but this title, I trust, still helps to keep matters in proportion.

*Peter Sutcliffe, The Oxford University Press; Nicolas Barker, The Oxford University Press and the Spread of Learning; Jan Morris (ed.), The Oxford Book of Oxford

Since the perfectibility of man seems, for the moment at least, to be a little beyond our reach, it may be better to concentrate on the perfectibility of books. And here the signs are excellent. It is impossible to imagine anything ascending nearer to the top-most peak of perfection than the *Oxford English Dictionary*, and yet in the past few years the Oxford perfectionists have dared to pile three brand-new supplements upon their towering pedestal, and there is still one more to come and no hint whatsoever that the whole contraption may come tumbling down. Or consider the Oxford University Press itself, now allegedly celebrating the five-hundredth year of the printing of books in the dreaming city. Not every modern product from the same press deserves its place on the same shelf with the dictionary, but the miracle is that many of them do. Somehow through the centuries some presiding genius with an infallible typographical eye has insisted that books are intended not merely to be read, marked and digested but also to be fondled, gazed upon, things of beauty, capable forever of defying their detractors face to face. Oxford has understood that better than anywhere else.

I once bought, some fifteen-odd years ago (for £7.15s), the three lovely folio volumes of the first edition of Clarendon's *History of the Rebellion and the Civil Wars*, printed at Oxford in the year 1704. It was, I now learn, the first bestseller which the Press ever had. Overnight the money poured in, although not alas into the University chest, since the Vice-Chancellor of the day, a certain William Delaune, President of St John's (where else?) pocketed the proceeds from the first two editions, and soon found himself pitched out not merely of his college but his rectory as well. A congenial light, however, is cast over Queen Anne's Oxford, by the further intelligence that the defrocked Delaune was not merely soon elected Lady Margaret Professor of Divinity but appointed Delegate to guard the University Press Accounts. He did it to such effect that his fellow Delegates were soon constructing a new printing house called the Clarendon Building, and some part of the credit for

Delaune's rehabilitation, one feels, must have been due to the beauty of that priceless book. From that day to this, I have blithely supposed, the Clarendon Press happily and devoutly poured forth its treasures into the lap of an admiring public.

Nothing of the sort! Academic spite, myopia, rivalry and incompetence are such that the real miracle is the survival of the University Press in any form and, what's more, there is no secret about the cause of the miracle. The don-piloted shipwreck has always sailed safely to port on a sea of Bibles, Bibles by the million in every shape and size. No degree of absurdity in the way the enterprise was supposed to be run – by a Board of Delegates who knew nothing of the business – could ever succeed finally in ruining the argosy. Peter Sutcliffe tells the whole story with a never-failing clarity and wit, and a necessary resolve not to lapse into hyperbole; everything at his disposal is as well-proportioned and appropriate as, say, Wadham College. 'The right to print money by printing Bibles,' he remarks, 'could not be questioned, for it had come from on high,' and the uncontrolled riches from these heavenly coffers confounded every other form of accountancy.

No one can say, however, that those University authorities didn't attempt some collective Benedictine vow of poverty. Scattered across Mr Sutcliffe's pages are references to some of the items which helped to squander the Biblical super-profits. He cannot resist rolling their titles round his tongue, and nor can I. Clarendon Press editions of the English divines 'took a little time to work their way out of the system', among them (a short list, I promise you) the work of Thomas Jackson (1579–1640) in twelve volumes; Sanderson (1587–1663) in six volumes appearing in 1854; Hall (1574–1656) in ten volumes, the third edition of that same century appearing in 1863. Bishop Smalridge's *Sermons*, produced on an equally lavish scale, sold one copy in ten years, another in 1885 and another in 1895, the last. 'It did not require any great flair,' writes Mr Sutcliffe,

> to recognise that Müller's *Passerine Birds* – the full title, *Certain Variations in the Vocal Organs of the Passeres (that have hitherto escaped notice)* – was going to be a slow seller. Nevertheless, its sales record was remarkable: 784 copies were printed and in the first year seven copies were sold (and forty given away): in 1880 one copy was sold, and in 1881 two copies, another in 1884, and three more in the 1890s. After twenty-five years it had sold twenty-one copies.

And Max Müller was, compared with some of the others, a charismatic figure, the equivalent of the twentieth-century 'television don'. He was, I am glad to say Mr Sutcliffe further reminds us, 'remembered as the man whose wife received the Imperial Order of Chastity, Third Class, after entertaining an Oriental potentate for lunch'.

Oxford's business acumen almost succeeded in dissipating its most precious asset, the King James's Bible, the Authorised Version, the matchless money-spinner of all time. Neglecting the wise maxim of the man who had said that what was good enough for St Paul should be good enough for anyone, the mid-nineteenth-century custodians of the Press embarked, with incredible energy and earnestness, upon the task of producing the Revised Version. Every scholarly precaution had been taken; every publishing skill was invoked – for example, for the purpose of simultaneous publication on both sides of the Atlantic, a ban broken only when the *Chicago Times* printed at a cost of ten thousand dollars the 110,000 words of the Gospels, the Acts and the Epistles, cabled from New York. But scoops or no scoops, the Revised Version of the New Testament had been grossly overprinted, and the moral could not be drawn in time to prevent a comparable overprinting of the revised Old Testament. And yet, eighty years later again, in the 1970s, on Oxford instructions with Cambridge participation in the folly, backed by a million-pound investment, the New English Bible was printed, not in the old Clarendon Building, not even in Oxford itself, but in Neasden, if you can believe it. Discretion briefly descends on Mr Sutcliffe's pages about the precise financial outcome of this risible venture, and it cannot altogether be accidental.

However, I have raced ahead to modern times and must retrace these steps, if a false impression is not to be left. Occasionally, throughout the centuries, the Oxford University Press seemed to be rescued by human agencies, and the moments should not be missed. One such was during the years of the Commonwealth when the Philosophical Society of Oxford met in John Wilkins's rooms in Wadham – they were called, or called themselves, the Wadham Group – and there was assimilated the new Baconian philosophy-cum-science, and John Wilkins, himself a kind of Barebones Maurice Bowra, wrote his *Coptic Gospels*, 500 copies of which were printed in 1716 and the last of which – a lesson to all impatient publishers – was disinterred from the warehouse in 1907, the paper hardly discoloured and the impressions still black and brilliant.

Another with comparably eccentric claims to immortality, although curiously not from Wadham, was Philip Lyttleton Gell, who still in the 1890s would arrive for his daily stint at the Walton Street office with a coach and pair, a luncheon hamper, and a bottle of champagne. Under his beneficent aegis the Press became the largest employer of labour in the city, and the danger was courted of a final escape from the Laudian Statutes of 1636 which, as one Oxford sceptic said, 'had laid the foundation of that fatal divorce between the University and the national mind which has lasted ever since'. Lyttleton Gell, says Mr Sutcliffe, was cheated of his due by his jealous successors, and it is good to see the matter rectified. Moreover, Mrs Gell now secures her niche in history too. One of the bestsellers at the turn of the century was *The Cloud of Witness*, 'a daily sequence of great thoughts from many minds, following the Christian season', and sold in twenty different styles. Published in 1904, it went on selling into the Second World War, together with others of the same brand such as *The More Excellent Way: Words of the Wise on the Life of Love*, which one of Mr Gell's contemporaries in the office described as Mrs Gell's 'tosh-books'.

However, no one can disguise the fact that despite 'the spirit of dementation' which, in the words of Mr Gladstone, sometimes afflicted Oxford, despite all its fopperies and fatuities, something in the essence of the place did set in hand, in the year 1858, what *The Times* later and rightly called the greatest effort which any printing press had undertaken since the invention of printing itself. Furthermore, Oxford supplied the stamina to enable the work to be completed *seventy years later*. 'The national honour of England is engaged,' said Max Müller, the same whose wife's honour had also been implicated. It was not enough to ward off all manner of threats, the worst being the disease of 'gigantism', an occupational complaint of the dictionary makers who kept demanding more words, more quotations, more space, more volumes, more decades. Some score-keeper for thirty-two years estimated that the twelve volumes defined 414,825 words and contained 1,827,306 illustrative quotations, that the type laid end to end would have stretched 178 miles and that the debit balance would be in the region of £375,000. But, as Mr Sutcliffe so triumphantly concludes, 'nobody knew quite what that meant'. With Clarendon outdone, with Caxton excelled, with Dr Johnson superseded in his own university, with Webster walloped on both sides of the Atlantic, indeed, with every other dictionary in the world reduced to the status of stuttering dwarfs, who would dare breathe a word about costs and profits? Mr Sutcliffe treats this and all kindred topics with suitable scorn.

However, as ever tending towards gigantism, Oxford offers a companion volume to Peter Sutcliffe's informal history, *The Oxford University Press and the Spread of Learning: An Illustrated History* by Nicolas Barker. Charles Ryskamp, Director of the Pierpont Morgan Library, New York, tells in an introduction to the work how the Oxford University Press has 'accomplished more than rulers and diplomats, wars and treaties, to establish English as the common language of the world today'. Nicolas Barker, in texts and pictures thereafter, modestly and magnificently illustrates the claim, and incidentally rectifies any injustice which may have emerged earlier in this article towards Archbishop Laud and Bishop John Fell. It was Laud certainly who had the vision of a University Press, a thought which should not be stressed too strongly in this five-hundredth anniversary year, since it might lead to some confusion about dates, and it was Dr Fell (more famous, alas, as the hero of the rhyme, 'I do not love you, Dr Fell . . .') who introduced the Fell types which set the University Press on the path to greatness.

Not that Dr Fell tended much toward flamboyance; he knew better. A mid-twentieth-century Printer to the University, quoted by Mr Sutcliffe, shows how the tradition lives, and how indeed, as all good journalists should learn, the printer knows best. This, according to Charles Batey, is what a book should be: 'The type should be legible, properly disposed on the page, and well inked: the paper should be opaque, of a right colour, kindly to the eye and pleasant to the touch; and the leaves should be secured in a safe binding, suitably lettered with the book's title. The whole should be of convenient weight, not burdensome; the book should open easily, and without alarms or crackles, and lie quite flat: and to all demands it should respond in a quiet, gentlemanly way; and as we read on, it should withdraw itself from our consciousness, leaving us alone with the author.'

All these qualities, I am happy to assure you, are superabundantly present in *The Oxford Book of Oxford*, edited by Jan Morris, and

published as part of the same mythical five-hundred-year cele-
bration. The volume can be opened anywhere, and read forwards,
backwards, or even just straight through from beginning to end and
back again. Somehow my eye alighted on a description of John
Evelyn's visit in 1654, to dine with the same John Wilkins cited
above, who was protecting the Press in the years of the Protectorate:

> We all din'd at that most obliging and universally-curious Dr Wil-
> kins's, at Wadham College. He was the first who shew'd me the
> transparent apiaries, which he had built like castles and palaces, and
> so order'd them one upon another as to take the hony without
> destroying the bees. These were adorn'd with a variety of dials, little
> statues, vanes, etc. and he was so aboundantly civil, as finding me
> pleas'd with them, to present me with one of the hives which he had
> empty . . . He had also contriv'd an hollow statue which gave a voice
> and utter'd words, by a long conceal'd pipe that went to its mouth,
> whilst one speaks through it at a good distance. He had above in his
> lodgings and gallery variety of shadows, dyals, perspectives and many
> other artificial mathematical, and magical curiosities, a way-wiser, a
> thermometer, a monstrous magnet, conic and other sections, a ball-
> ance on a demi-circle, most of them of his owne and that prodigious
> young scholar Mr Chr Wren, who presented me with a piece of white
> marble, which he had stain'd with a lively red very deepe, as beautiful
> as if it had been natural. Thus satisfied with the civilities of Oxford,
> we left it . . .

Oxford, suggests Jan Morris more elegantly than I do here, is a
piebald prodigy, a vivacious shambles, a turmoil, always dis-
satisfied. It has a lush fascination, a grey velvety feel in the evening, a
sense of calm and elegy. It is notoriously bibulous. It is testy, ironic
and intolerant. It is courageous, arrogant, generous, ornate, pun-
gent, smug and funny, both consciously or unconsciously. And how
discerning Jan Morris can be (in someone else's words or, better
still, her own) about the individual colleges. Christchurch is 'big,
stern, rich, certain'; Balliol stands for 'brain, power and worldly
influence'; Magdalen is 'not so much regal as matriarchal'.

And, finally, thrust into proper pre-eminence, above all the rest
comes wondrous, exquisitely-proportioned Dr Wilkins's Wadham;
founded by a woman and thereby perhaps escaping the Oxford vice
of misogyny; the college which proudly admitted Carew Raleigh to
its civilities, just after the wretched James I had executed his father;

the school where Robert Blake learnt how to sail ships and Mr Chr
Wren how to build churches, and Maurice Bowra how to bestow
that most benign of Oxford blessings, a legitimate complacency:
Wadham, of all places the greenest and most gracious, the peerless
and the most perfect in the whole green glory of Oxford. Jan Morris
does not quite say that, but, for the rest, she tells the truth and
nothing but the truth in a manner which would have horrified
Archbishop Laud.

# THE RATIONALIST
# *Winwood Reade*

———⟶∘⊙∘⟵———

There's something sweet in my uncertainty
I would not change for your Chaldean lore.

Byron, *Sardanapalus*

I wrote this introduction for a new Rationalist Press
edition of *The Martyrdom of Man*. But various
editions, introduced by others, are among the treasures to be found, for a few pence, in the second-
hand bookshops.

Of all favourite books, *The Martyrdom of Man* can best be recommended with the simple instruction: read it. Or maybe, better still, read it aloud. It is an oddity, a mixture which no one can find entirely palatable, a single volume which alone of all the author's writings has any reputation at all. And yet, whatever it is or is not, no question is possible about its peculiar literary quality. Scenes depicted in a few paragraphs or single sentences linger in the memory like verses learnt in childhood, and the whole resembles an epic poem. I find it hard to believe that anyone would need to read more than the opening pages to become captivated, almost drugged, by its rhythms and aroma.

When first published – in 1872 – it was greeted with a burst of bitterness and contempt. As the author explains in his preface, he was urged by the publisher and others to strike out passages bound to give offence; pleadings which he resisted not merely from a stubborn allegiance to the truth, 'a Pharisee virtue, a spiritual pride'. Much more was at stake, as he argues at the end; his whole philosophy and purpose. But it is interesting to consider why he should have attracted more venom than many of his fellow disciples of the new religion of humanity who at least could not complain of the attention they received. It was the decade when Charles Bradlaugh could pack 5000 people into a mass meeting to debate whether Salvation through the Atonement was indeed an immoral doctrine. Why was Winwood Reade treated as an outcast? The answer must be sought, I believe, in the sinuous force of his argument. Often, the rationalists of that and other ages have been accused of being desiccated theorists, and occasionally the charge may have been justified. But no one could say that *The Martyrdom of Man* lacked human warmth and romance. The very title was an adaptation of Christian sentiment, and the style provoked angry protests precisely because of its appeal to those nurtured on the Bible. It was outrageous that the devil should have such a thumping good tune.

So, despite the scorn or possibly assisted by it, the book secured a steady readership. Secularists used it (says Mr Sylvester Smith in *The London Heretics*) as a kind of substitute Bible of their own. It had a subtlety and beauty more satisfying than the hard polemics required by Bradlaugh and Co. to pulverize their platform opponents. And it also has many other associated attributes which reveal a most original mind. When Winwood Reade died of tuberculosis in 1875, at the age of thirty-seven, his much more famous novelist uncle, Charles Reade, wrote: '. . . in another fifteen years he would probably have won a great name and cured himself, as many thinking men have done, of certain obnoxious opinions which laid him open to reasonable censure'. The patronage may be overlooked. With such a style at his command and with a knowledge and imagination shared by few of his contemporaries, it surely is true that, had he lived, he would have become one of the most eminent of Victorians.

A formidable list could be compiled to prove his astonishing foresight, the inventions he prophesied – the motor car, the aeroplane, chemical foods, man's exploration of the universe and the outlawry of war through the effect of a planet-destroying weapon. He anticipated some of the best-known anticipations of H. G. Wells and Bernard Shaw, and yet even this total might constitute little more than a series of lucky guesses. Much more impressive, it seems to me, is the combination of an excitement or foreboding about the future with a reverence for the past. Somehow while searching, maybe vainly, for a theory of man's development, he instils a deep love of history and for the many unlikely figures to whom he gives a special prominence in his richly-coloured pageant.

Most of what he sees is from a quite unorthodox angle. He set out, following his own explorations, to tell the history of Africa and then became drawn into the attempt to sketch a universal history. His aim slightly misfires in both cases; perhaps what he achieves with more precision is to see Europe (with a glance at America) through the eyes of Africa and Asia – surely a strange feat for a comfortable middle-class subject of Queen Victoria. I don't know enough about the state of historical knowledge at that time to be certain how truly original he was. But my guess is that few others would have dared such an assault as his upon European conceit: 'Asia taught Europe its alphabet; Asia taught Europe to cipher and to draw; Asia taught Europe the language of the skies – how to calculate eclipses, how to follow the course of the stars, how to measure time by means of an instrument which recorded with its shadow the station of the sun; how to solve mathematical problems; how to philosophize with abstract ideas. Let us not forget the school in which we learnt to spell, and those venerable halls in which we acquired the rudiments of science and art.'

He seeks to discover how new civilisations made their great leaps forward and how living societies were turned to stone. He shows the petrification which must follow when hope is torn from human life and men are forbidden to do any new thing. He describes how history is made to move afresh by a Boccaccio copying out Homer with his own hand, by a Prince Henry of Portugal staring out upon the ocean from his castle near Cape St Vincent, by the wild Bedouin of the desert who invented the idea of one god. All the great prophets were heretics. 'Doubt is the offspring of knowledge; the savage never doubts at all.' *The Martyrdom of Man* is the gospel for heretics. Nowhere is the case for heresy placed better in its historical setting.

H. G. Wells, to his honour, paid proper tribute to his forerunner: 'One book that has influenced me very strongly is Winwood Reade's *Martyrdom of Man*. This *dates*, as people say, nowadays, and it has a fine gloom of its own, but it is still an extraordinarily inspiring presentation of human history as one consistent process.' Another appreciative reader in the late 1890s was the young Winston Churchill, then a studious subaltern on the Indian north-west frontier eagerly striving to fill the gaping holes in his Harrovian education but able only to reach this uncharacteristically cowardly conclusion: Reade was right, but wrong to say it: the human race must be allowed to keep its illusions.

That is the plea to which the author addresses himself in his final pages, the most eloquent peroration in agnostic literature. One other writer, a kindred spirit, expressed a similar view: 'In the Dark Ages,' wrote Heinrich Heine, 'people found their surest guide in Religion – just as a blind man is the best guide on a pitch-black night. He knows the way better than the seeing. But it is folly to use the blind old man as a guide after daybreak.'

It is better to turn to those, like Winwood Reade, who saw the daybreak coming.

# Index